Towards the Museum of the Future

Towards the Museum of the Future reviews the major current concerns in European museums through a series of specially commissioned, authoritative essays. Written against a background of unprecedented change in museums and society, the essays explore how museums are variously attempting to maintain their role in a culturally and politically unstable world.

The essays present a wide range of sometimes contradictory views on museums, exhibitions and museum education. They embrace case studies, general reviews and theoretical analyses, and are written from a variety of practical and theoretical points of view. Areas covered include European museums and the people who visit them; museums and the media; museums and exhibition design; the educational significance of museums in formal and informal settings.

This is the first book to approach current problems from such a wide perspective. Its authors, from seven countries, provide comprehensive coverage ranging not just geographically across Europe, but over most types of exhibitions and audiences in science, history and art museums.

Roger Miles is Head of the Department of Public Services at the Natural History Museum in London, where he has been responsible for a long series of major exhibitions for the general public.

Lauro Zavala is Professor in the Department of Education and Communication at the Metropolitan Autonomous University at Xochimilco in Mexico City.

07/08

UNIVERSITY OF
WOLVERHAMPTON

Harrison Learning Centre
City Campus
University of Wolverhampton
St Peter's Square
Wolverhampton WV1 1RH
Telephone: 0845 408 1631

Telephone Renewals: 01902 321333 or 0845 408 1631
Please Return this item on or before the last date shown above.
Fines will be charged if items are returned late.
See tariff of fines displayed at the Counter.

Towards the Museum of the Future

of the Future

New European Perspectives

Edited by

Roger Miles and Lauro Zavala

London and New York

First published 1994
by Routledge
11 New Fetter Lane, London EC4P 4EE

Simultaneously published in the USA and Canada
by Routledge
29 West 35th Street, New York, NY 10001

Typeset in Sabon by Florencetype Ltd, Kewstoke, Avon
Printed and bound in Great Britain by Butler & Tanner Ltd,
London and Frome
Printed on acid free paper

British Library Cataloguing in Publication Data
A catalogue record for this book is available from the British Library

Library of Congress Cataloging in Publication Data
Miles, Roger S.
Towards the museum of the future: new European perspectives /
Roger Miles and Lauro Zavala.
p. cm.
Includes bibliographical references and index.
1. Museums–Europe. 2. Europe–Cultural policy. I. Zavala,
Lauro. II. Title.
AM40.M55 1993
069'.094–dc20   93–12788

ISBN 0-415-0949-84

Contents

Contents

Figures

Notes on contributors

Pere Alberch is the Director of the National Museum of Natural Sciences in Madrid. Trained at the Universities of Kansas and California, Berkeley, he is a specialist in embryology and evolution.

Ruedi Baur is the co-founder, with Pippo Lionni, of the Atelier Intégral in Paris and Lyons. Trained as a graphic designer at the School of Applied Arts in Zurich, he has won awards for his work in Kiel (1984), Lyons (1988 and 1990) and Montpellier (1991). He works regularly for the Pompidou Centre and the City of Science and Industry in Paris, and for the cities of Marseilles, Villeurbanne and Lyons.

Christian Bernard is the Director of the Villa Arson at Nice, which is a national centre for contemporary art and a national school of fine arts. Since 1991 he has been working on plans for a future museum of modern and contemporary art in Geneva.

Louise Boucher works at McGill University, Montreal, where she is preparing a thesis on the evolution of science museums in North America. She has a background in communications, and her published work deals mainly with questions of heritage and scientific and technical culture.

Bernhard Graf is a member of the Institut dür Museumskunde in Berlin, where he heads the departments of museum education and visitor research. He is joint editor of *Museumsausstellungen: Planning–Design–Evaluation* (1985) and the joint author of *Besucher im Technischen Museum. Zum Besucherverhalten im Deutschen Museum München* (1993).

Jan Hjorth is Head of Development and Research at Riksutställningar in Stockholm, Sweden's state-run travelling exhibits service. He is one of the founder members of Riksutställningar.

Eilean Hooper-Greenhill is a Lecturer in the Department of Museum Studies at the University of Leicester. She is the author of *Museum and Gallery Education* (1991), *Museums and the Shaping of Knowledge* (1992) and *Museums and their Visitors* (forthcoming).

Pippo Lionni is the co-founder, with Ruedi Baur, of the Atelier Intégral in Paris and Lyons, and Director of the Unité de Création at the Ecole Nationale Supérieure de Création Industrielle in Paris. His work has been widely noticed in professional journals, and was the subject of an exhibition at the Institut für Neue Technische Form, Darmstadt, in 1991. Among many awards, he was the winner of the 1989 competition to design a logotype for the French presidency of the European Community.

Robert Lumley is a Lecturer in Italian Studies at University College in the University of London. He is the author of *States of Emergency: Cultures of Revolt in Italy, 1968–78* (1990), and the editor of *Culture and Conflict in Postwar Italy* (1990) and *The Museum Time-Machine* (1988).

Paulette M. McManus is a freelance museum consultant in the UK specialising in the relationship between museums and heritage sites and their publics. She has worked and published widely in North America and Europe.

Roger Miles is the Head of the Department of Public Services at the Natural History Museum in London, where he has been responsible since 1975 for a long series of innovative exhibitions and education programmes. He is the chief author of *The Design of Educational Exhibits* (1982, 1988).

Melanie Quin is a member of the team developing the new NINT Technology Museum in Amsterdam. She was earlier the Director of ECSITE, the European Collaborative for Science, Industry and Technology Exhibitions, with an office in Heureka – the Finnish Science Centre, at Vantaa, Finland; and before that the Director of the Nuffield Foundation's Interactive Science and Technology Project, with a base in London.

Ian Ritchie is an architect with offices in London (Ian Ritchie Architects) and Paris (Rice Francis Ritchie). He was responsible for major structures at the City for Science and Industry, Paris, the Reina Sofia Museum of Modern Art, Madrid, and the Ecology Gallery at the Natural History Museum, London. Rice Francis Ritchie were structural consultants for the Louvre Pyramid in Paris. Ian Ritchie's current projects include the New Meridian Planetarium at Greenwich, London, and Cultural Centres at Vitrolles and Albert in France. His awards include the Italian Iritecna Prize for Europe 1991.

Bernard Schiele is a Professor in the Communication Department at UQAM (University of Quebec at Montreal) and Research Director of CREST (Centre de Recherche en Evaluation Sociale des Technologies). In recent years he has focused on the popularisation of science and on scientific museology, and has directed international comparative research on the organisational and communications aspects of scientific and technical museology in Canada, the United States and France. He is currently working with Jacqueline Eidelman of CNRS, Paris, on the role and impact of scientific museology and the scientific exhibition.

Roger Silverstone is Professor of Media Studies at the University of Sussex. He was earlier the founding Director of the Centre for Research into Innovation, Culture and Technology at Brunel University. He has written or edited *The Message of Television: Myth and Narrative in Contemporary Culture* (1981), *Framing Science: the Making of a BBC Documentary* (1985), and *Consuming Technologies: Media and Information in Private Spaces* (1992).

Gillian Thomas is an Assistant Director (Project Development Division) at the Science Museum in London. Before that she was the Director of the new children's museum, Eureka!, in Halifax, UK, which opened in 1992. Earlier she was the Head of the Inventorium, the children's space at the City for Science and Industry in Paris.

Peter Vergo is Reader in Art History and Theory at the University of Essex, where he directs the Gallery Studies Course. He is the author of *Art in Vienna 1898–1918* (1975), translator and editor of Kandinsky's *Complete Writings on Art* (1982), and editor of *The New Museology* (1989). He was responsible for the exhibitions *Abstraction, Towards a New Art* (1980), *Vienna 1900* (1983) and *Expressionism. Masterpieces from the Thyssen-Bornemisza Collection* (1989–90).

Lauro Zavala is a Professor in the Department of Education and Communication at the Metropolitan Autonomous University at Xochimilco (UAM-X) in Mexico City. He is the author of *Material inflamable* [*Flammable Material*, film criticism, 1989], *La Seducción luminosa* [*The Luminous Seduction*, film theory, 1992], *Laberintos imaginarios* [*Imaginary Labyrinths*, postmodern culture, 1992], *La Literatura como espacio fronterizo* [*Boundaries of Literature*, 1992], and editor of *Teorías del cuento* [*Short Story Theories*, 2 vols, 1992], and *Posibilidades y límites de la comunicación museográfica* [*Possibilities and Limits of Communication in Museums*, 1992].

Photographic acknowledgements

The editors and publishers wish to express their thanks to the following for permission to reproduce illustrations: Richard Rogers Partnership, Fig. 1.1; Archipress, Figs 1.3, 1.7, 1.9, 1.10; Richard Meier & Partners, Figs 1.4, 1.16; Office for Metropolitan Architecture, Fig. 1.5; M. Keinefenn, Fig. 1.11; Claudio Piersanti, Fig. 1.12; Fundacion Coleccion Thyssen-Bornemisza, Fig. 1.14; Museo Nacional de Arte Romano, Fig. 1.15; Instituto Valenciano de Arte Moderno, Fig. 1.17; Atelier Intégral and the Villa Arson, Figs 2.1, 2.2, 2.3; Riksutställningar, Figs 7.1–7.5.

Introduction

Roger Miles

The speed and scale of recent political changes in Europe have been so astonishing that one hesitates, for fear of seeming too self-absorbed, to claim surprising and widespread changes in museums too. Yet, as a body, western Europe's museums have undergone profound changes in the last twenty years. These have tended to affect all aspects of their existence and operation, and are but imperfectly captured in bald statistics such as the doubling of the number of museums in the last thirty-five years, and a more than commensurate increase in the number of visits. Nevertheless, these statistics give at least a hint of the magnitude of the changes. And it is not too fanciful to see connections between political change and change in museums, as the growth of the UK heritage industry and current developments in reunified Germany make clear.

The authors of the thirteen essays in this volume were each invited to write on a theme selected by me, with the aim of reviewing some of the major present concerns in western European museums. Written from a variety of practical and theoretical points of view, the essays present a wide range of sometimes contradictory views on museums, exhibitions and museum education, embracing case studies, general reviews and theoretical analyses. They can be read as addressing themselves in one way or another to the problems of change, in the context of a consumer or post-industrial society. This is a science-based (some would say technology-dominated) society with pervasive media and advertising industries, instantaneous electronic communications, and a pluralistic culture in which the boundaries between high art and mass culture have been eroded. The essays variously reflect this society, as they show museums struggling to find a role for themselves in a culturally and politically unstable world.

It has not been possible to cover all aspects of European museums in these essays. Restricted to the public side, they have nothing to say about collection management, conservation and the like, and nothing directly to say about management and marketing. Regrettably, no room has been found for a discussion of the representation of women, minorities and non-European cultures in museums, or of that distinctly European phenomenon the ecomuseum, or of the current state of museums in eastern Europe. At least the first two of these topics already occupy a significant position in the current European museum thought.

1

The wide-ranging essays cover the deliberate building and marketing of museums and science centres in order to put cities and regions on the cultural map; the disputable development of heritage museums, particularly in the UK where their offerings can easily seem to be more histrionic than thèy are historic; and various efforts to make exhibits physically, mentally and culturally accessible to different sectors and subcultures of the population. These last efforts include the provision of more approachable buildings, travelling exhibits and help for local communities in making their own exhibitions, and the provision of museums and services for particular groups of visitors, especially schoolchildren and families on a day out. Such audience-led approaches bring museums closer to the mass media, with which, for good or ill, they increasingly share a dependence on their power to earn money.

While museums of the fine arts and history resist, on the whole, the urge to spread their message among the people, science and technology museums, and science centres, are responding vigorously to a felt need to teach ordinary people more science. Several of the essays touch on this subject. Although the outcome of this effort is uncertain and will be decided only in the long run, it is perhaps not surprising that empirical research on audiences and on the interaction between visitors and exhibits is concentrated in such museums. Much of the work is driven by the desire to produce better exhibits and services for the visitors, and, as several of the essays attest, the enthusiasm of museum practitioners who have first-hand experience of this approach is striking. Many museums yield nothing to the mass media when it comes to knowledge of their audiences.

Given the amount of change that is taking place in Europe's museums, it is small wonder that these essays present evidence of cultural clashes as designers, educators, curators and marketing specialists tussle to impose their own professional values on the physical form and running of museums and exhibitions. Nowhere is the struggle waged with more passion than in the clash between 'container' and 'contents', or design and information, and where simple answers are not likely to be found. And small wonder too, given that museums are set firmly within contemporary culture, that analyses of exhibitions in the light of, and with intellectual tools more normally associated with, the mass media, give us new insights into the creation and meanings of exhibitions. Several essays touch on this theme and are concerned with a variety of museums. These analyses draw more self-consciously on theoretical foundations than the empirical studies noted above and, among other matters, reopen the question of what is distinctive about museums in comparison with the mass media of communication. The answer seems to lie less in traditional notions about the use of concrete objects, which are signifiers rather than signifieds, than in characteristic manipulations of exhibition space and time, and the potential to combine many individual media of communication.

Museum developments are proceeding at different rates and, in detail, in different ways in the various countries and regions of western Europe. They are bringing with them new demands for professionalism and training, and new demands for skill and sensitivity in the discharge of duties. But as this collection of essays shows, they present as never before a stimulating intellectual challenge to all who concern themselves in this field.

This volume of essays will be published in Spanish by the National University of Mexico, and was originally commissioned by an interdisciplinary team working under the general co-ordination of Gerardo Portillo, former Director of the National School of Fine Arts in Mexico City. The team's project, 'The Museo-graphic Discourse: An Analytical Study and Some Practical Considerations', was set up in response to a call from the Rector of the National University to organise team-based innovations in research and teaching, and it has the support of the University's General Office of Scholarly Matters. This book is only one outcome of the team's work, which will also include further publications and the founding of a graduate programme of museum studies.

The editors are grateful to the National University of Mexico, and to their colleagues in the Museographic Discourse team, for the opportunity to publish this book in its present form. They are indebted to Naomi Lake, Fay Campbell and Ruth Champion for their invaluable help in preparing the work for publication.

Part 1
New worlds

Europe has seen a phenomenal resurgence in the building of museums during the 1970s and 1980s, exactly one hundred years after the last great boom which gave us, among many others, the magnificent buildings of the Victoria and Albert Museum in London (1876), the Rijksmuseum in Amsterdam (1885), and the Grande Galerie de Zoologie of the Natural History Museum in Paris (1889). We have long ago lost the certainty that neoclassicism is the 'correct' style for museum buildings, despite its ghostly reappearance in recent work such as the Sainsbury Wing of London's National Gallery. Ian Ritchie discusses in Chapter 1 the recent boom in new buildings and major refurbishment programmes in terms of today's pluralism in architecture as, throughout Europe, key cities compete to establish their individual identity through museum culture.

'Identity' has become a keyword in the way museums present themselves in today's complicated world, in which museum functions have also become increasingly complex. Ruedi Baur, Pippo Lionni and Christian Bernard discuss the role of a graphic identity in establishing a corporate spirit, which serves both to unify diverse functions within a museum and to present them as a coherent whole to the outside world. This leads them to views on the relationships between the museum as image, container and contents – central concerns of Ian Ritchie's contribution – that signal continuing debate on the proper balance between these aspects of museums and their functions. These are long-standing topics of discussion which, it seems, recent developments in Europe have done nothing to resolve, and may even have exacerbated. The subject is taken up by Jan Hjorth in Part 2 of this book (Chapter 7), with the thought that exhibitions, if they are not to abuse their visitors, should strike a balance between education and design.

Despite the construction of many new buildings, perhaps more than half of Europe's museums are housed in buildings that originally served other functions. There is a touching belief among planners and architectural historians that almost any redundant building can be made usable, and therefore 'saved', by converting it into a museum. Enthusiasts wishing either to start up or expand a museum, and having no money to do otherwise, are forced to go along with this notion, notwithstanding the problems it causes them. Thus science centres (though there are a few outstanding exceptions such as Heureka in Finland) have generally, on account of their financial precariousness, had to house themselves where they can. Nevertheless, as Melanie Quin makes clear in Chapter 3, science centres have developed with great vigour in Europe over the last ten years, propelled by the example of the United States and a concern for the public understanding of science. Their strong community spirit, reflected in the sharing of ideas and in the formation of ECSITE (European Collaborative for Science, Industry and Technology Exhibitions), contrasts strongly with the situation among more traditional museums, where separate development is still the order of the day.

The heritage debate centres on English attempts to turn history into an experience, to make the past knowable by, characteristically, making displays out of the people as well as for the people. England, with its huge voluntary membership of the National Trust and its official conservation body, English Heritage, and with its new cultural ministry, the Department of National Heritage, provides fertile soil for this approach and for the critical discussion that has come with it. As Robert Lumley explains, 'heritage' served as a metaphor for England's troubled identity in debates of the 1970s and 1980s (see Chapter 4). However, it would be wrong to view this as a uniquely English subject, for questions about the presentation of history to serve political and ideological purposes are never far below the surface in museums, regardless of type or country. This is particularly true of open-air or folk museums which, since their origins in Scandinavia (Skansen in Stockholm dates from 1891), have spread throughout Europe, and in which, in former Soviet-bloc countries such as Yugoslavia and Rumania, folk culture was celebrated to keep alive a sense of national identity. Europe's many current uncertainties over nationalism and nationality suggest that the heritage debate has far to run.

1

An architect's view of recent developments in European museums

Ian Ritchie

Introduction

There is little doubt that the Pompidou Centre in Paris (Figure 1.1), 1972–7, represented a dramatic shift in museum design and the *image* of museums in contemporary cultural life. Conceived as a technically and spatially flexible *container* for art, books, research and exploration, it provided, on an enormous scale, the opportunity for virtually any cultural *content* to be housed, including small objects, paintings, sculptures, site happenings, music, etc. This approach produced very large floor plates, whose intrinsic spatial characteristics were uniform although far from 'neutral', with the presence of the large-span beams and colour-coded servicing elements dominating the spaces.

However, this internal architecture was not necessarily the most significant aspect of the Pompidou Centre. The very nature of its entrance and its celebratory escalators took away the 'front steps' to high culture. It was, in its very essence, populist and freely accessible, and the strength of the public piazza in front of the building gave additional emphasis to the informality of the concept. There was no longer any notion of having to be 'educated' to participate in culture. The polemic created by the Pompidou Centre was not only architectural but also political. It represented the beginning of a renaissance in French government policy towards expressing belief in its own time and culture. This renaissance is still active today, having enjoyed the support of three French Presidents, opposing political parties in government, and the introduction of a certain autonomy for Paris through the re-establishment of the City Council and role of the Mayor. This renaissance is significant in as much as Paris was already, together with London and New York, a traditional centre of museum culture.

In 1978 the city of Frankfurt, co-ordinated by the Mayor Walter Wallman and the two main political parties (the Social Democrats (SPD) and the Conservatives (CDU)), agreed to redefine the *image* of Frankfurt and to promote the city as being much more than a financial centre. The key component of this change was the renewal of the urban landscape, into which would strategically be placed cultural institutions. Within the following decade, thirteen such institutions have been conceived, often by internationally renowned architects, and not without controversy.

This city of 500,000 people, in spending 11.5 per cent of its budget on culture, succeeded in transforming and enhancing its urban fabric and in completely changing the international perception of Frankfurt. Thus Frankfurt has, more than any other European city not previously a cultural centre, influenced through political will other non-capital European cities to invest in culture, and in particular in museums. This phenomenon has swept through Spain and, to a lesser but still significant degree, Italy. It is perhaps pertinent to ask why, in the last decade or so, European cities, one after the other, have decided to invest in museums. It is clear that these cultural typologies have become the kings, queens and sometimes aces in each city's hand as they vie with each other across Europe (and the world) for attention. France, largely through its museums, has been in the vanguard in implementing a 'cultural industry', first and foremost in Paris, but also in the provinces.

Thus three factors – the need for cultural facilities responding to our own age; the desires and quest for public awareness of recent cultural developments; and the desire for national and capital identity in a rapidly shrinking world – have also created an industry in both an economic and social sense. France, recognising the tendency of a leisure-orientated society in the 1960s along with many other western countries, constructed a coherent strategy which has resulted in Paris remaining at the top of the world's cultural capitals; its major provincial cities emerging strengthened in the wider European context and its smaller towns sharing in the cultural facilities boom of the 1980s.

It is certainly the European context which has become the challenge for many cities. Europe, whose identity is an ongoing accident of history, is in a sense no longer an embryonic community of countries, but has become one of the world's primary geographical zones, in which the principal players are now, and in the foreseeable future, the cities within it. The political power of the elected mayors in France, Germany and Spain, married with their respective visions to improve the quality of life, has led to the combination of urban design and public buildings as a major vehicle to carry forward these political objectives into reality.

New museums

To place in perspective the recent developments in museum design, it is first necessary to recall, with a precise but brief note, the development of European museums up to recent times. In essence, they began with collections, and if we go far back to the sacking of Corinth (AD 146) and Syracuse (212), the plundering of artefacts was on such a scale that apparently an entire area of Rome was set aside for trade in these art objects. This trading inevitably led to the arrival of collectors. It is the collector who began the process which led to the notion of museums. It is equally true that the nature of the collections subsequently conditioned the physical and spatial qualities of the buildings in which to house them. There is no denying that museums initially evolved as a result of the individual collector's wishes and demands, and not those of the public who first

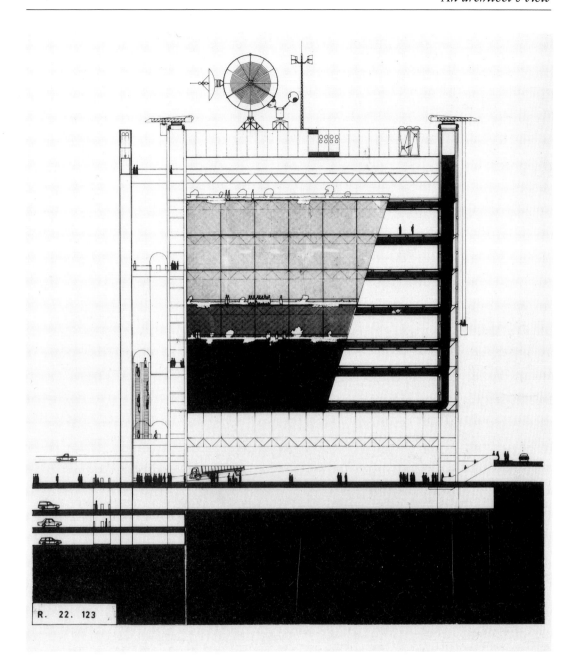

R. 22. 123

Figure 1.1 Pompidou Centre, Paris

came to visit these collections. Initially, these collections were in 'houses' (for example, Medici in Florence, François I in Paris). As their collections grew, the 'professional curator' appeared (Donatello at the Medici's, Leonardo da Vinci in Paris). In 1780, Grand Duke Leopold brought together the extensive Medici collections at Uffizi, which was opened to the general public in the 1830s (Leopold II), at which time it took the name Museo degli Uffizi. The physical nature of the display space at the Uffizi was a series of corridors. Throughout Italy during the early 1800s, the 'grand families' of Italy (e.g. the Borghese, Franese in Rome, the Dorias in Genoa, Este in Ferraza, etc.) vied with each other through the qualities and size of their respective collections which embellished their *palazzi*. Each in turn found the necessity to create a 'display nucleus' – gallery(ies), curator, restorer and collector. This nucleus is essentially still present today.

In parallel, in England, notable families were behaving in a similar way; and in 1757 the British Museum opened in Montague House. It was an assembly of private collections made over to the realm. Only after this stage did the very first signs of purpose-designed galleries appear: Sir John Soane's Dulwich Gallery (1814) and Sir Robert Smirke's British Museum (1823). A number of European capitals enlarged their 'houses' or 'palaces' with specific galleries (e.g. the Egyptian Wing of the Louvre, 1823) over the next few decades. In fact, the desire of the educated European to visit these collections became insatiable. The museum had arrived, and was a place where you studied and *learnt from the past*.

It was in 1851, with the Great Exhibition in the Crystal Palace in Hyde Park, London, that the first 'display' (and on a huge international scale) of the *present* with suggested interpretations for the *future* first appeared. This was very significant in that it was a purpose-designed public exhibition space which did not have the decorated facades of classicism, which had already been the 'norm' with public museums and galleries during the nineteenth century (Figure 1.2). I suggest that because of the historical nature of the museum collections, a classical architectural facade in front of enfilades of rooms and corridors was deemed culturally appropriate. In fact, the world exhibitions that followed in Paris (1867), Philadelphia (1876) and Paris again (1878) illustrated very clearly through their pavilion buildings an architectural taste for style, often quite independent of the *contents* on display. National identity was often expressed through each pavilion's architecture.

This short digression is relevant in highlighting certain characteristics of the nineteenth century in coming to terms with an architectural expression of its own modernity, but equally, in that many of the international exhibition pavilions remained and were transformed into public culture houses. However, museums (and museum architecture), despite their increasing number, were servants to an age of scientific, technical and geographical discovery.

In 1859, Sir Richard Owen laid down very clear guidelines for the design of the proposed Natural History Museum to be built, following an architectural

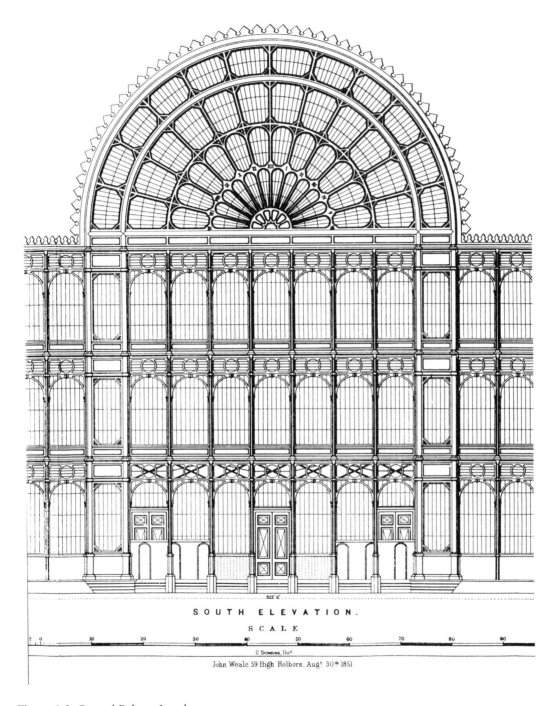

SOUTH ELEVATION.

SCALE

C Downes, Dir.ᵗ

John Weale. 59 High Holborn, Aug.ᵗ 30ᵗʰ 1851

Figure 1.2 Crystal Palace, London

competition, in London. In commissioning the building, which was to bring to the general public, in a *modern* way, the latest understanding of the natural world, he specified that natural lighting should be from the top, not directly overhead (cf. Soane's Dulwich Gallery) but from the junction of walls and roof, and that the spaces be column-free. These two design elements in his brief were extremely articulate architectural statements, one being specifically related to the quality (and probably the intensity) of light and the other to functional space. However, together they suggest a desired spatial quality which remains today; a primary concern for achieving the 'balance' between architectural space and exhibits.

In reviewing a number of recent European museums, this 'balance' has created much outspoken opinion, notably in the field of the art gallery/museum. In summary, this 'balance' can be considered as the relationship between *container* and *content*. The external expression of the container (its facade architecture) is not specifically part of this relationship unless by its very nature it is both the interior surface of the container and facade. The external appearance, *image*, of the container is, as we shall see, an active ingredient in the 'battle of the cities' currently being waged throughout Europe. It is in the context, then, of these three components – *image*, *container* and *contents* – that I shall focus my review on recent European museums.

These three components are reflections of a natural and recognisable hierarchy of perception. First, there is the intimate scale of personal and private contact with the objects (*contents*) of the museum's collection; then the internal spatial experience (*container*) usually shared with others and often very much part of the visitor's experience; and finally the public architecture *image* of the museum building, which by its very importance as a municipal or national repository of artefacts for private study is more often than not sited prominently, and as such is a dominant component and even generator of a particular urban composition.

Recently, museums have served as the stimuli for the regeneration of local areas as well as city monuments, and as important venues for social encounters. However, some recent museums and exhibitions have questioned the historical model of museums as storehouses. The traditional notion of the museum is being challenged by *contents* becoming events and *container* becoming catalyst, which, in turn, is leading the contemporary museum to become the place not of study, but of provocation and debate (e.g. the Pompidou Centre, Paris; the Ecology Gallery at the Natural History Museum, London). This can be restated as a decision on the part of museum directors for the museums to be part of today's real world and to be an active educational ingredient in our thoughts about the future. This is true for many museums of art, natural history, science and technology.

The design and building of the Museum of Modern Art (1987–91) in Frankfurt by Hans Hollein (Figure 1.3) continued the architect's challenge of the traditional museum:

> since sculpture has broken away from its pedestal, the picture has dispensed with its isolating frame and the installation (environment) has come to

Figure 1.3 Museum of Modern Art, Frankfurt

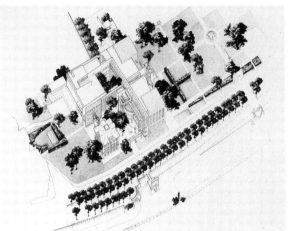

Figure 1.4 Museum of Decorative Arts, Frankfurt

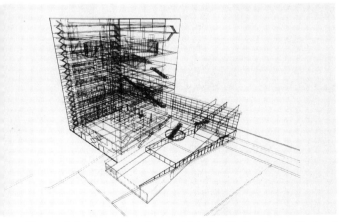

Figure 1.5 Centre for Art and Media Technology, Karlsruhe

13

represent a spatial totality which goes beyond an additive series of works and exists in a specific dialogue with the space containing it.

(Klotz 1991)

We now require museum presentation beyond linear or chronological enfilades – 'no artists, no museum'. One is reminded of the artist Robert Filliou walking the streets of Paris in 1962 with his 'museum in a hat', in order to show that the art museum (nineteenth-century version) had become completely unnecessary.

The architecture of the Frankfurt museum has its origins in Hollein's stated desire to create spaces within which contemporary artists feel that it is their art which is on display, and they can, if motivated, carry on a dialogue with the container. As regards the image, Hollein appears to have responded to the triangular site and its position as an entrance to the historical part of the city, near the old town wall and cathedral, through the use of materials evoking *gravitas* – red sandstone and render. This museum, as a triangular urban block, is expressive of modernity as process – researching and redefining gallery space, while at the same time responding in a distinctive yet compositional way to the urban texture of this part of Frankfurt.

By contrast, Richard Meier's Museum of Decorative Arts (Figure 1.4) engages the urban context by means of a two-dimensional grid, while not seeking *gravitas* through colour and material. Here the collection is domesticated within 'rooms' and precious items are placed in intimate niches. In recalling Frankfurt's intense programme of museum building, one is drawn to the conclusion that this new collection of museums is the new *image* of Frankfurt, and not any of the individual buildings. This new image is unquestionably one of expressive modernity and has revitalised the heart of Frankfurt, bringing people back to the city at weekends, along the River Main, the commercial district and old town.

The buildings read as built essays on the contemporary interpretation of modernism. Meier's interest in abstraction, Kleihues' search for texture and meaning, Behnisch's reinterpretation of organicism, Unger's primeval reductivism, Hollein's expressionism, Scheffler's tectonic classicism, or Peichl's and BJSS's monumentalism are late 20th century readings of different strands of the modern movement.

(Burdett 1991)

In Karlsruhe the project for the Centre for Art and Media Technology (ZKM) can be seen to crystallise a view of modernity as process and creative connectivity between two contemporary social facts, art and technology (Figure 1.5). In this centre, the element of debate, rather than the study of collections, is paramount and 'will have to pave new ground in terms of its substance and organisational structure' (Klotz 1991). By its very concept it will be experimental, both as a place and through its research in the collaboration of art and science. As a place, the visitor will inevitably be challenged as to his current opinions and views of the place of art and science in the contemporary world, but also will not necessarily find defined views as to what this contemporary world is or should be. The visitor will become part of the process of gaining insights and helping to anticipate the needs of the next century. In defining the programmatic concept for the centre, there is also a proposed Museum of Contemporary Art. This will focus more on traditional art as against media (ephemeral) art.

Heinrich Klotz (the appointed Director) puts forward his view:

> A Museum of Contemporary Art must consider the most recent phase of the history of artistic production over the last twenty to thirty years in its exhibitions and collections. Adjusting for the latest 'has beens' and the newest avant-garde implies a retrospective covering a short period. This comparison of styles and directions in the arts is an essential premise for setting up a collection. As soon as single pieces of venture art are recognised and become classics, they should no longer be exhibited and could be given to other state or municipal museums. It cannot be the objective of a Museum of Contemporary Art to earn itself a reputation by accumulating a collection of classics.
>
> (Klotz 1991)

The interpretation is one of creating spaces for temporary exhibits, hence the very strong need for the container to allow, and even encourage, change, whilst providing the servicing flexibility of such containers. When the media exhibition area, the media theatre, and the temporary contemporary art spaces are brought together in one building, together with experimental workshops, one begins to find a new definition of the contemporary art museum as one of an 'experimental stage – where presentation to the public is the ultimate proof of achievement' (Klotz 1991). In this project, the media content is both undefined in terms of scale and composition, it is ephemeral yet requires spaces that allow the contemporary expression of 'connected art and science' (Klotz 1991).

In designing this Museum of Contemporary Art, the architect Rem Koolhaas will be involved, as we saw through the projects in Frankfurt, in the process of modernity, but with the knowledge that as an experiment in itself the centre's container and image may well be dynamic. In this way it offers the possibility of being a 1990s witness to the evolution of a cultural architecture of change so powerfully stated by Renzo Piano and Richard Rogers at the Pompidou Centre in the 1970s.

> If the museum becomes the place where, without commercial pressure, one can obtain information about the world-wide developments of our own time, then the museum realises its most valuable function. I can say that culture consists of three pillars: art, science and spirituality. Bring all three into the museum and show the similarities of development within the different fields. Only then can the museum remain the temple of culture that we expect it to be.
>
> (Wijers 1991)

The reference to 'commercial pressures' is pertinent to this review of European museums. The desire, indeed the perceived need, to attract as many visitors as possible has revolutionised most museums. The days when they were frequented by the researcher, the odd school party and the Sunday family are very distant indeed. Today, clean shoes become trainers; the walking stick becomes the rucksack. This revolution has had a dramatic impact on the spatial programmes of museums, on the very nature of their organisation and indeed, in many instances, on the very role for which they were created. Most dramatic, perhaps, is the ability of these buildings simply to accommodate the flow of visitors and, from a marketing view, to hold them long enough (without boring them) to spend money at the book store and shops, but short enough to allow fresh visitors in.

For existing museums, accommodating all these visitors has meant extensions, remodelling, renovation and refurbishment. Entrance lobbies have become *Acceuils*, i.e. welcome halls to collect and distribute the visitors; cloakrooms have become 'hangers', preceded by security-check lines and the ticket desk; information centres and toilet facilities have assumed sizes normally associated with stadia. And all 'serious museums' boast their own restaurant, cafeteria, temporary exhibition galleries, lecture auditoria and conference facilities. And these, in turn, dancing to the market clock, are available out of hours for private use and city functions. Temporary exhibition space and marketing leads to greater transportation needs within the building: wider corridors, packaging and unpacking areas, transitory storerooms, increased media space and publications libraries. Truck parking, increased public access, and transitory artefacts lead to increased security arrangements and security accommodation. Security leads to more sophisticated technical installations, which lead to increased staff and maintenance costs. The upward spiral of complexity, of skilled management resources and, ultimately, of revenue to compete nationally and internationally, demands very serious and immediate appraisal. Such a revolution, in the last twenty or so years, if it continues, must lead to a certain level of saturation, and of cultural institutions becoming bankrupt or becoming public companies quoted on the stock exchanges of the world, and subject to the vagaries of such markets. Museums have become such big business that some of the larger ones are inevitably going to lose all sense of direction and of their intrinsic value.

In looking at Paris in particular, the phenomenal programme of museum growth has, at its roots, the recognition of Paris as a world city for tourism and as the centre of the French-speaking world. The financial investment in museum culture is seen as maintaining the former and as a witness to the vitality of France. Who would have thought that the largest abattoir in Europe, less than twenty years old, would become the largest science centre of the world (Figure 1.6). The competition, held in 1980 when Giscard d'Estang was President, included two interesting 'requirements'. One, overtly economic, was to keep the primary reinforced concrete and steel frame of the abattoir; and the other, more covert, was his request that visitors should not come to the centre in 'trainers'. Both are about conservation, the former economic, the latter social. This social conservation is partly a reaction to the populist approach of the Pompidou Centre and partly a desire to reinstate the classical status quo of high culture. However, with the socialist government, headed by President Mitterand, in

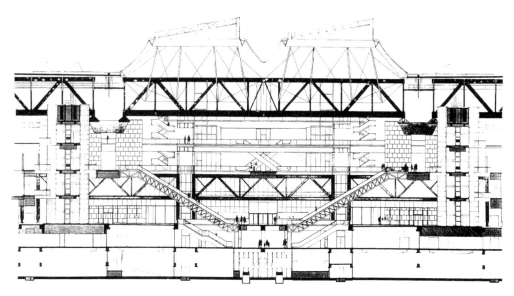

Figure 1.6 City for Science and Industry, La Villette, Paris

Figure 1.7 City for Science and Industry, La Villette, Paris

power throughout the rest of the 1980s, the social component became a desire to respond to the present in order to provide for the future.

Modernity had replaced historicism, not formally in the image of the museum, but in the desire to 'connect' the youth of France through schools and universities to the contents of the City for Science and Industry, and in particular the mediatheque. The permanent contents are arranged in four main sections: 'from earth to universe'; 'the adventure of life'; 'matter and the work of man'; and 'languages and communication'. These are supplemented by exhibition space for industry. To provide a visual reference point within this vast building (nearly 40,000 m^2) an enormous entrance hall of 100,000 m^3 was created, naturally lit by a translucent fabric roof and two 17 m diameter rotating domes (Figure 1.7). These domes, visible from the park and the surrounding urban landscape, together with the Geode and the three large bioclimatic facades, created the image of transformation.

President Mitterand, at the beginning of his first septennate in 1981, instigated the renovation and regeneration of the Louvre, and personally chose I. M. Pei as architect. More than any other architectural intervention since the Pompidou Centre, and more powerfully symbolic to many more people worldwide, has been the realisation of the 'Pyramid' at the Louvre (Figure 1.8). It represents the symbolic, luminous tip of the iceberg of a major restructuring of the Louvre Museum, concealing below ground 50,000 m^2 of new space. Moreover, the pyramid's political *image* belongs to all French people, despite stylistic controversy between historicists and modernists. At the time of the full-scale mock-up in Kevlar cable in 1985 (Figure 1.9), the 'symbolic message' remained largely subliminal. The mock-up would offer the opportunity for critics from all fields to realise exactly what was proposed for the Louvre's central urban stage and whether or not it was a viable proposition to celebrate the 200th anniversary of the Revolution, being placed in the very heart of pre-Revolution France (Louis XIV who began the Louvre as a palace and who stated that 'The State, it's me').

Two other Parisian projects are worth observing, both being conversions: one on a grand scale by Gae Aulenti, the Musée d'Orsay (Figure 1.10); the other more subtle and discreet, the Jeu de Paume by Antoine Stinco (Figure 1.11). A few years separate these two projects, but both are inextricably part of the French reinvestment in its cultural base. The Musée d'Orsay, a personal initiative by Giscard d'Estang, sought to rehouse together the French figurative arts of the eighteenth century in the nineteenth-century disused railway station. The Jeu de Paume, by contrast, creates for the first time in Paris a gallery for contemporary art, as against the Museum of Modern Art at the Pompidou Centre. These two projects, along with the Pompidou Centre, have physically manifested the Parisian rearrangement of its art collections; the Pompidou Centre being sourced from the Palais de Tokyo (Old Museum of Modern Art complex) now the Photography Museum, and the Musée d'Orsay emptying the Jeu de Paume of its Impressionist collection. The architect Stinco has created a series of studio *containers* at the Jeu de Paume, whose spatial neutrality is ambiguous in the

Figure 1.8 The Louvre, Paris: the Pyramid

Figure 1.9 The Louvre, Paris: Kevlar mock-up of the Pyramid

Figure 1.10 Musée d'Orsay, Paris

Figure 1.11 Le Jeu de Paume, Paris

Figure 1.12 Museum of Natural Science, Faenz, Italy

Figure 1.13 Centro de Arte Reina Sofia, Madrid

sense that he accepted that 'contemporary works of art are either totally incongruous or thoroughly traditional in appearance. Whenever you see contemporary works on show in places that weren't designed expressly for them, it is the space that comes across first' (Stinco 1991: 10).

The graphic signage of several of the new museums in Paris is the work of the graphic artist Jean Widmer, whose initial contribution in creating a 'corporate identity' at the Centre de Création Industrielle (CCI) helped establish in France the importance of the design discipline. His work is also seen at the Musée d'Orsay, Jeu de Paume, Institut du Monde Arabe, new National Music Conservatory at La Villette, and Pompidou Centre. Although not specific to content, container or image, graphic design crosses the boundaries of all three and has a significant impact on public perception of these cultural institutions.

In Italy, just north of Florence, there is the Contemporary Art Museum at Prato, not state-directed but developed on the initiative of an industrialist, Enrico Pecci, very much in the Prato tradition of private collectors donating to the city. This project, designed by Italo Gamberini, addresses the spatial questions of contemporary art, initially through the three key components of the brief: the museum/gallery; the CID (Centre of Information and Documentation on the visual arts, architecture and industrial design); and studios for artists to work at the museum. The museum/gallery container is conceived as a static structural grid of 12 m × 12 m, resulting in an interior space which is akin to an eighteenth-century enfilade, or suite of rooms. The intent at one level is the well-serviced industrial container, with regular top lighting capable of a degree of modification. The three components appear physically separated, arguably as a response to the site where an intersection of two important avenues occurs, and result in the creation of landscape spaces which influence subtly the rationalism of the structural grid design of the museum.

To the north-east, at Faenz, a delightful Museum of Natural Science to house the Domenico Malmerendi natural history collection has been realised in the solitude of one of the town's parks (Figure 1.12). It is a compact (36 m × 18 m), geometrically well-defined object, with no attempt at camouflage or historical pastiche. It sits calmly as a pavilion. However, the internal spaces surprise in the interesting rhythms, originating from the winding ramp giving access to the open central gallery, and from this to the side rooms. This image is modern, reminiscent of early modernist designs, that of simple geometric volumes, an understated formal composition and refined details. The inside of the apparent neutral container is, by contrast, dominated by primary-coloured vertical elements, showcases and screens, and is a rare example of exhibition space with no provision of zenithal light.

Carlo Scarpa's sensitive handling of the Castelvecchio Museum and Gae Aulenti's more modest refurbishment with Piero Castiglioni of the Palazzo Grassi both demonstrate a belief in the notion that old buildings are palimpsests upon which the contemporary architect makes his or her mark. Their approaches differ in the degree of sympathy each architect feels for the original, are undeniably contemporary and manifest some change from what was there, thus distinguishing those moments in history when social or economic need demanded architectural intervention.

New museums in Spain have largely been renovations of or additions to historical containers, or both. The diversity of design approaches reflects the prevalence of architectural pluralism, and the questioning of the functional and social role of museums. Spain has not yet undertaken the realisation of new museums on a scale comparable with that of France or Germany. Totally new museum buildings have been rare, such as Valencia's Museum of Modern Art and the Madrid City Museum, although several more are being advanced – Museum of Contemporary Art in Barcelona and the provincial museum of Leon. However, the investment programme has not been modest.

The Centro de Arte Reina Sofia (CARS), restructured from an eighteenth-century classically baroque general hospital in Madrid, compares in scale and cultural intent to that of the Pompidou Centre. Regarding the creation of a new *image*, the problem was publicly to overcome the immense solidity and history of the existing building. This was very successfully achieved by placing the main public vertical circulation (outside the main facade) in two transparent, yet structurally audacious glass towers (Figure 1.13). The design inspiration was drawn from Picasso's *Guernica*, and from a desire for lightness and minimalism in contrast to the *gravitas* of the existing building. Internally, the challenge was to create more exhibition space, and sufficient natural lighting and climate control within the rigid, yet sometimes elegantly proportioned structure of the building. The architects José-Luis Iñiguez de Onzoño and Antonio Vázquez de Castro achieved major structural and environmental improvements which are virtually invisible; in fact their whole internal architectural approach was minimalist, leaving vast white containers free for art and installations. A regret is the very limited public access to the generously proportioned landscaped courtyard, containing a magnificent Calder mobile.

A few hundred metres from CARS, and opposite the Prado, the industrialist Baron Thyssen and his wife have selected an early nineteenth-century classical palace, once a bank, to house their enormous art collection of some 700 paintings (Figure 1.14). They chose the Spanish architect Rafael Moneo to remodel the palace which opened in 1992 (Madrid's year as European City of Culture). The choice of site is significant, in that it may reveal part of the nature of Baron Thyssen. A new building was initially proposed in Lugano by the English architect James Stirling. The site then shifted to England (a Manchester Ship Canal site), and finally to the agreed site in Madrid's museum-mile. Here it benefits not only from a city population of 4 million (estimated 6 million by the year 2000), with a tourist influx of 40 million, but also from the fact that paintings in the proposed collection significantly 'compete' with the weaker areas of one of the world's great collections at the Prado (seventeenth-century Dutch and the twentieth century). However, according to Thyssen, at the end of ten years the paintings will become part of the national patrimony under current Spanish law.

Moneo's architecture is a stately modernism (cf. his architecture at the

Figure 1.14 Thyssen collection, Madrid

Figure 1.15 Roman Museum, Mérida, Spain

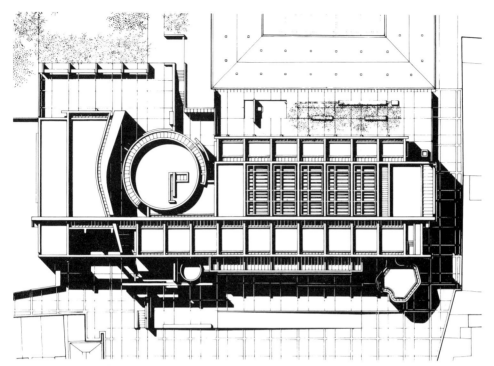

Figure 1.16 Museum of Contemporary Art, Barcelona

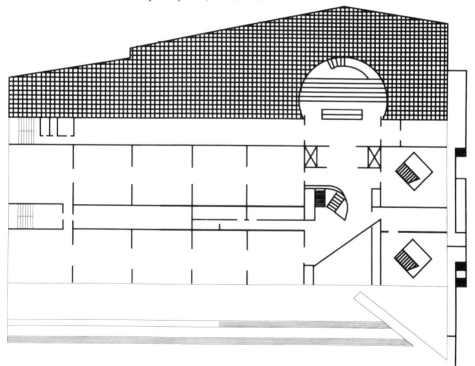

Figure 1.17 Institute of Modern Art, Valencia, Spain

remodelled Atocha Station at the end of the Castellana opposite CARS, and his Roman Museum at Mérida (Figure 1.15). In contrast to the 'neutrality' of most national and private galleries, Thyssen has made a significant and personal expression on the colour scheme of the *containers* – there is green (old masters), burnt sienna (modern) and red (for eighteenth and nineteenth centuries); this with his extraordinary collection and museum location suggests that it will prove hugely popular.

Barcelona is a 'city of Olympian projects', with architects of international stature designing them. Behind this resurgence of the Catalan capital is the city council and its dynamic Mayor, who is quoted as saying that 'the public facades of buildings and external spaces they create are the property of the citizen'. It is in this context that Richard Meier, on a site adjacent to the University and the Ramblas, is creating the Museum of Contemporary Art (Figure 1.16), but there will also be libraries, symposium centres, exhibition venues and other cultural institutions knitted into the existing fabric of the old quarter. True to form, Meier has produced a signature *image* for the MCA. It is organised on three main levels and a basement. On ground level there will be sculpture and industrial design – revealing the evolution of Catalan forms; on the first level there will be later twentieth-century avant-garde art; and on the naturally lit upper level, temporary exhibitions for works of living artists in more generously proportioned containers. The spatial architecture – white, shadows on white, solid and void – is Meier's oft-repeated formula for museums, whether in America or Germany, although there is a rigour to the rectilinear geometry of the medium-sized galleries at all levels, as against the 'rooms' in his Frankfurt museum. Its success will owe as much to its location as to the flow of the public spaces created through the museum, and the concentrated richness of the neighbouring cultural activities.

As mentioned, the new building, the Valencia Institute of Modern Art (IVAM), follows the late twentieth-century contemporary art museum typology of 'neutral' rectilinear containers with zenithal lighting where possible giving 'flexibility' to the display of the works of art (Figure 1.17). There are many more provincial museum projects completed and proposed in Spain for art, archaeology, and for science and technology (Cataluña's Generalitats' museum network dedicated to science, technology, industry and labour, and the Caixa de Pensions' Museum of Science in Barcelona) which, through technological gadgetry, are very popular with children. However, there is a lingering feeling that in Spain the museum phenomenon, particularly in the world of art, is possibly over-ambitious, leaving the question of the contents, their acquisition, display and management, to be more fully resolved.

Returning to England, three London museums, the Sainsbury Wing at the National Gallery (Venturi Scott Brown & Associates), the Sackler Galleries at the Royal Academy (Foster Associates) and the temporary Ecology Gallery at the Natural History Museum (Ian Ritchie Architects), have made differing architectural and museological statements, all financed privately. There is no major government commitment to new museums in Britain.

Venturi, at the press opening, said of his architecture that 'it would be hard to take for both classicists and modernists' (Figure 1.18). It has received enormous press exposure, being published in all the main national, architectural and art magazines. Internally, through an enfilade of rooms, all of neutral grey colour (the Gallery Director's wishes), naturally lit by the 'token daylight' (Venturi) inspired by Soane's Dulwich Picture Gallery (plus balance by artificial lighting), it provides containers for viewing a superb collection of early Renaissance paintings. The architecture of the containers is so subtle as to be almost absent to the average visitor – in Venturi's words 'their symbolism refers to the kind of spaces the painters were painting for Tuscan fifteenth-century palaces'. The result is a marked disassociation of the container from the contents, as if the container were attempting to camouflage itself. This is not the case with Soane's Dulwich Gallery, where the spatial pleasure is in harmony with the contents. The external image of the Sainsbury Wing has been much criticised at many levels, not least the imposition of a philosophical programme based on a personal reinterpretation of classicism, and an imposition of an intellectual symbolism. There is a strange banality and inelegance of the extension seen against the National Gallery, and for me there remains no enjoyment from the architecture, internally or externally, but a lot of pleasure in seeing the qualities in the paintings.

At the Sackler Galleries, Foster Associates have achieved the renovation of the old top-floor studios of Burlington House by an astute exploitation of the vertical space of a small, naturally ventilated void at the back of Burlington House and the later main Royal Academy galleries (Figure 1.19). The success of the project lies in the 'route': the vertical ride in the lift from the low-light levels at ground floor to the generous diffusion of natural light at the new gallery level. This offers a short but welcome moment of contemplation of space and time. The modest-sized galleries, barrel-vaulted, are almost 'neutral', the plastered white walls and pale wood flooring suggesting that the contents of most traditional art collections would be at home here. The zenithal light coming through the generous rooflights is not as calm as one would wish, owing to the continuously adjusting and somewhat noisy light-control louvres, which with the narrow linear air-conditioning slots disturb the initial impression of serenity.

Finally, at the Natural History Museum, the Ecology Gallery has, through its intended aim of challenging 'ecological preconceptions' and knowledge, attempted both to give a factual base to the essence of ecology as well as to provide an exhibition to encourage debate (Figure 1.20). The controversial design of the exhibition container is daringly contemporary, and creates another image within the magnificent romanesque building. This image, a spectacular asymmetric glass chasm crossed by four bridges, is also a symbolic element of the exhibition content. The glass enclosure, as exhibition route, attempts to cross the conventional boundaries of image, container and contents, whilst permitting the more programmatic contents the 'privacy' and 'individuality' to convey the detailed messages of ecology in a sequential manner.

In conclusion, from this short architectural review, I hope to have illustrated the

Figure 1.18 Sainsbury Wing, the National Gallery, London

Figure 1.19 Sackler Galleries, Royal Academy, London

Figure 1.20 The Ecology Gallery, the Natural History Museum, London

plurality of proposals prevalent in European museum design during the last few years.

In art, the 1960s artists left the museums – the avant-garde (minimalists, land and conceptual artists), who pronounced museums as art graveyards, have been followed by a museum resurgence through the heightened commercialisation of art in the 1980s. This has challenged architects to redefine, for their own time, the character of the container, between specific and generic space, or expressive and neutral galleries. When the content is known, the design of the container has a starting point, and architects can vary their bias towards or away from the content's influence as a means of creating not only the container's relationship to the content, but also the museum's character. When the content is unknown, or there is no collection as such, the tendency is towards the notion of the 'workshop', whether within a repainted factory space (e.g. the Saatchi Gallery in London), or a new container for experimentation (ZKM). Each generation of designers must determine its own solutions to the architectural space, both externally and internally, which is ideal for the presentation of the art, science and technology and issues of its own time.

This is in the spirit of modernity, which is at the very core of western civilisation, the research without preconceived formulas or stylistic prejudices; the creation of the most appropriate solutions to improve our understanding of ourselves and our environment.

References

Burdett, R. (1991) *Architecture of the Public Realm*, London: Architecture Foundation.
Klotz, H. (1991) 'Zentrum für Kunst und Medientechnologie, Karlsruhe', Statement, reprinted paper, London: Royal Academy of Arts.
Stinco, A. (1991) Interview in *Architecture d'Aujourd'hui*, September.
Wijers, L. (1991) Paper presented at the Third Annual Academy Forum, Royal Academy of Arts, London.

2

Some general thoughts on corporate museum identity: the case of the Villa Arson, Nice[1]

Ruedi Baur, Pippo Lionni and Christian Bernard

The brief and its requirements

A retrospective view of the situation by Christian Bernard who commissioned the visual identity programme

When I came to the Villa Arson there were basically two fundamental objectives: the first was the unification of all the activities that took place in the institution. This unification was carried out at all levels and I feel that the graphic treatment provided the framework within which everything was tied together. We've established a visual identity side by side with a financial management system: we tackled everything together. The graphics made 'visual' all that we were doing. Its primary role was to represent for us our own immediate, pragmatic, short-term goals. The second objective was to create a 'concept' for the Villa Arson: this would be a product of the process outlined above. At the outset the graphic designer had to identify something rather vague. He then had to find a graphic image which would provide the imaginary space or enclosure for the myth that I wanted to create. This was the point where we really had to plan and work out our ideas.

At the third stage we had to ensure that the planning of artistic events had its own rationale and ethic.[2] I had to have therefore an identity ready to hand which would be a kind of 'space–time' enclosure for the project and its development. I needed a fairly strong identity that would continually attract attention. It is, after all, only the next page of the same book and not a completely different book.

And a final point: we have a remarkable building, not particularly well known, which needed an image as abstract as possible yet in harmony with the architecture.

How it operates – the basis of the brief

It was a question of providing the Villa Arson with a working tool that would allow us to produce, if necessary with the later involvement of other graphic designers, all the communication elements necessary for the running of the organisation,[3] together with the marketing and publicity for exhibitions and other activities (Figures 2.1–2.3). Our contribution was limited to the presentation of the concept and the way it was to be used for each element.

The approach adopted

Rather than set out all the necessary visual constraints in a manual which said what you can't do, we have chosen, on the other hand, to set out the limits which define the spaces where there are no visual constraints.[4] We did not say 'This is what you can't do', but rather we defined a framework within which one can work. This framework is at the same time the corporate identity, the point of departure and the grid from which the Villa Arson could project an image specific to each exhibition and which would respond as closely as possible to the sensibility of the artist. Because they are structural, the elements of our identity are not felt to be obstacles; rather, they are creative tools. The typography, although it's everywhere present, is straightforward, and is standardised throughout.[5] It is part and parcel of our identity and is a creative tool for use as the context requires it. It does not play a part in the visual character of each exhibition. Colour, on the other hand, is one of the important variables and is therefore a means of expression specific to each event.

Corporate identity and the functioning of a contemporary art centre

CB: I want to emphasise the point that visual identity is not solely a means for communicating to the outside world. It's something in use here every day, creating a sense of belonging, of involvement and collective identity. I'm well aware that the house style has imposed a certain discipline. There are some things we cannot do with it; its function is to control, to regulate, to standardise. It's even a way of looking at the Villa Arson itself; and because it resembled the Villa Arson in many respects, it even had affinities with the institutional structure of the Villa Arson. Finally, I was aware that, as we went along, we adapted more and more to our house style: there was an interactive effect.

In spite of the abstract nature of corporate identity, I'm convinced that people who have received our catalogues, posters and packaging over the years and who come here for the first time, will discover that our visual identity will have prepared them for their first response to the building; less a case of 'So this is it?' than 'Of course, this is it!' This doesn't mean to say that there's a reflex action, but rather something very much like it. And whenever I present my business card, people see something else besides my name, they receive an image of the whole enterprise. I feel that this small bit of card encapsulates an enormous information network.

We've also used the house style in the computerised production of catalogues

Figure 2.1 Invitation card, Villa Arson, Nice, France

Figure 2.2 Reverse of invitation card, Villa Arson, Nice, France

Figure 2.3 Exhibition poster, Villa Arson, Nice, France

and other material, and at the same time, we've adopted certain guidelines covering the layout of correspondence. Thus, all the staff at the Villa Arson are involved daily with the implementation of the house style, not just a graphic designer who occasionally sends us something from his studio. Everyone – secretaries, typists, ancillary staff – needs to be aware of the house style. This immediately ensures that in their daily work, a bond is created between people that cuts across the usual boundaries. From the point of view of management, there's no doubt that this improves teamwork. When I came here I thought that all that was needed to identify an institution was to have a good image and stick with it; I never previously suspected the importance it was to have in organising our ideas, creating a collective spirit and identity at the heart of the organisation.

Identity – of the curator or institution

CB: I don't know how to explain why, at any given moment, a visual identity appears to cling so well to an object. It's true that, as the first to use our corporate identity, I felt that it attached itself naturally to the establishment and my planning objectives. In any event I was already convinced of the need and that it provided a kind of emotional support.

It's true that I've asked myself the question: 'If I went somewhere else, would I take the graphic identity with me?' The answer was 'no', yet at the same time the kind of work I might be doing elsewhere would have much in common with what I have developed here, and thus with its identity. So there'd be some point in taking it with me. But, in fact, I find that this visual tool becomes more and more inseparable from the entity, that is, the building, the locale and the people who work in it. When the time comes for someone else to take over, it's important that the house style is not changed overnight. In using it he would find plenty of advantages and possibilities that he could develop in his own way.[6] In France, particularly where an institution has recently been established, it's common to see new management taking over, changing the staff and the corporate identity even when these are already doing a good job.[7]

Graphic identity and flexible planning

Starting from the same point of departure, we should be able to use the house style to express very different aesthetic and artistic experiences. It is the constancy of that point of departure that matters and not the metamorphosis of the subject. The visual identity favours encounters between mutually antagonistic objects, which, juxtaposed in any other context, would not be perceived in the same way. Now, what interests me at any given moment is to show that there are questions that the artist tries to tackle, and, no matter how they are posed, these questions multiply, superimpose and cut across one another.

Graphic identity and interior space

One of the problems that affects the unity of image, place and programme is that the interior architectural space is rarely worked out in relation to the identity of the place. Any plan to devise an identity, even if it manages to get through the front door of the museum, might get as far as the directional signs, whereas it should really extend to the captions and to all the other elements that contribute to the protection of works, to the display cases, seating and lighting. We've got to be able to anticipate the totality of aesthetic and functional experiences in the context of identity and relate these experiences to the idea of visual communication.

Graphic identity, architecture and museography

CB: At the Villa Arson we have to think very carefully about what the building itself will allow us to do, about what will best harmonise with the building; in other words, we should not do anything that will compromise the architecture. There are probably some works which we wouldn't think of displaying because they just wouldn't work here. Conversely, some things obviously work here which we wouldn't try elsewhere. So, for a building as special as this, we had to produce, as I've said, a graphic identity, an image which is as abstract as possible yet which respects the architecture. When you live with this house style, when I look at my letterhead, for example, it's almost as though I'm seeing a photo of the Villa Arson. Our identity thus works in two ways: functionally and as a means of looking at the Villa Arson itself.

A building implies a whole range of qualities and constraints, as does a house style and a museographic programme. Everything has to pull together. Architecture, environment, context and site – all have hidden potential when it comes to the visual identity of a museum. When the graphic identity is based on some notable architectural and urban feature, that aspect of the identity which does not change will be more easily perceived because the image received beyond the museum and that received on the spot will reflect each other. However, if the architectural statement makes no reference to the museographic function, or does so as an afterthought, this contradiction will be likewise carried over into the identity. The architect must be aware that his contribution is an integral part both of the way the building works and of its identity. In the same way, the graphic designer who creates an information and visual recognition programme should know how to make the building reveal its museographic intentions. And he should be modest enough to do more than just create the image; he's also got to help to make it work.

I think that the main difference between the concept of identity – whether 'graphic', or even three-dimensional – and architecture resides in the fact that for architecture each new stone added is part of something which you're building up as you go along and which you can't change. Identity is something that's mobile, variable, and has its own rules, while for architecture, you're setting in stone, you're constructing more than a container, you're constructing pure and simple. How do you get to the point where this entity can be at the same time a place for creative activity, a place which, while neutral, will accept change, a place with some kind of ambience yet which remains unpretentious?

Many of the things about art that interest me are those that react with the already existing and not the things that present new conditions of existence. So I have difficulty in imagining what would be the most appropriate kind of architecture for this. If I had twenty-five or forty paintings to hang I would be able to imagine the walls around them. But that's not the kind of museum I want to create.

If I hang a Mondrian in Le Corbusier's Villa Savoye, I suspect that the Villa Savoye would overpower the painting itself. Even though I love Mondrian's work, the Villa presents another dimension. As a seminal work encapsulating the modern idea of beauty, the Villa establishes a model which will endure for some time. There is this difference of degree between that which is great architecture and that which architecture can bring into play in the twentieth century. It's true that twentieth-century art is often happier in nineteenth-century than in twentieth-century buildings. Only a supreme piece of twentieth-century architecture would be able to rise above artistic forms.[10]

But there is another side to this. Architecture is necessarily concerned with the townscape, while the kind of museum I'm talking about is more concerned with the space it encloses. I'm very conscious of this when I'm in the gallery here: you can see the town from some of the rooms yet, in spite of this, you can concentrate on the art and there's no conflict. But this does not mean you've got to be systematic about it. It's a good way of handling the problem. The Pompidou Centre, in its early days, was the antithesis of this. You were always aware of an ambiguous relation created by the interface between the work of art and the city on the outside. Most of the time the architect is concerned with the relationship with the immediate townscape. My kind of museum is concerned, above all, with the objects in it and the conditions that present them to best advantage. This has little to do, directly, with the town on the outside.[11]

Notes

1 A contemporary art centre and school with artists in residence, housed in a 1960s building overlooking Nice.

2 This is based on two premises: an art centre doesn't have collections in the conventional sense; so an art centre has to be a 'collection' of experiments and souvenirs. It is a 'theatre of the memory'. And it's also an exhibition which develops in time, in both a continuous and discontinuous manner: this is where 'memory' comes in. And so, what I call the logic of the programme arises from an ordering process which is not just chronological but a kind of spiral movement in the artistic domain; this is a part of what lies in the future and of which I am not yet aware. It repeats and restates those things on which I base my love for, and my thoughts about, art. What I also refer to as the ethical dimension arises from the fact that we ourselves produce most of what we show here, that is, we work with the artists and not with middlemen, working

rigorously with our own resources in well-defined conditions. Artists come here, live here, work and create here. That is to say, two-thirds of what is shown here has been conceived and made here for exhibition here.

3 Administrative paperwork, signs, labelling and particularly posters, information leaflets, invitations and exhibition catalogues.

4 Every item in (3) has a border of constant width. This border is both the symbolic definition of the creative space of the Villa Arson itself, and its identity. The logo and the typography are tied together and controlled by the grid.

5 Helvetica bold, positioned according to the grid.

6 The fact that the identity of the Villa Arson is based on parameters that allow a certain freedom, means that a new curator could probably develop a different visual specificity within the existing identity, without appearing to follow in his predecessor's footsteps.

7 *Ruedi Baur and Pippo Lionni*: there's an important question here for the designer who's in a position to design a visual identity for a cultural institution. In working out some ideas, should he refer solely to the place (i.e. the architecture and the immediate environment) or should he take into account the cultural objectives of the curators? This is particularly relevant in medium-size institutions where a forceful personality or team can have a profound influence on policy.

Should the identity be understated and appear sufficiently neutral so that it will work with any policy objective, or should it, on the other hand, be concerned, in the medium term, with the existing programme? The solution probably lies in an identity that is adaptable at three levels: a strong recognisable image which relates to those aspects of the place that do not change; a 'second-level' of identification relating to medium-term objectives; and lastly a 'third-level' relating to a particular activity. The separation of these visual pointers should allow the essential link between the various elements to be apparent irrespective of change; it should also allow for the expression of any particular objective. Significant architecture, a situation or a specific environment can all reinforce the idea of three levels of 'identity' through graphic treatment.

8 There can be no other building in the world quite like the Villa Arson in its complexity and in its commitment to art. We have here 17,000 m^2 devoted to art. It's a place for exhibition, a place for the making of art, a place for teaching, and a theatre. It's not actually a functional building even when we consider it in the context of modern culture which, generally speaking, is that of brutalism. Moreover, it's a building which harks back to Mediterranean architectural themes, from Babylon by way of Egypt, Crete, Greece and the Maghreb . . . it's not postmodern but rather 'pre-postmodern', a whole mix of historical, aesthetic and architectural motifs. It's often felt to be too complex, too difficult to 'read', and for this reason I believe that the house style brings out all the characteristics of the building: terraces, barriers, verticals, pillars, decks, etc.

9 From the point of view of art, the most responsive buildings are *not* the purpose-built museums. In many cases where an architect designs a building, art does not come into it. It's quite evident that during the 1980s, throughout Germany for example, architects designed museums primarily for themselves and for political reasons. These were political statements in the context of the city, for the benefit of politicians and collectors, and certainly not for art. There are few examples where the architect has placed himself at the service of the museum. We've got to find architects with a genuine love of art, and who don't simply want to make an architectural statement.

10 The purpose-built museum is something quite recent, a nineteenth-century concept. An architectural form for the museum, developed in the nineteenth century, hardly differed from any other public building. They were not necessarily monumental buildings: there's not much difference, from the outside, between a museum and a *préfecture*. On the other hand, once inside the museum, all is lucidity and clarity, there's hardly anything else you can compare it with. It's a very functional model that works very well, even for contemporary art. That is to say, if you look at Richard Serra's work at Baden Baden, it works very well even though it is a nineteenth-century museum. Like any other architectural form, it won't last for ever but at the moment it is holding its

own. Architects have become innovators, which was certainly not the case with most of the architects of nineteenth-century museums. And they have become innovators who want to promote a certain kind of architecture whether or not it met the needs of a museographic programme. Indeed, the very idea of a museographic programme is only about twenty years old. Museology is a recent science. It's only in the past few years that museums have given some thought to the way they function so it's difficult to come to firm conclusions. Certainly there are distinguished architects who wanted their names to be associated with great museums, but they still all want to make the great architectural statement.

11 Most of the objects I'm talking about and with which I work are objects outside the domain of everyday experience, objects which sharpen our view of reality, throwing into relief objects in the real world. These objects are thus located on the periphery defined by the architecture, which is of necessity a construction in the domain of the 'real'. And this is just the challenge I would want any publicly commissioned work to meet: what I would want art to do is to have it mimic architecture, that is, to have an authoritative presence in the world.

3

Aims, strengths and weaknesses of the European science centre movement

Melanie Quin

Origins

Despite their considerable variety, interactive science-technology centres share two essential characteristics: their emphasis is contemporary rather than historic; the majority (in some cases 100 per cent) of their exhibits are specially constructed, interactive devices which encourage visitors to investigate natural phenomena and experiment with technology.

Fragments of the interactive approach have existed in major museums since early this century: the handles and buttons in the Science Museum Children's Gallery (opened in 1931, London); the chemical demonstrations at the Palais de la Découverte (1937, Paris); and industrial engines, in action, at the Deutsches Museum (1925, Munich).

For those at school in England in the 1960s, whether as pupils or teachers, the interactive approach will also be familiar from Nuffield science. They, and others, may also have visited Philips' Evoluon exhibition in Eindhoven before it was finally closed in 1990.

The London and Deutsches Museums inspired Frank Oppenheimer. But the Exploratorium he founded in San Francisco in 1969 – and the Ontario Science Centre that opened in Toronto also in 1969 – were the first of a completely new kind of institution with a truly hands-on approach to exhibition/education. Their examples have provided the catalyst for many groups throughout the world that have since produced demonstrations and exhibits with an open-ended outcome dependent on the visitors' input.

The growth in number and popularity of interactive science-technology exhibitions in Europe is one of the success stories of the last decade: the number in Britain alone jumped from four in 1987 to sixteen at the time of writing. The Nuffield Foundation established a three-year, in-house project (the Interactive Science and Technology Project) in October 1987 to help the development of interactive exhibitions – by providing a focus for information exchange both in the UK and internationally – and to promote the development of 'hands-on' ideas and methods. The Nuffield project served as a resource for the science centres and, building a strong network of contacts stretching from the BBC and

British Association to science centres worldwide, itself served as a launch pad, in 1989, for ECSITE – the European Collaborative for Science, Industry and Technology Exhibitions.

The science centre movement of this chapter's title is, however, greater than the sum of its constituent institutions. As the cycle of development comes full circle, historic museums are themselves drawing on the experiences of the new interactive centres, and the flavour of interactivity is pervading the formal education system. The foundation of ECSITE thus reflects on the one hand a mushrooming of new institutions, and on the other hand a growing interest in a new medium of science communication. The pan-European Collaborative embraces science centres and museums committed to the interactive approach in their exhibitions, and also individual science teachers, researchers and designers.

It has been my good fortune, first while running the Nuffield Foundation's Interactive Science and Technology Project, and more recently as Director of ECSITE, to visit a large number of science centres and to talk to an even larger number of inspirational people. My intention, therefore, is to present not a formal evaluation of the science centre movement – the field is evolving so rapidly that such an attempt would at best be out of date by publication day – but verbal snapshots: the visions of individuals, the mission statements and success stories that are shaping the movement's evolution. Most of the quotations appearing in this chapter are therefore personal communications, recorded during interviews with various policy-shapers behind the European science centre movement. Two case studies are presented for two very different institutions; and some pointers offered to the questions of 'where?' and 'what next?' for the movement as a whole.

Invitation to participate

The new interpretative medium

Science centres the world over share the aim of increasing public understanding of science, but their precise 'mission statements' vary. And whilst all include interactive devices in their exhibitions, the design style of each centre and its programme of educational activities and special events are finely tuned to the country's culture and to the needs of the local community.

On a wet Sunday, the family group on a casual visit may be looking for an alternative to the cinema. They are unlikely to be searching for the meaning of Life, the Universe and Everything. And yet, however subtly, they are influenced by the science centre's mission statement since this affects both its contents – from tutti-frutti amalgam to thematic structure – and design style. The extreme design types might, pejoratively, be labelled: 'scientist's workshop', 'technological trade fair', 'historical storehouse', 'adventure playground'. The popularity of interactive exhibitions attests to their designers' ability to mix elements of these four, to animate them with events and activities and to create a stimulating experience in visitor-friendly surroundings.

Snapshots

In vox pop interviews, respondents frequently identify art, literature, music, cinema and sport as the facets of our culture. Yet, despite daily contact with electric lights, gas boilers, microwave ovens, cars, telephones, televisions and hi-fi equipment, science and technology are rarely included in the list. As a result, a common mission statement for science centres is 'to alter the general public's perception of science'.

Peter Briggs, Director of the British Association for the Advancement of Science, summarizes the rationale as follows:

> Living confidently with the 'appliances of science'; decision making in a society where most issues have a scientific or technological dimension; making choices about personal lifestyles; increasing job prospects; improving the health and prosperity of the nation – all these and more are advanced as reasons why better understanding of science is needed in our society. . . . Promoting public understanding of science has, in effect, become a good cause in the world of science and one with which many different groups can identify.

Roger Lesgards – past President of the massive City for Science and Industry in Paris, and President of ECSITE (1990–2) – affirms that science is not a natural subject for exhibitions, but that modern science centres can effectively translate and mediate science for the lay public. Implicit in his opening question is his mission for the City for Science and Industry:

> How can one ensure that scientific museums provoke joy, dreams and emotions, but at the same time promote the desire to go 'back to the sources' of science, to reasoning, to rigorous approaches, to knowledge, and to the research method? This is no simple matter, particularly in our time. We live in a period of the history of humanity where science has covered immense tracts of knowledge, moving towards the infinitely large, the infinitely small and the infinitely complex. Scientific research today is focused on the observation of chaotic, unpredictable and discontinuous phenomena. And each area of research requires extreme specialisation, access to which is limited to the specialists alone. At the same time, multi-disciplinarity, the interlinking of scientific disciplines and systematic approaches, becomes indispensable. Hence scientific museums, which must reflect this situation, are condemned paradoxically to becoming both increasingly ambitious and increasingly modest in their aims.

> [Two ambitions extend the museum's mission beyond the walls of the exhibition.] Firstly, a scientific museum should be designed as an element

within a wider geographical context, as a place within a regional, national or international network. By creating an intermeshing of establishments, exchanging information with one another, the resources of each will be enhanced. Secondly, a scientific museum is a springboard for various initiatives which should go beyond the exhibition field and bring into play as wide a range as possible of other media: books, magazine articles, television broadcasts, films, video cassettes, educational toys and games, debates, conferences, seminars, career presentations, theatre, music, the plastic arts. . . . Science, in order to be understood in all its strength and relativity, can only benefit from being seen in a variety of lights.

Ian Russell, UK interactive-interpretation consultant, eloquently expresses the opinion of many individual science centre staff:

It would be wonderful if every single visitor emerged into the daylight an hour or two later with a totally altered world view, a life-changing passion for science, a profound understanding of the nature and process of scientific discovery, and a detailed factual knowledge of science, say to level-10 in Britain's National Curriculum (i.e., the top level, achievable by a clever minority of 16-year-olds).

Although undeniably worthy and desirable, these are not practical things for us to aim for. An hour or two is not a large proportion of a person's lifetime educational intake.

Motivation is a good, practical, educational starting point. Interactive centres have proved to be overwhelmingly effective in this. Following group visits, sensitive primary-school teachers have been staggered by the clamorous interest and frantic activity on returning to the classroom. Parents have reported similar excitement and follow-up experimentation on the part of their children. Interactive centre staff commonly overhear youngsters muttering: 'I'm going to be a scientist when I grow up!' Such motivation frequently seems to extend considerably beyond the brief duration of a visit in ways that must have a major positive influence on subsequent education. Motivation is proving to be a supremely cost-effective objective.

Wonder, curiosity, interest, eagerness to learn, intellectual self-confidence, 'liking science' and 'wanting to become a scientist' are all palpably real and important. One suspects that they are seldom stated as formal educational objectives because they are so difficult to assess and quantify.

The aims of the European science centre movement can thus be set in the context of growing concern with public awareness of science. In the USA this is labelled 'science literacy'. But in France it bears the considerably more appealing title of 'culture scientifique', encompassing the whole realm of scientific appreciation as well as the 'learning' and 'understanding' commonly associated with formal science education.

A cresting wave

Vigour

First and foremost, yet often taken for granted within the growing community of science centre professionals, is the very fact of its vigorous growth and the enthusiasm with which exhibitions are welcomed. The following comments have all been recorded in the TECHNIQUEST visitors' book:

'It's brilliant – much better than a museum – because you can touch everything'

(Kelly, aged 10)

'I'm enjoying myself so much, I must come back without the children'

(Grandmother)

'My pupils got a tremendous amount out of it, even children who get bored easily have thoroughly enjoyed themselves'

(Comprehensive school headmaster)

'A marvellous place for all the family to play and learn together'

(Mother)

Science is on the road in the UK and in Spain, and ECSITE (see below) is planning a European science circus. La Carpa de la Ciència set off from Barcelona's Museu de la Ciència at the end of 1990, taking exhibits from the science centre itself round the country in a 542 m² relocatable octagonal structure. There are 'hands-on' experiments and classic museum pieces such as a Foucault pendulum and 80,000-volt electrostatic generator. The idea is to take the participatory style to people who, for geographic reasons, are unlikely to visit the Museu de la Ciència. The enthusiasm emanating from Barcelona (where Spain's first science centre opened in 1980) has fuelled developments nation-wide: Casa de la Ciències opened in La Coruña in 1985, Acciona in Madrid in 1993, and a major project is under way in Valencia.

The proliferation of science centres in the UK is largely attributable to the catalytic effect of the Discovery Dome. Travelling since summer 1988 from Orkney to sites in Belfast, Cornwall and Cambridge, the geodesic tented exhibition has introduced families, school groups (and even TV viewers, through the Big Top Science BBC programmes) to optics, mechanics, meteorology and more, through engaging 'hands-on' exhibits.

Heritage

This affects on three levels: the historical heritage of European history; the heritage of the North American science centre experience; and the influence of the encyclopaedic curricula common to continental European schools.

Europe's rich cultural heritage finds physical expression in the historical collections of its science museums. The Deutsches Museum, Munich, for example, covers the development of science and technology from its origins to the present day, and sets out to present the great inventions and results of research against a general background of the history of civilisation, and to explain their significance and effects. The scope is vast, embracing most fields of technology and aspects of natural science from mining to astrophysics. Besides historical artefacts – among them some valuable originals such as the first motor car and first diesel engine – the museum offers over 1,000 models, experiments and demonstrations that the visitor can operate by hand or by pressing a button.

For such a museum, interactive exhibits offer a new communication medium for interpreting their collections to a public that is ever more media-sophisticated. At the Greater Manchester Museum of Science and Industry, the involvement of visitors with interactive exhibits in the Xperiment! gallery is a natural extension of the policy of operating historic machinery on a large scale, and of the education department's work in the use of hands-on activities such as calico printing, paper making and the operation of electrical apparatus in classes linked to gallery visits.

Even the dwarf sees a long way, standing on the shoulders of a giant. The experience of North American science centres, accumulated since the early 1970s, has provided invaluable guidance to the good, the bad and the potential pitfalls. It is almost *de rigueur* for the senior staff of new science centre projects to make a grand tour of major US institutions. The clear gain is an accelerated learning curve. The flip side, for the European movement as a whole, is the consequent cloning syndrome – the copying, without question, of exhibits that are known to work with American visitors. In publishing three excellent *Cookbooks*, the Exploratorium in San Francisco has a lot to answer for. The *Cookbooks* give detailed exhibit recipe plans, and hence both confidence and know-how for setting up an interactive exhibition. Yet this also gives a 'sameness' to the exhibitions. 'See the Light' at the New York Hall of Science, is almost identical to 'La lumière démasquée' at the City for Science and Industry, Paris, and both are polished versions of about eighty exhibits first developed at the Exploratorium – exhibits that are also found in science centres large and small around the world, their details refined to conform with the institution's house style.

Formulated by Aristotle and legitimised by the Catholic Church is the theory (in a nutshell) that a good general education can be provided through seven 'liberal arts': grammar, logic and rhetoric, arithmetic, geometry, music, astronomy. This theory became enshrined in the highly specialised curricula of schools in England and Wales (not supplanted by the broad encyclopaedic National Curriculum till 1989).

The most widely accepted alternative theory, advanced by eighteenth-century French social and educational reformers, suggests that *all* knowledge should be included in the school curriculum. The explosion of scientific knowledge over the last 200 years and the development of mass communications have undoubtedly created problems for knowledge-based encyclopaedic curricula, but the commitment to a broad approach remains.

As a result, 'science' means physics – perhaps supplemented with some technology, chemistry and biology – in English-speaking countries. And exhibition contents reflect this interpretation. However, in continental Europe the definition is much broader, and it comes as no surprise to local visitors to find natural history and earth science at the Museu de la Ciència in Barcelona, to find anthropology and political history at Museon, Den Haag, or linguistics and archaeology at Heureka, Vantaa.

Heritage gives the European science centre movement a potential for cultural richness greater than that in North America. Developing science centres in Latin America and Asia share the European potential.

Networking

ECSITE (the European Collaborative for Science, Industry and Technology Exhibitions) was founded on the initiative of the City for Science and Industry, Paris, with the support of a launching grant from the Nuffield Foundation, a major British charitable trust. ECSITE members are European science centres and museums whose exhibitions present science to the public through a combination of traditional displays and interactive exhibits.

The only equivalent organisation – the (American) Association of Science-Technology Centers – is based in Washington DC, and was established in 1973. However, by 1989, twenty-three European institutions felt the time had come to concentrate on the specific needs and interests of European exhibitions, rather than looking across the Atlantic for guidance and co-ordination.

The role of ECSITE is therefore to facilitate and co-ordinate members' activities, particularly by means of developing multilingual travelling exhibitions. The Collaborative offers a unique information network and a focus for European initiatives to raise public understanding of science, industry and technology.

In January 1991, the Collaborative was constituted as a non-profit-making international organisation of scientific purpose. ECSITE is governed by Belgian law and its registered office is hosted by the Belgian Minister for Science Policy. The executive office was first hosted by Heureka, the Finnish Science Centre, and now by the Museum of Science, Barcelona.

The volume of correspondence, by mail and FAX, and the busy telephone line bear witness to the dynamism of an expanding community of science centre professionals. A ripple of innovation is spreading, via ECSITE's associate members, to institutions as widely spread as India, New Zealand, Korea and Canada, and to individuals representing the full range from exhibition product manufacturers, to curators of historic collections, to professors of science education.

Insecurity and self-doubt

Managerial style

Every country in Europe has its own business culture, with its own ideas about management, structure, roles and organisational behaviour. The stereotypes contain as much accurate observation as caricature: the British proceed sequentially, while the Italians do everything at once and all speak at once. The French have reached a decision if the senior person present doesn't disagree with the thrust of a meeting; the Germans only believe a decision has been made when someone authoritative stands up and says so. But underlying such national variations are organisational issues particular to interactive science centres.

The key people in the development of a new science centre are inspirational, with the vision, charisma and determination essential to get the project off the drawing board. Yet such missionary figures are by nature transient, and the science centre must make the transition from project phase to operation, and must face the regular problems of any business: accountancy, staffing, premises, marketing, and R&D costs.

The issue of 'Explainers' serves as an example. 'Helpers', 'Pilots', 'Hosts', 'Guides' – the variety of names provides a clue to their subtly different roles in different science centres. They are an essential ingredient of the visitor experience, the human face beside all the clever gismos, yet – almost by definition – not part of the project development team. Their recruitment swells staff numbers just before opening day, causing an instant them-and-us divide with ensuing problems of morale in the months ahead:

- What is the optimum number of Explainers?
- How much do they cost?
- From which departmental budget?
- How many spend how much of their time doing demonstrations? running workshops? running planetarium shows?
- What effect does that have on their morale?
- What training does a new Explainer need?
- What ongoing training is required to keep the jobs interesting/rewarding/ challenging?

Financial precariousness

In the USA, the strong support from National Science Foundation funding, the encouragement provided by the charitable contribution law, and the fragmented administration of school science education, all contribute to a healthy level of financial support for science centres. The situation in Europe is less secure, less predictable, and enormously variable from country to country.

The City for Science and Industry, opened in 1986, is already Paris's third biggest tourist attraction, after the Eiffel Tower and the Louvre. The government put in the FF3,000m it cost to develop the science centre in the carcass of a former abattoir. It also pays FF720m a year towards running costs. In the UK, there is government funding for national museums (which may indirectly fund the development of interactive exhibitions, such as 'Launch Pad' and 'Flight Lab' at the Science Museum, South Kensington) but the major support for independent science centres has come from charitable foundations, supplemented by industrial sponsorship and visitor-generated revenue. The two case studies (pp. 48–53) provide further comparative data.

Are they learning or merely playing?

Is the science centre a circus or a serious educational initiative? Arguably, the question should be reversed: 'Are they playing – developing an exploratory approach to life itself and the basis perhaps for a career in scientific research – or merely learning facts and figures?'

Curiosity killed the cat but made the scientist, and the challenge of those who value measurable cognitive gains over long-term affective benefits sends ripples of self-doubt through the science centre movement. The most recent spasm was set off by an article in *New Scientist* (Wymer 1991). The response (correspondence column, and Quin 1991) acknowledged that little real learning can be achieved in the short duration of a visit to a science centre. The criticism, and implied weakness of an interactive exhibition, is its superficiality: what deep understanding can the visitor gain in a few hours of hands-on experience, with the inadequate support of exhibit text labels?

The answer is that the exhibits themselves are but the tip of an iceberg of science communication. The best science centres – the best endowed, the most carefully researched, and those well integrated into the formal education system (on the one hand) and the national mass communication media (on the other) – all offer more than just exhibits; and their programmes of special events and activities are finely tuned to the needs of their communities.

Professor Richard Gregory, founder of the Exploratory in Bristol, UK, is ready to admit that there is a danger of interactive science centres trivialising science: 'Should we indeed speak of a "science centre" which lacks the rigour of science?' he asks:

> Science is a slow, often tedious, business, with most experiments being controls designed to show that in certain conditions nothing happens. . . .
> Is it simply that science museums seldom attempt explanations because explaining is not their traditional aim? Or have they found it impossible to present ideas in a museum context? Are the concepts and principles underlying appearances just too hard to present without the kind of background knowledge instilled over years, in courses in schools and universities?
> We may need somewhat separated, more thoughtful 'Explanatories'.

Possibly existing schools and universities are the explanatories we need. But in schools and universities explanations are built up gradually on a carefully planned, slowly growing basis of knowledge. Can we speed this up? Can we introduce sometimes difficult concepts of physics, chemistry, life, time, symbols, intelligence, chaos or whatever, in minutes rather than years? This is the challenge.

I return to this theme below.

Case studies of two contrasted science centres

Techniquest, Wales

The Techniquest story

Cardiff Bay, once the red-light docklands area, is today the home of Techniquest and focus of Baltimore-style development plans. A dream of informal science education, a helping hand from the USA, and a clearly focused business mind, are the key ingredients in the Techniquest story to date.

In early 1985, a brainstorming group was set up by Professor John Beetlestone to refine his dreams of a science centre for Wales. In September that year a Finance and Management Advisory Group was formed from committed people in the business community. And in October a 'Boffin' Advisory Group of scientists, engineers and designers was formed.

The two were merged in the Techniquest Action Group in June 1986, with Rudi Plaut as Chairman. By that time British Gas Wales had offered their showroom in the Cardiff pedestrian shopping precinct, rent free, for a temporary exhibition opening in November 1986; and the Gatsby Foundation had awarded the project an £83,000 launching grant.

Techniquest was established as a company limited by guarantee with charitable status in July 1986; and the first Exhibits Director, appointed from the USA, arrived to direct the design, fabrication and display of the first exhibition. Forty organisations and 100 individuals contributed to transforming the first phase of the dream into reality.

By the time the exhibition closed in August 1987, the Gatsby Foundation had already approved a grant of £600,000 for phase-2. The following March, Cardiff Bay Development Corporation (CBDC) authorized the release of funds for the purchase of a building to be sited on land made available by the National Museum of Wales, opposite the Industrial and Maritime Museum on the Cardiff Bay waterfront. The 1,000 m^2 exhibition was opened to the public – in its modern industrial shed – in September 1988, and the 100,000th visitor arrived in October 1989.

Techniquest submitted proposals for its phase-3 development, as a major science-based attraction, in October 1988. Prospects then yo-yoed from bright to gloomy. The future of the science centre appeared to be in the lap of politicians and property developers, sidelining the visionaries into the role of a pressure group.

Finally, after appointing consultants to examine the proposals, the Development Corporation Board chose the science centre as its lead project in November 1991: the funding and site were approved for a threefold expansion of Techniquest opening in Autumn 1994 in purpose-built accommodation adjacent to the historic docklands and a modern motorway extension.

Strong point 1: populist appeal

The exhibition unashamedly adopts the tutti-frutti approach. The initial display of exhibits selected from the *Exploratorium Cookbooks* was a surefire success and has since been augmented by innovative designs developed in the Techniquest workshop – the programmable hydraulic Welsh dragon has become a favourite with locals and tourists alike. The strategy works and, combined with bright primary colours, rounded corners, and welcoming 'Helpers', a happy hubbub is generated in cheerful, comfortable surroundings.

Strong point 2: organic growth

Starting small and developing in an entrepreneurial fashion permitted extremely tight management control. The trustees were closely involved and committed, providing the necessary expertise for setting up and running a new business (albeit with charitable status). The Director's idealism was thus complemented by his Chairman's commercial realism. (See also weak point 2, below.)

Strong point 3: customer-led programmes

Following the introduction (for the first time in 100 years) of a National Curriculum in the UK, Techniquest has become a valuable educational resource. The development of the Kits Programme, for example, is a direct response to primary-school needs: after visiting the exhibition, teachers can borrow a kit containing all the equipment necessary for simple practical science activities in class. The science centre thus maintains its educational integrity whilst also operating as a popular tourist attraction.

Weak point 1: difficulty of attracting capital investment

In common with all successful small businesses, Techniquest has faced the problem of attracting capital. The Gatsby Foundation grant, for expansion to phase-2, was made in expectation of an educational return: a gain in informal science education in South Wales. Techniquest's site in an area of urban regeneration presented the opportunity of financial support from CBDC. Capital investment will be supplemented by ongoing support for operational costs, provided by an endowment linked to commercial activity (shopping centre, etc.) in the area round the science centre. In return, the Development Corporation will demand a long-term influx of visitors to the site.

Weak point 2: initial credibility gap

What's a science centre? Why should Cardiff have one? Who are these wild-eyed enthusiasts?

The Techniquest Action Group – consisting of key local figures, all participating out of personal interest – not only provided essential professional expertise (often at no cost), but also established invaluable links with the local industrial, commercial and educational communities, and with local and regional government. The fledgling science centre's credibility was thus assured and a spreading network of goodwill has since built strong support in the city, leading Techniquest to become the regional base of the British Association for the Advancement of Science and the regional meeting place of the ASE (Association of Science Education).

Heureka – the Finnish Science Centre

How Heureka came about

A small core of enthusiastic science communicators, a simply produced, hugely successful physics exhibition, and the vision of a novel form of national institution, created the launch pad for Heureka.

Planning started in autumn 1981 and the Science Centre Foundation was registered in January 1984. In the next five years a succession of temporary exhibitions was held, on subjects as varied as water, medical science, and Finnish language and culture. All proved essential for generating popular support and for the process of prototyping and modifying exhibit ideas and display techniques. Over 1,000 scientists participated in the planning stages, donating valuable time and expertise.

An architectural competition was held and two rising architects were awarded the building contract. (Total capital costs were FIM120m (US$30m), of which 60 per cent was for the building itself, contributed by the City of Vantaa, the Finnish state, and corporate sponsorship.) From the start of site work in February 1987 to the public opening in April 1989, things moved fast. And since the opening, regular visitors have been rewarded by a changing programme of (750 m^2) temporary exhibitions and special events, supplementing the basic exhibition of 2,300 m^2.

In the park surrounding the science centre, outdoor exhibits include samples of Finnish bedrock (from Helsinki to northern Lapland) and ten stations on an Environmental Trail, for example: measure aeroplane noise, or examine the damaging effect of acid rain on the spruces by the river bank.

Indoors, Heureka also includes a lecture hall, science shop, cheerful café, stylish restaurant, and the geodesic dome of the Verne Theatre. With a hemispheric screen of almost 500 m^2, and seats for 197 spectators, the Verne Theatre is equipped for multi-slide projector shows, planetarium programmes and hemispheric film.

Heureka is located in the city of Vantaa, 15 minutes from Helsinki's central railway station, or about ten minutes' drive from the airport.

Strong point 1: new national attraction

Heureka has the cool clarity and simplicity characteristic of modern Finnish design, making the building a place to visit in its own right. The science centre is the first of a completely new type of institution in Finland, and a bridge from the post-industrial age into the information age. The many computer simulations and information technology exhibits support this image.

The building itself is a beautiful mathematical sculpture. Reflective surfaces shy away from the vertical, like building blocks transformed by Computer Aided Design. Interlocking volumes are joined by ramps and tantalising views through internal 'windows'. Computer programs mix happily with classic hands-on exhibits and with static displays, all monochromatic or shiny, bathed in cool daylight, spotlit with halogen bulbs.

The design style, though no key to the science centre's operation, created huge publicity and immediately established Heureka as a national attraction.

Strong point 2: thematic coherence

The broad themes of the exhibition are the universe, life, human society, technology; and exhibits in the main Cylinder Hall and outer Pillar Hall are displayed in such a way as, subtly, to draw intellectual links. Stronger story lines, and the fruits of current research, are presented in the series of temporary exhibitions.

Visitors during the summer of 1990 found a real hands-on portrayal of the Iron Age, complete with a full-size replica of an Iron Age house based on archaeological information from the Finnish island of Åland. They were encouraged to join in peat-laying and making reed bundles for the roof, or digging at the nearby archaeological site.

The theme from September 1991 to May 1992 was environmental. 'Balance?' challenged visitors to explore the global issues and to re-evaluate their own lifestyles.

The exhibition which opened in June 1992 took the 75th anniversary of Finnish independence as the opportunity to look back over more than a hundred years of history, examining the forces – social, economic, technical, cultural – that have forged the nation.

Strong point 3: links with the scientific community

Not only participatory, Heureka is also continuously evolving. The links established with scientists at Helsinki University, the Technical University at Otaniemi, and with a variety of research institutes have been maintained. Research scientists' input serves as a drip-feed to the main exhibition and a basis for developing the temporary shows. A later addition to the basic exhibition was a striking demonstration of chaos using a stream of water that fell on to a mirror and could be changed from smooth (laminar) flow to chaotic turbulence. As science and learning change, so do the contents of the Finnish Science Centre.

Weak point 1: financial precariousness

Comparative data table:

Deutsches Museum, Munich
Surface area: over 50,000 m^2
Visitors 1989 total: 1,400,000, including 18% in school classes
Total staff: 388, including 26 part-time and 2 volunteers

Annual budget 1990 total: DM44m including:

government and city funding	DM32m	
ticket sales	DM4.9m	(11%)
business activities	DM4.1m	
donations	DM1.7m	

Museu de la Ciència, Barcelona
Surface area:

Permanent exhibition	1,850 m^2
Temporary exhibition	400 m^2
Planetarium, lecture rooms and school workshops	1,350 m^2

Visitors 1989 total: 330,000, including 56% in school groups
Total staff: 36, including 32 full-time
Annual budget 1989 total: 300m ptas including:

funding from Fundació Caixa de Pensiones	200m ptas
income from visitors	100m ptas (33%)

Museon, Den Haag
Surface area: 5,500 m^2
Visitors 1989 total: 300,000, including 33% in school groups
Total staff: 60, including 55 full-time, 5 part-time, 40 volunteers
Annual budget 1989 total: 6.75m guilders including:

funding from municipality	5m guilders
sponsorship	1m guilders
income from visitors	750,000 guilders (11%)

Heureka, Vantaa

Total area:	8,200 m^2
Permanent exhibition area:	2,300 m^2
Temporary exhibition area:	750 m^2

Visitors 1990 total: 320,000, including 22% in school groups
Full-time staff: 45

Budget 1991 total: FIM 27m
including:

city of Vantaa funding	FIM 6m
visitor income	FIM 19.5m (72%)
corporate sponsorship	FIM 1.5m

The data tell their own story. In the USA, the Pacific Science Center's marketing strategy is held in high esteem: while the US average visitor-generated revenue is 35 per cent, PSC records around 65 per cent (ASTC 1987 survey data). The (predicted) dip in visitor numbers at Heureka, once the honeymoon period of opening was past, makes the current financial position untenable in the long term.

Weak point 2: uneasy transition from project phase to operation

Common to all dreams that become real science centres is a charismatic leader. Heureka is no exception. When Hannu Miettitnen moved on, the then Science Director was invited to accept the Chief Executive position. Per-Edvin Persson now faces the challenge of building a revolutionary project that took off in a blaze of publicity into an influential national institution.

Still moving in the twenty-first century?

'One day, every city will have a science centre, just as today most cities have a library, art gallery, theatre and sports arena', wrote Stephen Pizzey in 1987. That dream is coming ever closer to reality. But is the proliferation of science centres an expression of fashion or a genuine response to society's needs?

Roger Lesgards is in no doubt: 'The number of scientific museums is increasing all over the world. They must therefore reflect a real need.' Certainly the levels of funding, together with the level of public support, indicate that the French government (and to a lesser extent those of other continental European countries) see value and prestige in major centres affirming science as part of their culture.

Will there be evolution or stagnation? Will these newly created national institutions become modern dinosaurs, or vigorous hybrids? In the sense that every new science centre is to some extent a clone of those that opened before, the spread of the movement is an enormously successful example of niche colonisation. It is not self-evident that individual science centres, or the movement as a whole, will evolve further. Yet discussion on the pages of the ECSITE Newsletter, and at the conferences of the international science centre community, reveal an active search for the 'next generation'. Three thinkers offer instructive pointers.

Ilan Chabay (President of the New Curiosity Shop, Californian consultants in creative science education) is seeking to develop conceptual frameworks through exhibits:

> The wonderful experience of being a 'barefoot empiricist wallowing in the facts' of science is not sufficient to develop a conceptual framework in

which to arrange and use those facts and predict the behaviour of systems. We need to develop means, in and out of the classroom and museum, that allow people to rationalise their observations and develop a coherent model. They also need to understand that the model is subject to constant revision and improvement. . . . One concern therefore is to develop sets of closely related exhibits in a single theme. In the museum setting, the physical layout and proximity of the exhibits can further reinforce a sense of the relationship between elements in each exhibit and the conceptual unity among them.

Tom Semadeni (Science Director at Science North, Sudbury, Ontario) places the emphasis on the experimental process, encouraging people to become scientists themselves:

By and large, what a visitor experiences at Science North is real science, the science of the here and now, investigations into what is going on around us and, sometimes, within us. This may be the single most significant characteristic which sets Science North apart from other science centres. Much of our power comes from the fact that we are real scientists doing real science.

Illustrations of this are found at every turn:

- weather radar tracks rain and snow in northern Ontario
- the ham radio provides a communication window to the world
- real music is composed on the computer-based instruments
- blood samples are tested and typed
- woven goods are being turned out on looms
- binoculars and field guides encourage informed observation of the clientele at the bird feeders
- a snake is shedding its skin . . .

These are but a few examples. This even ignores the smaller stuff that goes on in the individual labs, like growing crystals, or measuring the microclimate of the building, or fiddling with superconductors, or testing blood samples in a centrifuge. And, at the risk of sounding whimsically optimistic, real science at Science North can often be fun, as well it should be.

James Bradburne, architect and exhibit designer, sets the scope most ambitiously:

The next generation science centres are second order experiences – the interaction of interaction. Their approach is fundamentally 'meta-hands-on'. It strives to make every part of the visitor experience, from the moment of their arrival until the moment they step out of the door, contribute to a total, integrated understanding of the doing of science as a fundamental human activity.

Whilst physics is ideally suited to interpretation with interactive exhibits – it is practical to design exhibits that demonstrate real physical phenomena – other sciences deal in phenomena that are non-reversible, non-repeatable, happen too slowly or too fast, on a mega or micro scale, and may be demonstrated only (in an exhibition gallery) by means of simulations. There is a strong case for searching out new media of science communication and adapting them to the science centre. Interactive exhibitory is but one, extremely seductive medium. It cannot, alone, tell the whole story. Science, especially environmental science, doesn't fit neatly into air-conditioned exhibition galleries.

My personal dream is of a science centre where you can do science as well as find out about science; a science centre that is both multi-media and multi-dimensional. It offers interactive exhibits and a lending library; interactive software and television programmes; Meccano and Lego kits; planetarium shows and laboratory experiments; teacher-training programmes, kids' science camps and field trips. It publishes posters and books and work sheets. There are opportunities to carry out personal research and to plumb the depths. There is science drama and an annual kite festival.

The aim is to communicate science, not build scientific cathedrals: a network with 'science events centres', not institutions. However beautiful, architectural plans are but a means to an end.

Select bibliography

ASTC Science Center Survey, 1989, Washington DC: ASTC.

Gregory, R.L. (1986) *Hands-on Science: An Introduction to the Bristol Exploratory*, London: Duckworth.

National Council of Science Museums, India (1990) *Museums without Walls, 1988 Conference Proceedings*, Delhi.

National Science and Technology Centre (1991) *Interactive Exhibits Relating to the Environment, 1991 Workshop Proceedings*, Canberra.

Nuffield Foundation (1989) *Sharing Science. Issues in the Development of the Interactive Science and Technology Centres 1989*, London.

Pizzey, S. (1987) *Interactive Science and Technology Centres*, London: Science Projects Publishing.

Quin, M. (1990) 'The interpreter's role in an interactive science and technology centre', in S. Goodland and B. Hirst (eds), *Explorations in Peer Tutoring*, Oxford: Basil Blackwell, pp. 194–202.

—— (1991) 'All grown up and ready to play', *New Scientist*, 26 October, pp. 60–1.

Shortland, M. (1987) 'No business like show business', *Nature*, 16 July, pp. 213–14.

Wymer, P. (1991) 'Never mind the science, feel the experience', *New Scientist*, 5 October, p. 53.

4

The debate on heritage reviewed

Robert Lumley

> To be is to have been
>   *David Lowenthal*

For over a decade now there has been a lively and sometimes bitter debate in England over the question of 'heritage'. It is not an entirely new discussion in that an anxious preoccupation with the nation's past and its material (and spiritual) legacy dates back to at least the late nineteenth century. However, it has acquired a particular salience since the 1960s. A 'transplanted' North American academic noted then a people deeply imbued with historicity:

> English attitudes towards locale seem permeated with antiquarianism – a settled bent in favour of the old or the traditional, even if less useful or beautiful than the new . . . all arts and the whole built environment reflect this bias. Delight in continuity and cumulation is integral to English appreciation of *genius loci*, the enduring idiosyncrasies that lend places their precious identity.
>
> (Lowenthal 1985: xviii)

In the 1970s and 1980s, 'heritage' became a key word in a wider debate about the nation's identity. It stood as a metaphor for the English condition with some commentators referring to the 'national necropolis' or 'museum society'.

To non-English readers, the very framework of the debate might confirm their image of the 'insularity' of what Winston Churchill called 'this island people'. The imagery used as well as the neuroses of a nation coming painfully to terms with its European future after an imperial past suggest peculiarity. Hopefully, all this will not appear irrelevant. After all, it is but one example of the difficulties of living in an 'old country' in a period of dramatic historical transition. And, as will be shown, concern with 'heritage' is increasingly international in scope and reveals the impact on local cultures of the forces of globalisation. The search for authenticity and roots gets more intense the more cultures become placeless.

Heritage undefined

What is 'heritage'? Look up the *Shorter Oxford English Dictionary* and you will find the following entry:

1 That which has been or may be inherited.
2 The fact of inheriting; hereditary succession.
3 Anything given or received to be a proper possession.
4 An inherited lot or portion.

It does little to help analyse the phenomenon which this chapter will examine.

A better starting point is a passage from Patrick Cormack's (1976) *Heritage in Danger*. One particular extract is cited by at least four of the main books involved in the heritage debate. I propose, therefore, to quote Cormack first, and then various comments on him.

> When I am asked to define our heritage I do not think in dictionary terms, but instead I reflect on certain sights and sounds. I think of a morning mist on the Tweed at Dryburgh where the magic of Turner and the romance of Scott both come fleetingly to life; a celebration of the Eucharist in a quiet Norfolk Church with the medieval glass filtering the colours, and the noise of the harvesting coming through the open door; or of standing at any time before the Wilton Diptych. Each scene recalls aspects of an indivisible heritage, and is part of the fabric and expression of our civilisation.
>
> (Cormack 1976: 14)

> The interpretative stress on the senses, on the experience of meanings which are vitally incommunicable and undefinable may only seem clear as an example of what Hermann Glaser once described as the 'deadening of thought through mysticising vagueness' . . . a kind of sacrament encountered only in fleeting if well remembered experiences which go without saying to exactly the extent that they are taken for granted by initiates, by true members of the ancestral nation.
>
> (Wright 1985: 81)

> Equally ineffable is the concept of national heritage, normally evoked with sublyrical vagueness. . . . Those who drafted the National Heritage Act confess they 'could no more define the national heritage than we could define, say, beauty or art . . . So we let the national heritage define itself.' That heritage 'includes not only the Tower of London but agricultural vestiges visible only by the aid of aerial photography'.
>
> (Lowenthal 1985: 36–7)

> This pastoral, romantic and religiose evocation, not far from a Hovis bread commercial, in fact defines a very specific view of heritage – but we can expect quite different sights and sounds at the Beamish Open Air Museum Geordies' Heritage Day.
>
> (Hewison 1987: 32)

This is heritage at its most pretentiously reverential, drawing on art, religion and rurality in ways unlikely to connect fully with a broad popular response, despite their continuing potency within the codes of narrower (though influential) versions of national identity. Such versions often have strong imperialist assumptions, giving their rhetoric a white racial character which either ignores, or openly rejects, the nature of Britain as a multi-racial society.

(Corner and Harvey 1991: 51)

It should be evident from these quotations that the debate about heritage in England has had strong political connotations. The past has been, and continues to be, a vital source of legitimation for both Left and Right. However, the struggle to define heritage has involved a range of actors from museum professionals and academics and critics to amateur collectors, with lobbies and voluntary organisations playing central parts. Political parties have been relatively marginal to the defining process. Moreover, the steady broadening of the concept of heritage to include natural as well as human phenomena, and the increasingly anthropological (as opposed to art historical) definition of culture are long-term developments not reducible to political explanation. In the face of such fundamental cultural changes, it was perhaps wise (tautologically) to 'let the national heritage define itself'.

The 'heritage debate' has had many aspects and a full account would need, above all, to examine its consequences for what has or has not been conserved and preserved. My aim is the more modest one of introducing some of the main features of the debate under three headings: its recent origins in the context of economic decline; the connection between heritage and enterprise; and, lastly, the problem of interpreting history through the idea of heritage.

Heritage and decline

The coupling of the two terms 'heritage' and 'decline' is most explicit in the subtitle of a book which did a great deal to popularise the debate, Robert Hewison's *Heritage Industry*; it reads 'Britain in a Climate of Decline'. For Hewison, heritage entailed the promotion of a culture that is backward-looking rather than future-oriented, fearful of the present and therefore escapist, and incapable of innovation. It focuses on a Britain that is post-imperial and steadily losing out to other countries in the struggle for industrial and commercial competitiveness.

Hewison cites Neil Cossons, then newly appointed Director of the Science Museum and formerly of the pioneering Ironbridge Open Air Museum, as saying: 'There is an anti-industrial, anti-technological feeling which has grown up enormously in the last 20 to 25 years. . . . We're an industrial nation desperately pretending not to be one' (Hewison 1987: 104). Hewison goes on to refer to the vogue for historical re-enactment as 'evidence of the persistent fantasy that it is possible to step back into the past. Museums and fashion exploit the same nostalgic drive; the most contemporary attitude is a disdain for the present day' (ibid: 83). The tremendous growth in museums and museum visiting, the development of open air museums concentrating on industrial archaeology, the fortunes of the country house conservation lobby, the popularity of Civil War re-enactments, the marketing of Victoriana in modern dress by Laura Ashley – all these are symptoms of a life-forsaking nostalgia for the 'glorious' past. Because the British (it would be more accurate to say 'English' as all Hewison's examples are drawn from England) are unable to face the present, they turn for consolation to the past.

A commentator, Patrick Wright, whose book, *On Living in an Old Country*, first initiated the wider debate (Wright 1985), has a more subtle approach but finds an overarching connection between decline and the contemporary obsession with heritage: 'This sense of history as entropic decline gathers momentum in the sharpening of the British crisis. National heritage is the backward glance which is taken from the edge of a vividly imagined abyss, and it accompanies a sense that history is foreclosed' (Wright 1985: 70). If decline, and anxiety about decline, can be traced to the late nineteenth century (coincidentally, the National Trust was founded in 1895), it grows in strength in the decades following the Second World War. The supremacy of science; the attendant disqualification of everyday forms of knowledge; the rise of bureaucracy and the economics of scale – these are all developments common to industrialised countries. Disenchantment is not, argues Wright, peculiar to Britain, but it has taken a particular form in which historical consciousness has been dominant:

> History becomes, more urgently, the object of ceremonies of resonance and continuity when it seems actively to be threatened and opposed by an inferior present epoch – when, to put this differently, society is developing (or 'receding') in a way that cuts across the grain of traditional forms of security and self-understanding. More strongly still, we turn to the past when the future seems unattainable. . . . We have in the modern period conceived the future through progressivist philosophies of history. In terms of these philosophies, history is less and less intelligible. . . . In the [postwar] British experience, the idea of 'progress', linked as it has been to the development of liberal market forces, or, under Labour, to a statist social democracy, has failed to deliver the promised land.
>
> (Wright 1985: 166)

The seminal texts in the debate belong to the mid-1980s, but the theme of heritage as an aspect of a society pathologically obsessed with tradition recurs subsequently (Samuel 1989). Drawing on psychoanalytic terminology, Kevin Robins uses the concept of 'protective illusion' to analyse the 'prevailing concern with the comforts and continuities of historical tradition and identity' that 'reflects an insular and narcissistic response to the breakdown of Britain' (Robins 1991: 22). The British problem is seen to be about 'recognising the overwhelming anxieties and catastrophic fears that have been born out of empire and the imperial encounter', and coming to terms with 'other cultures, other states, other histories, other peoples'. The alternative is a 'retreat into cultural autism and of a rearguard reinforcement of imperial illusions' (Robins 1991: 22–3). The whole national response to the Falklands/Malvinas war, brilliantly explored by Wright through the media coverage of the raising of one of Henry VIII's warships from the bottom of the Channel (Wright 1985: 161–93), revealed the power of such illusions.

The linking of heritage and decline is seen, therefore, as fundamental to the English case – the result of epochal and structural factors given a sharp twist in the conjuncture of the late 1970s/early 1980s. A phenomenon that is quintessentially cultural but simultaneously a matter of economic and psychic health. However, during the debate, the nature of the connections has frequently been asserted rather than closely examined within a framework of causality. Hewison's approach of juxtaposing information on economic decline with facts about the growth of heritage tends to *assume* connections and not demonstrate them. Wright's use of micro case studies provides greater insights into the *experience* of protagonists, but the economic dimension remains nebulous.

Heritage as enterprise: imagineering

The fact that something new was happening provoked the debate on heritage. Even if that 'new' was dressed in old clothing, its novelty was striking. Suddenly, it seemed, England was being covered with heritage sites. This paradox (and paradox is the rhetorical figure most often employed in the language of commentators) is contained in the very title *Heritage Industry*, two words which, Hewison argues, are in conflict with one another. However, in the early stages of the debate, Hewison and Wright both stressed the heritage–decline couplet, leaving other aspects in the margins.

The idea that the heritage boom was a sign of change and innovation rather than of decline was noted by Peter York as early as 1984. He writes of the Covent Garden development:

> Everybody in Covent Garden, consciously or not, is doing their bit in the *grand tableau* – their contribution to what Walt Disney called 'imagineering' – the professional dreaming up and execution of three-dimensional fantasies. The new Covent Garden is one vast designers' world. . . . It is clearly the newest of a series of new urban theme parks: areas planned, reconstructed, laid on, for total experience.
>
> (York 1984: 47)

Heritage, in this perspective, comes to be seen less as an inability to come to terms with change (escapism, nostalgia, etc.) and more as a strategy for enabling change. Heritage also gets reinterpreted as a sign of postmodernity rather than as the downside of modernity with its failures and disappointments (Lumley 1987, 1988).

It is not that industrial decline has not taken place. John Urry refers to the profound sense of loss that accompanied the 'remarkably rapid deindustrialisation' of the early 1980s, especially in Northern England, Scotland and Wales. However, he goes on to show how conditions were created for an economic restructuring in which heritage often played a key role. Local authorities, taking advantage of vacant inner-city premises and the rise of small businesses, tended to lead initiatives in regeneration. A city like Bradford was exemplary in investing in museums and historic sites in an attempt to change its image and attract tourism together with new investment. Similar local ventures have had a knock-on effect, whereas Britain 'within a global division of tourism' has come to 'specialise in holidays that emphasise the historical and the quaint' (Urry 1991: 108).

Note that we are no longer dealing with a phenomenon that is seen as exclusively or pathologically 'British', but with one in which the British case represents a variant of a general development. Tourism, the motor force, is a global industry growing at a vertiginous pace. By 1984 international tourism was the second largest item of world trade. In addition, its internationalisation, especially in Europe, means that every tourist site can be compared with those located abroad (Urry 1991: 48). Note also the pioneering role played by the USA with the mall and the waterfront development, with ever more frequent references to Disneyland as the model for Europeans and others (ibid: 119–20).

The radical implications of the globalisation of the economy for notions of cultural identity is interestingly examined by Kevin Robins. The language of heritage ('heritage-speak') is, of course, shot through with essentialism, with the idea of roots suggesting a deeply physical belonging to a place. Although this can have exclusivist and racial connotations, it does not follow automatically. As Wright insists, a sense of place can also be understood as an attachment to everyday historical consciousness in the face of dislocation and the experience of modernity (Wright 1985: 86–7). However, heritage is increasingly a construct in a world of rootlessness; as 'the old order of prescription and exclusive places and meaning endowed durations is dissolving', we are faced with 'the challenge of new self-interpretation'. For people living in a region, this can often mean reconstructing a sense of place within a context in which giant corporations, such as Sony, transform a previous situation. Regional identity can grow while national identity becomes less encompassing: 'in order to position itself in the new global context, the region must re-image and, ultimately, re-imagine itself' (Robins 1991: 39). The North East of England is a case in point. The region's history has had to be reassessed to stress the 'special relationship with Japan' now that over forty Japanese companies are located there. New open-air museums, such as Beamish and Ironbridge, have been important in attempting to re-create identities for whole areas, promoting a local or regional form of patriotism and aiming in the process to make them more attractive to investors. The degree to which the image produced by the image-makers corresponds to the self-image of the inhabitants is more difficult to assess (West 1988; Bennett 1988). However, for Robins, this capacity to reinterpret the self is not seen negatively as 'fabrication' or 'false history' but as a form of adaptation. Potentially it entails freeing the (national) self from the burden of a past formed in defence of an essentialist identity designed to exclude 'the other'.

Heritage versus history: a case study

A recent book on tourism has suggested that the very term 'museum' has ceased to be useful in describing the new phenomenon of heritage, even if the label continues to be used:

> It is clear that museums cannot be created about anything anywhere. But a museum on almost any topic can be created somewhere. A lot more museums will emerge in the next few years although whether we should still refer to them as 'museums' is increasingly doubtful. The very term 'museum' stems from a period of high art and auratic culture well before 'heritage' had been invented.
>
> (Urry 1991: 134)

One of the features of postmodernity is said to be the collapse of older cultural hierarchies and the replacement of canons of taste by a spirit of relativity (Perniola 1990). In this perspective, differences between museums, heritage centres and theme parks cease to be very significant. Ironically perhaps, the insistence of certain populist Marxists that culture should be seen in terms of 'industry' rather than of the authors and artists so central to auratic notions of culture converged with the ideas promoted by the *laissez-faire* school of thinking. Attacked from all sides, the so-called paternalist, elitist model of culture lost its ascendancy.

So far I have presented a sort of overview of the heritage debate in order to identify its main contours. I want now to look at the heritage phenomenon by examining its manifestation in a particular instance, an example small in itself but revealing in miniature of attempts to redraw the cultural map. The micro study will open the way for some more general observations. The example in question is a real one and all the documents quoted are genuine but I shall invent names and alter some details to disguise the identity of the place and people involved.

Oldholm is a small country house in northern England which includes some original medieval parts but which is largely early nineteenth-century neoclassical. Architecturally, it is interesting but not a landmark. Rather, the fame of the house is due chiefly to the celebrated playwright who lived there and whose name attracts visitors. Oldholm now belongs to the local authority who took it over in 1980. My story begins in 1988 when two members of senior management from the local authority Arts Department visited the house and wrote a report. That report and the reply to it by the curatorial staff form the basis of this account.

The report contained a number of criticisms and recommendations. The criticisms concerned 'legibility' – the lack of signs and consequent difficulty for visitors to get an overall idea of the house; poor labelling; an excess of objects on display – and the problem that 'the house has an exceptional collection of furniture but lacks the sense of people. The danger is that it may acquire the air of an expensive antique shop'. The uniforms of the attendants, it was said, created a 'barrier'. The major thrust of the criticism, however, was that the presentation as a whole lacked the theatrical touch of the playwright himself.

As for the recommendations, these started with the call for a 'clear concept', and went on to suggest a relevant visitor survey. The stress was very much on dividing the house into different areas, in some of which visitors could sit on replica furniture, giving the house that 'elusive quality of being "lived in" ', and on including an 'interpretation centre'. The report also proposed the use of details of everyday life, such as unmade beds, which would draw attention to the famous playwright himself, and the production of audio tapes with sound effects including 'replicated dialogues and correspondence, plainsong, the roar of boars and howl of wolf-dogs, the sound of unearthly footfalls following the listener'. Whereas the National Trust property of Erdigg (a country house entered by the servants' hall) provided the report with a model for paying greater attention to the humble and daily aspects of history, the Warwick Castle *tableaux*, using wax figures, represented a more accessible approach to the past. In order to help implement such changes, an Education, Interpretation and Events Officer was said to be required.

The curators responded to the assessment report by noting first of all that the assessors had at no point consulted them about their current plans and work-in-progress; i.e., they had parachuted in, making a brief visit based on little knowledge of the house and its history. They claimed that many of the proposals (e.g. concerning labelling) were already under way. Moreover, they rejected the suggestion that there was a lack of 'concept': 'a clear concept does exist in the sense that we have a clear idea of why Oldholm is important and of what we are doing, why we are doing it and how it should be done'.

It is evident from the reply that fundamental differences divided the curators from the assessors. Some of these can be grouped under the heading of 'workplace knowledge' and professionalism, and primarily concern the practicability of the report's recommendations. But more is at stake. There is a conflict over their very desirability. At one level there is know-how: 'Do the assessors know what they mean by replica furniture and what it would cost?'; 'Do they realise the difficulties in supervising differentiated areas of access?'; 'Do they have any ideas of the costs of *tableaux* which Warwick Castle can afford to use because of its ownership by Madame Tussaud's?' Again and again the assessors reveal their ignorance of crucial technicalities. They come, moreover, with preconceptions derived from the latest fashion for market research, multi-media events or displays and for showing the social history of under- or un-represented groups (such as domestic servants). These interests are, of course, entirely valid. The problem in this instance is that the assessors start by ignoring or failing to value, and hence fail to connect with, the very considerable experience, knowledge and commitment of curators who are in daily contact with the house and its visitors.

The differences in terms of presentational strategies is dramatic. Take the proposals for *tableaux* and for sound effects: 'The introduction of *tableaux* would be obtrusive and most inappropriate. Oldholm is a reality and its effective presentation demands only the most subtle forms of illusion'; 'A theatrical approach does have a place, especially given the playwright's eccentric use of the house and work habits . . . these can be suggested using props in his study for example, but the theatrical approach must be backed up by sound research. It should entertain but never mislead or misinform'; 'We are sceptical about the use of sound effects and if incorporated they would need to be very carefully selected and well researched.' It is tartly pointed out, for instance, that a recording of singing in the plunge-bath might be rather anachronistic as there would only have been cold water in it! The curators observe twice that the intelligence of the public should not be underestimated and they note the interest in the restoration of the library: 'Visitors are fascinated by the detective work.' The report's conclusion is unqualified: 'If Oldholm were to be developed along certain of the lines suggested by the assessors, its character would not only be trivialised but destroyed.'

The 'concept' (or should one say 'theme') of the assessors is clearly not shared by the curators. The clash between them can be explained in a number of ways. There is a difference of work culture; the assessors are an Exhibitions Officer and an Education Officer who are not tied to any particular historical site and who work from the offices of the local authority; the fact that the exchange took place in 1988 is important to bear in mind. Local authorities, under pressure from central government, were then showing a new interest in the management and exploitation of their resources, including cultural ones, and a new breed of professionals (notable in marketing, advertising, public relations and design) was emerging in the public as well as the private sector. The language of reports, such as the one referred to here (and the sheer number of them!) reflects the impact of economic and management terminology with its 'concepts' and 'corporate planned approach'. Furthermore, the idea of heritage as enterprise and as the means of regenerating areas, of attracting tourism and putting places on the map, was being actively promoted by local authorities.

However, the clash has a wider cultural dimension. On the one hand, there are the assessors who adopt a new brand of heritage centre approach. They stress the importance of entertainment, accessibility and the use of *mise en scène* designed to make history visible and audible. They want to play on the public's fascination with the private life of great men, simultaneously provoking awe and deconsecrating the act of worship. For them, it does not matter so much whether reconstructions are historically accurate in every detail: the problem of immediate visitor enjoyment and identification is paramount. On the other hand, the curators belong to an older tradition associated with the work of the National Trust, in which the organic unity of the house and its preservation for future generations are cardinal concerns. They insist on the 'appropriateness' of the relationships between object, context and display – an appropriateness guaranteed by the historical truth provided by scholarly research. The authenticity of the house and its contents furnish the unique experience to which visitors accede through guidance but also through intellectual effort.

Many of these issues of interpretation will be familiar to readers who work in the museum sector. They have been at the centre of debate for some time. In

Britain at least one director of a national museum has provoked controversy by speaking of the need to learn from Disneyland. In this context, I want just to conclude by linking the issues more closely with the whole heritage debate. In this sense, the Oldholm example is useful in illustrating a number of key points: the multifaceted and internally divided features of the heritage phenomenon; the increasingly conscious orientation towards the public; and, lastly, the intellectual questions posed by how to represent 'history'.

History and myth

Robert Hewison's *The Heritage Industry* (Hewison 1987) had presented heritage as a monolithic phenomenon in which diverse manifestations from museums and the National Trust to fashion revivalism were said to be engaged equally in producing 'bogus history'. Likewise, Hewison seemed to assume that the public was a credulous mass, easily seduced by the sirens of nostalgia. However, this analysis, even though of polemical value, reproduced a Frankfurt School conception of mass culture incapable of grasping the complexities of the situation. Critics of Hewison have drawn attention to the differences within the so-called 'heritage industry' and to the need to make assessments and judgements accordingly. Patrick Wright, for instance, contrasts the work of the National Trust with the historical speculation of property developers engaged in 'imagineering' and underlines the democratic impulses in the museum world:

> If you look at the open air museums, you are looking at people whose intention is extremely worthy. It is democratic, connected with adult education, about reaching new constituencies, giving people a way of thinking about what had been the domain of exclusive professions.
>
> (Wright 1989: 52)

He also provides an appreciation of latterday antiquarians, such as the much maligned metal detectorists, busy reinventing cabinets of curiosities at a time when museums have been banishing aura and magic from their collections in the name of science and education (Wright 1991: 139–51). Clearly heritage cannot be adequately understood as the product of museum professionals and businessmen when it is defined and redefined 'from below' as well as 'from above'. It is better analysed as a field in which competing groups and interests seek to establish or undermine orthodoxies (Bourdieu 1980).

The second question – the relationship between visitors and heritage – has witnessed an equivalent critique of Hewison's earlier formulations. Whereas he identified the new promotional strategies at work, he failed to allow visitors the independence of perception and judgement, which he evidently found in himself. More recent contributions to the heritage debate have suggested that audience research should be the starting point for proper enquiry. How else, it is asked, can one know what effect is being achieved? As Adrian Mellor observes of the Albert Dock in Liverpool, some of the questions that might be asked concern the social groups who visit and their relationship to their localities:

Why are there so few black people, or people by themselves? Is dock visiting more of a middle class or working class pursuit? Is it perhaps that people now have to seek through communal visiting the neighbourliness they feel they have lost from their real communities?

(Mellor 1991: 114–15)

Museum curators themselves have shown a much greater interest in how visitors perceive displays in the wake of the concern with the 'consumer' generated by the new heritage sites. A particularly insightful comment comes from an assistant keeper at the Victoria and Albert Museum in London who notes the importance of ambience as opposed to individual displays:

Since all the surveys of the patterns of museum visiting demonstrate that visitors spend extremely little time inspecting any of the contents, except in the museum shop, it is arguable that the overall environment is of greater importance than what is actually displayed. This is not as straightforward an issue as curators are likely to think. I certainly do not visit botanical gardens, which I like and enjoy, for the plants on display, in which I have little interest.

(Saumarez-Smith 1989: 18)

In this perspective, the public ceases to be divided into the discerning few and the ignorant many, and is seen as complex and differentiated, requiring subtle and carefully calibrated strategies in order to have its attention engaged.

Finally, the heritage phenomenon has put questions of historical representation firmly on the agenda. The desire to 'show' history by making the past into an experience was the key ingredient in the new generation of museums, such as Jorvik Viking Centre in York and the Beamish Open Air Museum. History had to be brought to life in 3-D and to include the everyday life of people, whether ordinary or great. The desire to create this illusion has had remarkable influence, gaining ground outside the new museums and penetrating places such as our Oldholm. The visitor-centred approach has reinforced this tendency, while the discrediting of a positivist conception of history has opened the door to a relativism according to which fact, like beauty, is in the eye of the beholder.

This experiential notion of history comes in for some fierce criticism from those few academic historians who have engaged with the issue. An excellent critique of museum practice, referring especially to the Jorvik Viking Centre in York and the London Museum of Childhood, is worth quoting:

There is a theory of history implicit in such claims [to provide a simulacrum of the past], and it hinges on our ability to use objects as means of entering into and living vicariously in a past time. Visitors are required to assent to the historical authenticity and reality of what they have seen, while they simultaneously recognise its artificial, fabricated nature . . . an exact facsimile is technically impossible, and many aspects of life cannot be conveyed through looking, smelling and listening – work, hunger, disease, war, death are obvious examples. We understand the past, not by spuriously re-experiencing it, but by turning over many different kinds of evidence relating to it and by generating from this an understanding which inevitably has a strong intellectual, that is, abstract component. What is present, like that which is omitted, is not accidental, even if the selection processes are largely unconscious. It is precisely in this way that historical myths are constructed – myths that express powerful, if silent needs.

(Jordanova 1989: 25–6)

Visit an English country house and you are unlikely to be confronted with previous ravages of hunger, work and war. Rather, the past is liable to be a 'place of rest, certainty, reconciliation, a place of tranquillized sleep' (Bennett 1988: 70). Visit a museum of rural life and you are more likely to learn about the workings of a plough than about those of the laws that governed life in the country. Jordanova's critique can be illustrated with innumerable examples. However, the hold that myths exercise on the imagination is such that they are frequently resistant to rationalist critique. The 'invention of tradition' has been related to the demise of liberal rationalist ideologies in the nineteenth century (Hobsbawm and Ranger 1984: 8), and we should by now have acquired a considerable respect for the power of myths. The problem for those who pit themselves against the facile forms assumed by history in the guise of heritage is not just to expose falsehoods, but to find a way to present a different history that is communicable to a wider public. Historical truths left in abstract form remain within the limited domain of the profession. The possibilities in the English case for reinventing heritage present particularly severe difficulties, as should now be apparent. A sense of national identity is at stake. However, there are many who work in museums and other cultural institutions associated with heritage for whom a less narrow and insular conception of the national past has undoubted attractions. A greater awareness of the constructed rather than natural character of heritage can help to loosen the grip of myth. For all its inadequacies, the heritage debate may have contributed to this process.

References

Bennett, T. (1988) 'Museums and "the people" ' in R. Lumley (ed.), *The Museum Time-Machine*, London: Comedia/Routledge, pp. 63–85.

Bourdieu, P. (1980) 'The symbolic production of belief – contribution to an economy of symbolic goods', *Media, Culture and Society*, vol. 2, pp. 225–54.

Cormack, P. (1976) *Heritage in Danger*, London: New English Library.

Corner, J. and Harvey, S. (1991) *Enterprise and Heritage*, London: Routledge.

Hewison, R. (1987) *The Heritage Industry*, London: Methuen.

Hobsbawm, E. and Ranger, T. (eds) (1984) *The Invention of Tradition*, Cambridge: Cambridge University Press.

Jordanova, L. (1989) 'Objects of knowledge: A historical perspective on museums', in P. Vergo (ed.), *The New Museology*, London: Reaktion Books, pp. 22–41.

Lowenthal, D. (1985) *The Past is a Foreign Country*, Cambridge: Cambridge University Press.

Lumley, R. (1987) 'Museums in a postmodern world', *Museums Journal*, vol. 87, no. 2, pp. 81–3.

—— (ed.) (1988) *The Museum Time-Machine*, London: Comedia/Routledge.

Mellor, A. (1991) 'Enterprise and heritage in the dock', in J. Corner and S. Harvey (eds), *Enterprise and Heritage*, London: Routledge, pp. 93–116.

Perniola, M. (1990) *Enigmi*, Genoa: Costa e Nolan.

Robins, K. (1991) 'Tradition and translation: national culture in its global context', in J. Corner and S. Harvey (eds), *Enterprise and Heritage*, London: Routledge, pp. 21–44.

Samuel, R. (ed.) (1989) *Patriotism: The Making and Unmaking of British National Identity*, London: Routledge.

Samaurez-Smith, C. (1989) 'Museums, artefacts and meanings', in P. Vergo (ed.), *The New Museology*, London: Reaktion Books, pp. 6–21.

Urry, J. (1991) *The Tourist Gaze*, London: Sage.

West, B. (1988) 'The making of the national working past', in R. Lumley (ed.), *The Museum Time-Machine*, London: Comedia/Routledge, pp. 36–63.

Wright, P. (1985) *On Living in an Old Country*, London: Verso.

—— (1989) 'Sneering at the theme parks', *Block*, Spring, pp. 48–56.

—— (1991) *A Journey through Ruins*, London: Radius.

York, P. (1984) *Modern Times*, London: Heinemann.

Part 2
New services

Perhaps the most striking fact about museums is captured in the single word 'variety'. Museums exist in diverse forms with multiple purposes and have heterogeneous audiences; they vary both in what they provide and in how they provide it. This variety often makes it difficult to generalise about museums, or to transfer information from one to another. On the other hand, it is a stimulus to empirical work, whether in the form of visitor surveys or exhibit evaluations.

Most western European countries have carried out some form of study on their museum visitors. Notable work has been done in Sweden, Holland, France and Britain, but nowhere in the world have museum visitors been researched and surveyed as thoroughly, year by year, as in Germany. Initially confined to the Federal Republic, visitor surveys have now been expanded to embrace the whole of reunited Germany, and, among other results, are giving a fascinating glimpse of changes in the museum-going habits of former Soviet-bloc citizens. In describing this work, Bernhard Graf shows how qualitative and quantitative studies, in all types of museums, are relevant to issues that are normally seen as disparate, such as marketing, defining the mission, and planning educational exhibitions.

The understanding of visitors that has come out of this empirical work, whether carried out for marketing or educational reasons, has led to more change in Europe's museums over the last fifteen years than in the whole of their previous history. Not only is the visitor's need for physical comfort now more likely to be recognised and cared for, but exhibitions are less likely to be designed on the false, if unspoken, assumption that the visitor is preparing to take a degree in the subjects on the basis of a twice-yearly visit.

It has been much easier for science and natural history museums to adjust to this more democratic world, in which, for example, the visitor is recognised as having the final say in whatever communication takes place. Such museums tend to have more representative audiences – though still strongly biased towards the better-off and the better educated, as Eilean Hooper-Greenhill reminds us – and more clearly defined missions. By way of contrast, art and history museums often seem, and indeed often are, elitist bastions of high culture. Thus it is not surprising that Paulette McManus's study of family visits (Chapter 6) is particularly relevant to science and natural history museums, where family groups may account for more than two-thirds of all individual visitors. Families may see a museum visit as primarily an opportunity to enjoy each other's company and cement family ties, but such visits also provide potent opportunities for education, with adults and children helping each other to learn from the exhibits.

On the evidence of their approach to local communities, democratic responsibilities are interpreted in strikingly different ways in museums in the United States and Europe. Less frightened of the demotic, United States museums make vigorous and impressive efforts to reach non-visitors, the disadvantaged and minorities, through outreach programmes, special events, educational programmes and exhibitions. Little of this is evident in Europe, despite the pioneering efforts of the Pompidou Centre in Paris to democratise access to high culture (see Chapter 1 by Ian Ritchie). However, some countries have attempted, with varying degrees of success, to set up touring exhibits services, notably the former Soviet Union, Portugal and Britain, where the subject has long been under discussion without bearing much fruit. ECSITE, described by Melanie Quin (Chapter 3), is an attempt to provide widespread good exhibitions by sharing costs, but will not necessarily reach those who do not already visit museums and science centres.

The case for touring exhibitions is that they can take a museum's message to a larger and more widespread audience. And it is not surprising that Sweden, with its small, widespread population and long history of social democracy, should have set the pace in Europe. Jan Hjorth gives an account in Chapter 7 of the origins, early struggles and development of Riksutställningar, Swedish Travelling Exhibitions, which was set up over twenty-five years ago as part of a government drive to make culture more widely available in all regions of the country and to all segments of society. But as he explains, the service has moved on beyond the rather patriarchal aim of taking exhibitions to the people, to also helping local communities produce their own exhibitions. Not hands-on exhibits, but hands-on exhibit making, and a model for all who care to follow.

Children, whether in organised school parties or as members of family groups, are an important part of the museum audience, particularly for science and natural history museums. How best to respond to their needs? Gillian Thomas in Chapter 8 rejects the 'ghettoisation' of museums, which results from setting aside particular areas and activities for children, and argues in favour of dedicated children's museums. But these, with the distinguished exception of Museon, the museum for education in The Hague, have not until recently taken on in Europe. Perhaps this is because there was, until recently, no widespread dissatisfaction with Europe's school systems. In describing her work in setting up exhibitions for children in France and Britain, Gillian Thomas shows how potential visitors are consulted and involved in the work, so that the educational approach takes their requirements into account. Bernard Graf describes parallel procedures for adult exhibitions in Germany. Both writers adopt a psychology-based perspective which is widespread among practical exhibition makers in the United States and Europe, and which most sociologists interested in these matters see as complementary to their approach. However, as Eilean Hooper-Greenhill reminds us in writing about educational theories that have informed museum practices (Chapter 9), some sociology-based writers in England see themselves in opposition, to at least their view of the practitioner's case. No doubt, as in many other instances, the truth will eventually be seen to fall between two schools.

5

Visitor studies in Germany: methods and examples

Bernhard Graf

Relations between marketing and museums

Most of Germany's 4,300 museums are non-profit-making organisations. This is true of both public (i.e. more than half of the museums in the west) and private museums. However, there are tax breaks for both the museums and for charitable donors, if it can be proved that the purpose of the income or gift is non-commercial. So the marketing policies and activities of museums must be developed within the constraints of running non-profit-making organisations. All marketing strategies must, for example, be consistent with mainstream museum activities. As far as the visitors and general public are concerned, these activities centre on the tasks of presentation and collection. In a qualitative, international study of selected museums, Schuck-Wersig and Wersig (1988) differentiated between (a) the marketing of means, and (b) the marketing of resources.

Schuck-Wersig and Wersig consider all the areas of activity and potential marketing models that exist between the visitor/customer and the holding organisation/sponsor. While it would be an unwelcome digression to discuss every element in this scheme, I would like to give an example of one of the consequences for German museums.

The mass media are nowadays probably the most important factor in marketing, because:

- For holding organisations and sponsors, mass-media-echo is an essential element of success, and
- as a result, a quantitatively measurable increase of attendance can be expected.

The Museum für Verkehr und Technik in Berlin is mentioned as the best German example of this effect:

Nearly every month one can read about a new exhibit or exhibition, a donation, a sponsored exhibition. Of course, one could say this museum is in its growth period – but growth periods are symbols for successful holder- and sponsor-marketing.

(Schuck-Wersig and Wersig 1988: 8)

This leads to a major principle: The museum's mission is an essential factor for any kind of marketing effort, or strategy for communicating with the general public, because it is the decisive factor for success. Every museum communicates ideas and messages, as well as objects, to the general public, which is generally a larger group than just the visitors. This is true for all types of museums. One important consequence for the external marketing of museums is, therefore, that one must discuss goals and concepts for the museum and for the staff, before developing marketing concepts. A second important consequence is that one must know as much as possible about the general public and the visitors, to find the right ways to communicate defined strategies.

Attendance data

What use are attendance data, and what are their limitations as aids to planning? As our institute (Institut für Museumskunde, Berlin) carries out the only author-ised attendance study for German museums (it is one of the reports of the federal statistical office in Wiesbaden as well as for most Bundesländer), I am naturally enthusiastic about the importance of this annual study and its weight in deter-mining cultural policy. It is quite impressive to be able to report more than 97 million visits to about 4,300 museums in Germany in 1990 (73.78 million in the western Bundesländer, and around 23.3 million visits in the former GDR). And it is, of course, of some interest to compare the data for 1989 with those for 1990, which show some effects of the reunification of Germany. As compared to 1989, the total attendance for 1990 shows that visits to museums have decreased by about 5.1 million. Taken by themselves, however, the museums in the 'old' Federal Countries show an increase of about 3.747 million (5.4 per cent) for 1990 over 1989, giving a total of 73.78 million visits. Museums in the 'new' Federal Countries (the former GDR), on the other hand, show a decrease of 8.86 million (27.5 per cent). This decrease can be attributed to the political and economic (social) changes in that region.

These results raise questions regarding the impact of the political changes on the role of museums in the so-called old and new Bundesländer. Two-thirds of the 719 museums that responded to our survey from the former GDR reported a significant decrease in attendance. In addition to the most frequently cited reason for the decrease – political and social changes and growing unemploy-ment – there was a significant decrease in organised group visits (i.e. holiday camp visitors from the eastern European countries). Furthermore, new tourist destinations had become available which hitherto had been inaccessible. When announcing an increase of visits, the following main reasons were listed by the museums of the 'old' Federal Countries: great international or national exhibitions; public relations or educational activities in museums; and the (re)opening of museums.

Based on our annual attendance study for all museums in Germany, we have started a comparative research programme. This uses the annual data of museums over the last ten years to create a time-line and find groups of museums that show an increase/decrease of attendance in their summarized attendance figures. Together with Professor Heiner Treinen, who has the Chair for Methodology and Statistics in Social Science at the Ruhr University, Bochum, and Professor Helmut Kromrey, we found that the permanent increase in summarized attendance figures as a whole (from about 54 million visits in 1981 to over 70 million visits in 1990 for the former West Germany) was due to the effects of new or reopened museums. In 1981 we addressed our questionnaires to approximately 2,200 museums; in 1990 to about 3,300 in the 'old' Bundesländer. There was not a steady increase over all of this time: we found a slight decrease in the first years after 1981, but then a more or less stable increase until 1990. If we compare only those museums which could report attendance in all, or at least in all but one, of the years between 1981 and 1991, some interesting results can be seen:

- In most large museums we have no increase, in some important cases even a slight decrease of attendance.
- The increase in summarized attendance figures for museums as a whole was caused by a relatively small number of very important and very active museums, which presented remarkable exhibitions or extended their permanent exhibitions.
- Museum-related activities, such as exhibitions, the extension of collections, new museum buildings and so on, are much stronger indicators of increased attendance than atypical activities which could be housed elsewhere (theatre, movies, concerts, etc.)

These findings are interesting enough – leading the museum back to its own goals and concepts. But these results do not tell us anything about the variety of different target groups, or about the general public and its broad variety of interests, background, and cognitive and affective concepts and expectations towards the ancient institution 'museum'. Some results from several studies which our institute has carried out, or supervised, will be mentioned next.

Analysing attendance

There are two main ways of analysing museum attendance. The first is the so-called omnibus-pool method, in which a randomly selected number of persons, representative of the population, is asked a variety of questions on several topics. These studies are usually done to predict the outcome of elections or to study opinions on, or attitudes towards, important political questions. Questions about museum visits – as well as questions about the use of, or interest in, other cultural institutions – serve sometimes to monitor the socio-cultural levels of the respondents. The advantage of omnibus studies is that they can tell us something about the general public, and not only about people who already visit museums. The disadvantages are of relatively uncertain data and of a rather general level of content, only scratching the surface of interesting hypotheses. Nevertheless, these studies are the only way to collect quantitative data about non-visitors and potential visitors. Therefore we plan to co-operate with two German institutes carrying out such studies. The first project will be carried out by the IFO (Institut für Wirtschaftsforschung, Munich), and will investigate economic relations between cultural and political developments. The second project, 'Kultur-barometer', will concentrate on the cultural patterns of people in the old and new Bundesländer.

The second method of obtaining valid information about the attendance structure of a museum, or a group of comparable museums, is the controlled entrance study. Visitors are asked, before visiting the exhibitions, who they are and where they come from; what their museum-related interests are; how they got their information about a special exhibition or about the museum; and so on. The first systematic entrance study was done in Munich at the Deutsches Museum in 1974, when Professor Günther Gottmann became second Director General and was responsible for the education department and public relations. The results of this study allowed the Deutsches Museum to define its target groups for educational planning and visitor services.

The Institut für Museumskunde has carried out several entrance studies since 1982. One project, 'Besucherstruktur-Analyse', includes twenty-eight museums of different types and size all over the former Bundesrepublik. Results have been published as vol. 9 of our *Materialien aus dem Institut für Museumskunde* (Klein 1984). An important result of this study was the realisation that each group of museums has a typical attendance profile. Furthermore, we found that only one-third of the visitors on average see the museum as an institution where they expect to be educated. One-third want just leisure and pleasure, and one-third expect both fun and education.

The next study was done as a phased entrance-interview-study in about forty museums during three periods each year for three years. It involved thirty-six museums in Nordrhein-Westfalen, and – as a control group – four museums in Berlin. The results of this study were published under the title: *Der Gläserne Besucher* (Klein 1989). It is not possible to summarize the whole study here, so let me give just one example. Science museums had the relatively lowest percentage of frequent museum visitors (defined as having made more than four visits to the museum in question), whether visiting as individuals or in groups (9 per cent individuals and 5 per cent in groups). The reason may be that some highly successful museums, such as the Berlin Museum für Verkehr und Technik, already mentioned for its marketing success, were not part of the study; but nevertheless other prominent museums were chosen, such as the Deutsches Bergbaumuseum in Bochum. A high percentage of the visitors to science museums are not museum experts. What do we expect them to do there? And what do they do, once they are in the exhibitions? These are questions we should always keep in mind.

Visitor behaviour

In 1979 Heiner Treinen and I began a research project in the Deutsches Museum in Munich. We carried out a combined observation and interview study in five exhibition areas, starting with two sections of the former aviation hall, then testing a special exhibition on Frauenhofer, and finally studying two parts of the physics exhibition: mechanics and nuclear physics. This study, *Besucher im Technischen Museum* (Graf and Treinen 1983), proved that several of the educational theories and approaches transferred to the museum by curators and designers did not work.

In the decades between 1960 and 1980, most curators and museum educators based their exhibits and educational programmes on school-orientated learning theory. But in a museum the visitor behaves in a mass-media manner. This typical behaviour is characterised in two provocative terms by Heiner Treinen: 'active laziness' and 'cultural window-shopping'. These terms describe the usual situation of a museum visit, which is a leisure-time experience. The indicators, observed in all kinds of museums, lead to the conclusion that most visitors do not want to study in a goal-oriented, systematic manner. They 'shop' around. That means that visitors regularly do not study or read the exhibition, they play or move around, guided by the attraction of single highlights, or extrinsic elements of the exhibits, as well as by their own interests and background. They do not necessarily want to learn in a museum, but they expect a museum to be a scientific, historically and technologically profound, institution. Visitors may attend to hands-on devices and push buttons, turn cranks or use computers. But they do not necessarily understand the reaction they have started. Sometimes they do not even wait for it.

So what are the possible consequences of these results? Is the plebiscite for museum exhibits something like: the noisier the better? Of course not. One must be aware that the image of the institution 'museum', as a scientific-historical research centre, has to be fulfilled, and this will be expected by the general public. But one should translate the messages in the exhibits, which the curators have already formulated, for the visitors. One should offer explanations and basic information for different levels of education and interest, in order to provide an opportunity for most of the general public to understand a fair part of an exhibition. One should not necessarily reduce the number and length of labels, or define general limitations for reading-time based on the fact that the average reading time for one label is under five seconds. One should structure labels like an article in a newspaper, using headlines and advance organisers. And one should accept that some visitors will still not read them. This is just one example of research which facilitates visitor-oriented exhibition planning, which in turn is connected with formative evaluation during the planning process. This user-oriented approach is very popular in market research, but unusual in museums. There are, however, a number of relevant studies from England and the USA, e.g. by Ross Loomis, Roger Miles, Chandler Screven and Harris Shettel, and some of this work is summarized in a publication from the Deutsches Museum, *Museumsausstellungen: Planung – Design – Evaluation* (Graf and Knerr 1985). A further project, which has still to report in full, involves formative and summative evaluation in the planning of new exhibitions in the Deutsches Museum, Munich, the Württemberg Regional Museum, Stuttgart and the Natural History Museum, Karlsruhe (Klein and Graf 1990). I must refer also to the results of Hans-Joachim Klein and Barbara Wüsthoff-Schäfer (1990) on the particular problem of elaborate installations and theatre-oriented designs in museums. One can never easily turn down an expensive exhibit after it has been finished, even if it is obvious that it does not communicate to the public, or at least not in the way originally intended. So it is also a form of cost-effectiveness to test roughly made models of exhibits before finishing them in their final form for the exhibition.

Thus, one can see that there are some interesting aspects and results of visitor-oriented research and marketing, which can be used in the museum as tools to serve the basic tasks of these ancient and traditional institutions.

References

Graf, B. and Knerr, G. (eds) (1985) *Museumsausstellungen: Planung–Design–Evaluation*, Munich: Deutsches Museum.

Graf, B. and Treinen, H. (1983) *Besucher im Technischen Museum. Zum Besucherverhalten im Deutschen Museum München*, Berliner Schriften zur Museumskunde, vol. 4, Berlin: Gebrüder Mann Verlag.

Klein, H.-J. (1984) 'Analyse der Besucherstrukturen an ausgewählten Museen in der Bundesrepublik Deutschland und in Berlin (West)', *Materialien aus dem Institut für Museumskunde*, vol. 9, pp. 1–220.

—— (1989) *Der Gläserne Besucher. Publikumsstrukturen einer Museumslandschaft*, Berliner Schriften zur Museumskunde, vol. 8, Berlin: Gebrüder Mann Verlag.

Klein, H.-J. and Wüsthoff-Schäfer, B. (1990) 'Inszenierung an Museen und ihre Wirkung auf Besucher', *Materialien aus dem Institut für Museumskunde*, vol. 32, pp. 1–141.

Klein, H.-J. and Graf, B. (1990) 'Visitor-oriented museum planning – a project in West Germany', *ILVR Review*, vol. 1, no. 2, p. 117.

Schuck-Wersig, P. and Wersig, G. (1988) 'Museen und Marketing: Marketingkonzeptionen amerikanischer Grossstadtmuseen als Anregung und Herausforderung', *Materialien aus dem Institut für Museumskunde*, vol. 25, pp. 1–112.

6

Families in museums

Paulette M. McManus

Introduction

Museums are a focal point for outings and 'places to go to' for the inhabitants in the cities and towns in which they are established, and for the visitors to those cities and towns. Most museums wish to encourage this state of affairs and nowadays many seek to describe their visitors so that they can serve them better. This description usually involves a demographic survey of visitors as they enter or leave the museum. Typically, regardless of country or type of museum, it reveals that a large number of people visit the museum as a member of a family group. Quite often, I suspect, this situation leads museum professionals to think 'Oh, we have to cater for a lot of children' and, I surmise, they often have mixed feelings about this conclusion.

Recent visitor research in European and American museums, which I shall discuss later, has shown us a different picture, in which the group of people making up the family is revealed as a social unit that functions in a remarkably consistent way in the museum environment. It functions as it does because of the presence of children, but we really have to cater for a particular cross-generational group of people, rather than for a lot of children with parents or relatives attached as 'extras'.

The family as the major part of the museum audience

A demographic survey will usually indicate that a large number of people visit a museum as a member of a family group. As such a survey is usually concerned with the responses of individuals, and as groups containing children are often the largest groupings of individuals visiting a museum, they actually under-estimate the number of people we need to consider when we are thinking about families in museums. Table 1 illustrates the way in which family members can be 'hidden' behind an individual representative of the family in survey work. The data are taken from a representative sample of visitors to the Natural History Museum, London (McManus 1987) and they include children in families,

Table 1 Representation of museum audience constituencies

Constituency	Visitor groups (%)		Visitor individuals (%)	
Groups with children	46.3	(n=297)	68.2	(n=1,072)
Singletons	31.5	(n=202)	12.9	(n= 202)
Couples	13.9	(n= 89)	11.9	(n= 178)
Adult group	8.3	(n= 53)	7.6	(n= 120)

children with teachers, and children with other children in a single category 'Groups containing Children'. It can be seen that 46.3 per cent of all the group types considered were groups containing children (297 of 641 groups, 133 of them family groups) and that the individuals accounted for in the category numbered 1,072, i.e. 68.2 per cent of all the individuals represented by that sample.

The table illustrates that the people that curators believe they are best able to serve – potentially informed or educated adults – make up just under one-third of the museum audience. Like it or not, we need to be proactive in trying to understand family attitudes, needs and behaviours with regard to museum visiting if we wish to satisfy the major part of our audience.

Family agendas for museum visiting

All the attitude surveys I have read or undertaken indicate that families seek pleasure or enjoyment from their visit to a museum alongside hopes for a generally informative or educational experience. That is, families have a dual agenda built into their visiting behaviour. In the past, we have put a lot of effort into trying to satisfy the educational agenda and have been blind to the fact that both agendas influence each other since they are in operation simultaneously. As a consequence, the educational agenda dominated the thoughts of museum professionals and many visitor studies were concerned with examination-like attempts to pinpoint learning from exhibits so that we could tell ourselves that we were succeeding on the educational front. This early research orientation is understandable when we reflect on the public education duty enshrined in the founding documents of our public museums.

The pleasure agenda

Over the past decade many museum researchers have begun to examine the interplay between the two agendas, at first seeking to find how the pleasure agenda might affect the educational agenda, but latterly calling on work from many disciplines to focus on understanding the pleasure agenda. It is becoming clear that the enjoyment that families seek is not to be derived solely from the exhibits in our museums, no matter how entertaining they might be, but also, and perhaps chiefly, from the enjoyment and pleasure to be found in functioning as an intimate social unit in a public place the family has freely chosen to visit.

Families now have more leisure, energy and money left over for family outings than in the past. It appears that they like to invest these resources in outings which serve to build and strengthen family ties. This is understandable when we consider that family domestic life can often become intense, especially when there is no extended family to relieve pressures and when everyone in the family may have a heavy and perhaps stressful work load which can tend to emphasise individual concerns rather than joint family concerns. Often, both parents have careers which take them out of the home and also, over the past fifty years, we have tended to place increasing formal educational loads on our children. In this context, it can be seen that the museum becomes an attractive destination for a family outing if it can be perceived as an easy, relaxing environment for social activity within the family.

The educational agenda

Children naturally strive to gain experience about the world while parents, motivated by love for their children, assist this process by seeking, providing and choosing safe, non-threatening experiences and environments for their explorations. One can see how a parent's perceptions of a museum as a mediated area for first-hand experience, offering real objects and repeatable phenomena from which to gain that experience, could prompt a museum visit for the whole family. If, in addition, personal interests can be harnessed – as when a particular museum can be seen as a place where one, some, or all members of the family can find a focus of fascination – then a museum visit can start to look like a successful outing even before it has begun.

I sometimes wonder how many families have been introduced to museums because of the fascination of 5-year-olds with dinosaurs. So, we need to provide our family visitors with exhibition environments which will maximise the opportunity for social interaction within the group and provide first-hand experiences of significant objects and phenomena.

Public perception of the educational validity of museums

Parents need to perceive the array of experiences they share with their children as worthwhile educational experiences on the grounds that they are validated by the research work that goes on behind the scenes in the museum. When parents have this perception, they set the tone of the visit so that children will appreciate the museum in a particular way and will behave and attend in the museum according to a schema communicated to them by their parents. For example, they will know that they are not in a theme park or an exhibition devoted to thrills, no matter how superficially similar some modern museum exhibits may be to exhibits in such places. I have come to this conclusion after listening to many recordings of conversations made in a museum. The way in which 'they' – meaning the museum or the people working in it – were referred to as if 'they' had a special authoritative status, which put the seal on exhibits, was very telling.

I have investigated the issue of perceived educational validity little by little over the past few years. My first findings indicated that visitors thought that educating the public should be the main job of people who worked in museums and that research on collections was perceived as a very much less important activity. Later investigations into the perceived nature of museum collections indicated that visitors might not rank research as an important museum activity because they could not imagine what it might entail – museum professionals have been too reticent about their work and people couldn't describe it to themselves. However, comments about collections indicated that people unconsciously assume a research process which makes the collections 'important'.

It is likely that families and others might get more out of their museum visits if we 'educated' them more about how museums work. The success of tours to the research departments of the Natural History Museum, London, and the popularity of the Natural History Centre at the Liverpool Museum, which allows visitors to handle and examine parts of the collections on open storage (very popular with families), may indicate the path to be taken towards increasing public awareness and respect for museums and museum work. When a museum has an image as a real, live part of the local and material culture, it is more likely to attract a wide audience.

Building a constant audience

If the family enjoys a good social experience while having an exciting educational experience, which is perceived as worthwhile, we are quite likely to have begun to build a future part of the one-third adult audience I referred to in Table 1. Bettelheim (1984), in discussing this issue, makes a plea to museums to maintain an impressive atmosphere which puts adults, and more especially children, in the mood to marvel and wonder, to expect rare experiences and to be prepared for them. He quotes a survey by Newsom and Silver (1978) which found that 60 per cent of adult visitors to an art museum attributed their interest in museums to the fact that someone in their family took them to visit a museum when they were a child. He concluded that sustained personal influences, initiated and repeated by the family, can account for a lifelong interest in museum-going.

The prosaic needs of the family when making a museum visit

Families have many of the everyday needs of other visitors when they are in the museum. The satisfaction of these needs is especially relevant to their comfort and pleasure because lack of provision, or poor provision, can lead to acute, and sometimes noisy, distress. Let us consider the family's prosaic needs by following a family into the museum and, for the moment, ignoring the presentation of exhibits.

The following discussion may appear to be as prosaic as the needs I describe. However, many national and local museums do not look at these situations from the visitor's point of view and so do not serve their visitors well. The satisfaction of the family's social agenda, and hence its educational agenda, is very likely to depend on a lack of stress concerning the topics I describe below. In Britain many museums have recently found that they must charge entry fees at the door in order to survive financially. It is surely significant that such hard-pressed institutions have usually found it expedient to upgrade the facilities I describe in order to ensure visitor satisfaction and pleasure and to encourage return visits.

Orientation

As the family enters the door, they will feel the need for simple, clear orientation to the museum spaces and facilities. The journey to the museum may have been a little hectic, the children will be excited, the parents will want to show that they are confident in this new, sometimes large and often very confusing space. If possible it is good to provide a calm good open foyer where they can get their bearings. It is absolutely essential that the parents should immediately be able to see evidence of a well-designed, comprehensive signage system the family can trust throughout their visit.

Museum orientation systems can be diabolically confusing. This happens because those working in a museum become familiar with the quirks of the architectural space and exhibition layouts and so cease to appreciate the confusion and frustration they can conjure up in the hearts of newcomers to the museum. I have been in museums where orientation systems have obviously been prepared on an ad hoc basis, so that later directions countermand earlier ones. I have been in others where several generations of signage exist side by side in confusing disarray. You only have to encounter one family which has struggled up the wrong staircase to take a child in a push-chair to a non-existent toilet to appreciate the resentment, exhaustion and anger created. It is well worth spending money on a survey of the use of museum spaces and the design of a suitable orientation system based on the survey findings.

Families appreciate the provision of a clear map of the museum spaces and facilities which they can carry round the museum with them. Nearly all of them will use one if it is provided. When a museum charges entry at the door, it is practical to give the map along with the ticket. Otherwise, leaflet maps should be provided in a well-marked, obvious position in the foyer.

Cloakrooms and lockers

Soon after their initial acclimatisation to the museum space, and with map in hand, the parents will begin to look for cloakrooms and lockers. Outings involving children, especially very young ones, can generate a large amount of hand luggage for the parents. In cold weather everyone will have heavy coats, hats and maybe outdoor shoes to leave in the cloakroom. If there is insufficient cloakroom or locker provision, the parents may end up carrying it all – a circumstance which is certain to shorten the visit to the museum. Having enough cloakroom space is not always sufficient. Some large museums have excellent cloakroom facilities but fail to staff them adequately during peak periods of demand. This is a false economy which is paid for by the museum audience in visiting time. Most museum visits last for one and a half to two hours, and it is unfair and discourteous to expect visitors, especially families, to give up a sizeable fraction of their visiting time in the cloakroom queue.

Toilets and baby-changing facilities

Clean, efficient toilet and hand-washing facilities, where people do not have to queue, are appreciated by all visitors and especially by mothers and fathers with young children. Many families visiting the museum are quite likely to include an infant and, inevitably, one of the parents will need to have a place at which they can attend to the baby with ease. It is best to have a specially organised area for this somewhere near the toilets rather than make do with some obscure, little-used room.

Drinking water

Many museums neglect to provide drinking-water fountains in their buildings. Depending on the climate of the area in which the museum is located, and the levels of temperature and humidity maintained in the galleries, I think that it is wise to provide a free drinking-water fountain in the museum. Young children are not as good as adults at maintaining bodily fluid and temperature levels and when they need a drink of water they really *do* need it – manufactured soft drinks may not suffice.

Food

Children inevitably get hungry and it is very stressful for their parents if they cannot adequately satisfy their children's needs in this respect. If we think about the overall family visit time, and add travelling time to the visiting time, we should expect to provide some form of refreshment suitable for children. Simple, reasonably cheap food in clean, cheerful surroundings, without having to wait too long to get it, is what is needed. The family is likely to extend their visit if they have a refreshing, relaxing break at lunchtime.

Families in exhibitions behave differently from other visitors

Research may show that families behave in consistent ways in different museums but this information would be of little use if they behaved like all the other visitors in the museum. When we are concerned with museum audiences we need to know whether families behave differently from other people and where the differences lie.

A study of 1,572 individuals in 641 visitor groups in the Natural History Museum, London (McManus 1987, 1988) demonstrated that the social context of visits did affect the learning-related behaviour of visitors and that families did behave differently from other groupings of visitors. As a part of the study, eight variables were recorded in the observation schedule, while the conversations of visitors were recorded while they were at five exhibits in the museum. The variables were: group type, group size, the nearness of strangers, the physical space maintained by people in groups, the use of interactive exhibits when they were available, reading behaviour, the duration of conversations, and the duration of visits.

Statistically significant relationships, of the order of p<14<0.0001, were found between the group type variable and the four measures related to interaction with, and learning at, exhibits – the use of interactive exhibits, reading behaviour, talking at the exhibit, and allocation of time at the exhibit. There appeared to be four distinct constituencies for reception of the museum message. The constituencies were, first, groups containing children; second, adult singletons of either sex; third, adult male and female couples; and, lastly, adult peer groups. The groups-containing-children constituency made up 46.3 per cent of the sample population and was composed of 133 family groups, 121 child peer groups and 43 teacher and pupil groups.

This evidence suggests that museum visitors bring with them, as a part of the social context of their visit, the propensity for different behaviours related to learning from exhibits. Each of us would behave differently when visiting a museum according to the social constituency in which we found ourselves. Since such distinctions can be drawn, it is worth examining the characteristics of the constituencies to see how family groups differ from other groups in behaviour and needs.

The singleton constituency

This constituency is characterised by brief visits to exhibits and the comprehensive reading of exhibit texts. Female singletons were just as likely to play at the interactive exhibits as any other visitor to the museum, but male singletons were twice as likely not to play at them.

The couples constituency

This constituency is characterised by a lack of conversation when compared to other social groups. Nearly half of the couples did not talk to each other at all when they were at the exhibits. They also tended not to play with any available interactive exhibits. They were likely to read the text labels comprehensively and to stay at exhibits for long periods.

The adult-social-group constituency

This constituency is characterised by the way time is spent at exhibits. Adult social groups were less likely than members of other constituencies to give exhibits cursory attention but very likely to leave them after 30 seconds. Overall, they were less involved with exhibits than those in other constituencies.

The groups-containing-children constituency

This constituency is characterised by the extreme likelihood of play at interactive exhibits and of long conversational periods within the group, with a strong tendency towards longer visits than those made by other visitors. The groups were likely not to be seen to read labels, unless adults were in the group (parents or teachers), when reading was likely to be glancing at text in character.

Within the constituency, three levels of descending social intimacy were observed – family groups, child peer groups and, lastly, teacher–pupil groups. The duration of conversations and visits paralleled this order, with family groups having the longest conversations and being likely to visit an exhibit for longer than one minute, child peer groups having shorter conversations and being likely to visit for longer than 45 seconds, and teacher–pupil groups having the shortest conversations and being likely to visit for over 30 seconds.

These descriptions of constituency behaviour found amongst groups containing children at the Natural History Museum parallel findings from American museums. Gottfried (1979), in a study at the Lawrence Hall of Science, found that children in peer groups approached exhibits at a physical level and did not overtly read texts or graphics. He also found a clear relationship between peer instruction and social interaction in his study, with peer dyads being the grouping which became most involved in exploration and discussion. These factors – exploration and discussion – are related to the measures of conversational and visit duration used in the Natural History Museum study. Rosenfeld (1980) found that adult–child groups spent more time together at the San Francisco Zoo than did child peer groups – the findings from the Natural History Museum would lead to the same conclusion.

Diamond (1986) found that most adult and child groups in a study she conducted in the Lawrence Hall of Science and the San Francisco Exploratorium did not read exhibit instructions before they began to play with the exhibits. The families preferred to try to understand how the exhibits worked by manipulating them, and they read instructions or looked at graphics only as a last resort. When this stage was reached, it was the parent who read text or consulted explanatory graphics. This finding is in accord with the findings from the Natural History Museum, where it was found that there were differences in reading behaviour in groups containing children when adults were present, as compared to the behaviour of groups containing children alone. When adults were present, reading behaviour involved brief glances at the label text. When children were alone, they were not often observed to read (although it should be noted that it is very difficult to tell when people are reading (see McManus 1989a)). If adults with children are to feed information from exhibit texts back into the conversations they have with their children, they need the texts to be arranged in small, subheaded chunks so that they can easily access the information they search for.

Families' behaviour in exhibitions

Several studies of the behaviour of family groups during their entire visit to an exhibition, as opposed to visits to single exhibits, have been made. Laetsch *et al.* (1980) provide a brief summary of whole-visit studies of child-dominated groups in zoos and science centres. I now discuss a study, referred to by them, of family visits to a science centre.

The teaching behaviour of families

Diamond (1986) was interested in the teaching behaviour of families. She recorded the interactions between family members and their responses to exhibits in two science centres. It was found that the average family visit lasted just over two hours and that the families visited an average of sixty-two exhibits during their visits. Between 80 and 90 per cent of the entire visit duration was spent at exhibits. The rest of the time was spent at the café, the shop, the toilets, or waiting for other family members.

The twenty-eight families in her study appeared briefly to review exhibits until they found one that especially interested them. Then they would spend much longer periods of time. The mother tended to approach exhibits at which other family members were present and the children were likely to manipulate exhibits by themselves while their parents might watch or read to them.

Behaviours indicating aggression or distress on the part of a family member were more common when the second quarter of the visit was in progress. Mothers managed the ending of the visit and did so by actively terminating interactions with exhibits more frequently than during the earlier stages of the visit.

Diamond observed family 'teaching behaviours', which included showing, pointing, giving someone something to look at, pulling someone across to an exhibit, telling another family member to do something, describing something, and raising questions. Children accompanied by their parents 'showed' things to them more often than did children with other adult relatives. Otherwise, there was no difference in child behaviour dependent on the status of an adult relative. There was no social role involved in the describing of things and the asking of questions. Parents were more likely to 'show and tell' and the mothers were more likely to name something. The parents used the text and graphics to supplement their own knowledge and, also, as direct teaching aids when they read them out to their children.

Diamond concluded that teaching occurs as a fundamental aspect of the spontaneous social interactions of the family group. Family teaching worked to aid learning as it modified sensory feedback from the manipulation of exhibits. Family teaching also modified the symbolic feedback from exhibit texts. Interestingly, she indicated that all members of the family appeared to benefit from the family teaching behaviour.

The strategies families use to enhance learning from exhibits

Hilke (1988) and Hilke and Balling (1989) observed forty-two families throughout their visits in a hands-on science exhibition and a traditional exhibition hall in a natural history museum. They set out to discover whether families act as if they were trying to learn from exhibits and to note what learning-support strategies were used. The families they observed maintained a high focus on the exhibits and engaged in behaviours that supported the acquisition and exchange of information about them.

Hilke and Balling found no age and sex biases in the deployment of the family strategies. Acquiring and exchanging information was the primary focus of activity and 66 per cent of all behaviours were accounted for by it. In all, 86 per cent of what was said and done during the visit was directed at the exhibits. The remaining 14 per cent of behaviours were related to waiting for other family members, talking with or looking at a stranger, and to moving between exhibits.

It was noted that there was a distinct tendency for individual family members to decide for themselves just what they would see and when they would move on to a new exhibit. Hence, most of the information-gathering activity was done by an individual family member as they read, listened, looked at or manipulated an exhibit. Parents tended to let their children choose the exhibits the family would attend to, and more than half of all movements between exhibits were undertaken alone.

Hilke and Balling describe the behaviours of their families as co-operative. The information each person was exposed to was heavily influenced by other family members. Personal strategies for information-gathering seemed to be pursued in the presence of other family members. Most information exchange occurred as the spontaneous, unsolicited sharing of salient aspects of the experience of the giver of the information. Parents and children gave and received information in this way to an equal degree. The information was mainly concerned with facts and, to a lesser extent, with accounts of experiences and personal interpretations. Children were more likely than adults to broadcast facts. This tendency to broadcast commentaries on individual experiences increased the information available to all family members.

It was noticed that interaction was usually between parent and child pairs rather than between parents or siblings. This ensured that the giving and receiving of information took place between the more knowledgeable and experienced and the less knowledgeable, and it provided the parents with the opportunity to teach and guide their children. Hilke and Balling concluded that their families were 'active discoverers'.

Interestingly, Hilke and Balling also noted that family learning behaviour differed little between the hands-on exhibition and the traditional display hall. This observation is in contradiction to the findings in two studies which examined behaviour at individual traditional and interactive exhibits (Blud 1990; McManus 1989b). Both of these studies reported heightened levels of verbal activity at interactive exhibits and concluded that interactive exhibits encouraged social interaction.

A model of family behaviour in museums

From the pictures of whole-visit family behaviour given by Diamond (1986), Hilke (1988) and Hilke and Balling (1989), and from my own research (McManus 1987, 1988, 1989a, 1989b), I can model a picture of the family during a museum visit. We can think of the family as a co-ordinated hunter-gatherer team actively foraging in the museum to satisfy their curiosity about topics and objects that interest them, and to satisfy their curiosity about the topics and objects which museum professionals collect and study. Their behaviour is practical and economical since the exploration and information-gathering is shared out between the family members.

The parents select the likely area of exploration. Since the visit will last about two hours, this might be the entire contents of a small museum or several exhibitions in a large museum. The family then purposefully moves in a loose formation to explore the selected area. The children may physically lead in this exploratory behaviour. As family members encounter interesting items they report back to the family group as they broadcast factual information to each other. The parents are likely to identify or name new items encountered by the children and, in teaching mode, to comment on, or interpret, the information broadcast by the children much more than the children are likely to comment on the information broadcast by their parents.

Hence, the family works collectively to build a 'family perception' of the communications from the museum. At the same time, each individual family member forms his or her own perceptions of the exhibition encounter. These perceptions are inevitably mediated and adjusted by the social filter of the family 'forage, broadcast and comment' activity. The more relaxed the family is, and the more harmoniously they function as a family unit, the more successful the family and the individuals within it will be in engaging with the messages offered by the display (McManus 1988).

Special provision for families

Discovery rooms

Many museums set up discovery rooms especially designed for families with children up to the age of around 8. In Chapter 8 of this book, Gillian Thomas describes the special needs of such young children. White (1990) discusses discovery rooms and offers a useful list of references concerning the discovery rooms set up in a number of museums. She describes the discovery room as a place where families can feel they are having a family experience while working together on activities unavailable in the traditional halls of the museum. White describes the discovery room as a 'recovery room' offering a change of pace from the rest of the museum – a haven for the young family.

White notes that families stay longer in discovery rooms than do other visitors. Children appear to initiate exploration of the objects provided, and interaction with another family member is likely to lead to a more sustained inspection of that object. She notes that experience has shown that it is important to offer a broad range of choices of activities designed to suit all family members.

Family activity packs

Many museums offer printed guides or activity packs for the use of families. Newbury (1987) designed family activity packs for several British heritage sites and their museums when she discovered that most guides were only suitable for adults and that most activity packs were prepared exclusively for children. She noted that most visits to heritage sites were made as a family visit and set out to cater for the family as a unit by working on the social dimension of family behaviour.

Her family activity packs contained activity trail cards, a wall chart, photographs, activities and recipes to use at home, maps, suggestions for resting spots and picnics, and instructions for making things. The separate activity cards for each family member are used on site as the family walks around a museum or heritage site. The family builds up an information bank as each family member makes discoveries as he or she undertakes an activity or solves a problem on his or her card.

The impact of family visits to museums

Stevenson (1992) investigated the long-term impact on family group members of the interactive science centre Launch Pad in the Science Museum, London. He noted the short time-scale of involvement with individual exhibits and the brief duration of museum visits as a whole, and wished to investigate the memories of such encounters. He wondered if the memories of family group members would be of the episodes, or events, attached to the visit; whether they would have had time to build memories containing meaningful constructs derived from the cognitive processing of evidence gained from experimenting with the interactive exhibits.

Stevenson tracked twenty families throughout their visit; interviewed 109 families as they left the exhibition; sent some of these people a follow-up questionnaire several weeks after their visit and, six months after the visits, interviewed seventy-nine individual family members in their family groups in the family home.

Most of the families spent around an hour in Launch Pad and most families looked at nearly all of the exhibits during their visit. Children spent 53 per cent of their time in active investigations (over twice as long as adult family members). Around 80 per cent of the time at an exhibit was spent in interaction with another family member or a nearby stranger. Other behaviours included watching other people manipulate exhibits and managing the movement of family members between exhibits. The children, contrary to received opinion, did not spend large amounts of time rushing mindlessly about the exhibition. Male and female family members behaved throughout their visits in similar ways. The families did not spend less time at exhibits in the later stages of the visit and the pattern of behaviours did not alter significantly throughout the visit. This whole-visit description is similar in character to the descriptions of Diamond and of Hilke and Balling discussed above.

The responses to the questionnaires which Stevenson sent out several weeks after the family visits indicated that 99 per cent of the family members had talked to each other, or to family or friends, about the exhibits after the visit had been completed. Stevenson found that, six months after the visit to Launch Pad, the visitors were keen to talk about their visit. Most of them could describe exhibits without prompting: 27 per cent of all the memories of exhibits were spontaneous; 61 per cent were prompted by photographs; and 13 per cent were prompted by the comments of other family members. Only 17 per cent of the exhibits in the centre were not remembered by someone.

Family members were able to remember much of their visit to the science centre in clear detail. In fact, the durability of museum visit memories is one of the remarkable findings from this study. Sixty per cent of the personal memories were descriptions of exhibits and how they were used, 26 per cent of them were of thoughts about, and reflections on, the science or technology behind an exhibit, and 14 per cent were about the emotional feelings attached to seeing and using an exhibit.

Stevenson concluded that most memories of the museum visit were episodic in nature (presumably memories of the episode would be available for integration with related later experiences). This finding is in harmony with that of Hilke and

Balling (1989) who noted that the majority of the broadcast comments they recorded from family members were factual in nature. Factual description would tend to help build a descriptive, episodic memory of an event. Stevenson also found that a significant number of the memories reported to him indicated that cognitive processing, related to episodes which occurred during the family visit, does take place. Discussion with other family members after the visit was suggested as a factor involved in the retention and formation of memories.

Gender and family behaviour

Conflicting evidence

Gender does not appear to be a factor in the determination of whole-visit family behaviour. Hilke and Balling (1989) did not note any gender influences in their study described above. On the contrary, they described family behaviour as egalitarian. Stevenson (1992) did not record any gender-specific behaviour in his memories study. The work of Diamond (1986) reported that mothers tended to name things for their children and subtly to engineer the end of the family visit. However, only seven of the family groups in Diamond's study contained mother-and-father partnerships. Of the rest, mothers and fathers either visited alone or with adult relatives or friends. This circumstance is likely to have affected this particular finding.

Two studies of family activity at individual exhibits have reported gender-specific behaviour. Cone and Kendall (1978) observed family behaviour at four exhibits in an anthropology hall. Less than half of the family groups contained both mother and father and most did not contain both boys and girls. They noted differences between boys and girls in eliciting information from parents and, also, in parental interaction with sons and daughters. The mothers were likely to be the initiators of conversations while fathers appeared to be rather reticent and directed most of their talk to their sons. Boys asked questions more frequently than girls.

Blud (1990) observed fifty family groups at each of three exhibits in the Science Museum, London. Some groups contained one child and one adult, otherwise the generation and gender composition of the entire sample of family groups was somewhat similar in distribution to that of Cone and Kendall, although it differed at each of the three exhibits. Blud's findings on gender influence were in contradiction to those of Cone and Kendall.

In Blud's study, fathers interacted with children more than mothers did, and daughters initiated more conversations than sons. Blud (1990) went on to look at small subsamples of six families containing mother, father, daughter and son at an interactive exhibit and five families of identical construction at a traditional exhibit. At the interactive exhibit, mothers initiated more conversations than fathers, while fathers interacted more with daughters than with sons. Behaviour was more egalitarian at the static exhibit, although the girls did not initiate much interaction there. The gender differences observed here seem to be determined more by the exhibits than by family composition. However, it must be remembered that these final sample sizes were very small.

Assessment of the evidence for gender effects on family visits

There is a justified interest in exploring the notion of how gender-determined behaviour might affect communication with boys and girls in science museums because of the perception that girls might be socialised away from an interest in science. At the moment, I find the evidence for gender influences to be, at best, inconclusive.

First, social dynamics within a family are very subtle and influential and I suspect that they cannot easily be smoothed away by constructing standardised descriptive measures when families are not composed of parents and children of both sexes. It would be very difficult, and even more time-consuming, but I would prefer to see more studies where mothers and fathers, sons and daughters were present at the same time and where variations in the ages of children, and therefore stages of development, were taken into account.

Second, the whole-visit studies we have examined do not point to gender influences on family behaviour. It may be the case that they are incidental at particular moments during the visit to the museum and become ironed out over time.

Third, we have noted in the examination of whole-visit studies that individual family members tend to broadcast facts to the family in general as a part of the family information-gathering strategy. This means that many factual statements are open to any other family member to comment on, if so inclined, or silently to acknowledge and accept without challenge or reply. Gender biases would upset this co-operative balance. In my own linguistic analysis of conversations at three exhibits in the Natural History Museum (McManus 1987, 1989b) I found that 15 per cent of conversational acts fell into the category of silent acknowledgement and acceptance by the group as a whole.

The studies at individual exhibits would not have recorded these acts as features peculiar to group activity in the museum since there is an assumption that there is an addressee and an addressor for every comment. That is, interaction in the family is here seen as taking place between individuals rather than as an open, co-operative, group-focused activity.

Weaknesses in the picture of family behaviour in the museum

At present, there are three main reasons for the fuzzy picture we have of family behaviour in museums, although the picture is getting clearer all the time. First, many of the larger research studies cited in the museum literature were conducted in zoos and aquaria and, although such places share some similarities with museums as sources of informal education, they are not quite the same as museums. Second, the research that has been done in museums has been conducted almost exclusively in science museums. We do not know if families behave in quite the same ways in history or art museums although, judging by their reactions to traditional exhibits in science museums, it is quite likely that they do. Lastly, human behaviour is extremely complex when looked at second by second and, as a consequence, the analysis of behavioural data is very time-consuming. This means that the sample sizes and numbers of events investigated in studies are typically very small in number – often around twenty-five families at perhaps three or four exhibits – so that we have to piece together a picture from the complementary parts of different pieces of investigation. However, I hope that you will agree that an interesting base, on which decisions can be made and further work undertaken, has been established.

References

Bettelheim, B. (1984) 'Children, curiosity and museums', in S. Nichols, M. Alexander and K. Yellis (eds), *Museum Education Anthology 1973–1983*, Washington DC: Museum Education Roundtable.

Blud, L. (1990) 'Family interactions during a museum visit', *International Journal of Museum Management and Curatorship*, vol. 9, no. 3, pp. 257–64.

Cone, C. and Kendall, K. (1978) 'Space, time and family interaction: visitor behaviour at the Science Museum of Minnesota', *Curator*, vol. 21, no. 4, pp. 245–58.

Diamond, J. (1986) 'The behavior of family groups in science museums', *Curator*, vol. 29, no. 2, pp. 139–54.

Gottfried, J.L. (1979) 'A naturalistic study of children's behavior during field trips to a free-choice learning environment', PhD dissertation, University of California, Berkeley.

Hilke, D.D. (1988) 'Strategies for family learning in museums', *Visitor Studies: Theory, Research and Practice*, vol. 2, Jacksonville, Alabama: Centre for Social Design.

Hilke, D.D. and Balling, J.D. (1989) 'The Family as a Learning System: an Observational Study of Families in Museums', Unpublished manuscript, National Museum of American History, Smithsonian Institution, Washington DC.

Laetsch, W.M., Diamond, J., Gottfried, J.L. and Rosenfeld, S. (1980) 'Children and family groups in science centres', *Science and Children*, vol. 17, no. 6, pp. 14–17.

McManus, P.M. (1987) 'It's the company you keep: the social determination of learning-related behaviour in a science museum', *International Journal of Museum Management and Curatorship*, vol. 6, pp. 263–70.

—— (1988) 'Good companions: more on the social determination of learning-related behaviour in a science museum', *International Journal of Museum Management and Curatorship*, vol. 7, pp. 37–44.

—— (1989a) 'Oh yes they do! How visitors read labels and interact with exhibit texts', *Curator*, vol. 32, no. 3, pp. 174–89.

—— (1989b) 'What people say and how they think in a science museum', in D.L. Uzzell (ed.), *Heritage Interpretation Vol. 2, The Visitor Experience*, London: Bellhaven Press.

Newbury, E. (1987) 'Something for all the family', *Journal of Education in Museums*, vol. 8, pp. 9–10.

Newsom, B.Y. and Silver, A.Z. (1978) *The Art Museum as Educator*, Berkeley, Ca.: University of California Press.

Rosenfeld, S. (1980) 'Informal education in zoos: naturalistic studies of family groups', PhD dissertation, University of California, Berkeley.

Stevenson, J. (1992) 'The long-term impact of interactive exhibits', *International Journal of Science Education*, vol. 13, no. 5, pp. 521–31.

White, J. (1990) 'What have we discovered about discovery rooms?', in B. Serrell (ed.), *What Research Says about Learning in Science Museums*, Washington DC: Association of Science-Technology Centres.

7

Travelling exhibits: the Swedish experience

Jan Hjorth

Introduction

I shall now tell you the thirty-year long story of the rise, but hopefully not the downfall,[1] of a state-run organisation built on a simple, ingenious idea: to put exhibitions on tour. This is also the story of technical production and design problems, and the big non-stop fight between three goddesses, named Art, Pedagogy and Science, strange names for goddesses but then it is a strange war, too. I know all about it, because I was there, right from the very first day, and I am still there. Or do I really know? To be right in the thick of it is perhaps the wrong location from which to understand and get a good perspective. So this is certainly not a scholarly essay.

Once upon a time all this started in a small yet large country called **Sweden**. Small yet large? Well, small because the population is only about 8.5 million people. Large because it covers a big area, hidden far up in the very north of Europe.

Few people and long distances: that's part of the very point of putting exhibitions on tour. Why should an exhibition produced in a museum, at great cost, be seen only by the people living near the museum? And why indeed should it be seen and enjoyed by only the wealthy and educated city people? The 1960s in Sweden was a decade in which cultural policy was subjected to a serious appraisal. Discussion books and articles were published dealing with the function of cultural life in society, the organisation of cultural amenities, and the conditions of cultural practitioners. Policy-makers and cultural workers were provided with figures and arguments by students of the sociology of culture, all of them showing the different cultural patterns presented by different social classes. A great deal of the discussion concerned ways and means of increasing the consumption of culture, possibilities of broadening the cultural environment, and the question of efficient cultural distribution.

Intellectuals and politicians, interested in long and theoretical discussions regarding **cultural policy**, coined two policy phrases (at least) for exhibitions in Sweden: geographical justice and social justice. This meant that it would be unfair for the cities and the capital to keep exhibitions to themselves. That would be bad economy, too. Put them on tour, to meet *more* people in *other* places; and, of course, it is unfair not to lure *new* groups of visitors, as they are also taxpayers and consequently economic contributors, even though they may not have dreamt of going to exhibitions.

I remember somebody ('the Man in the Street') who said: 'Culture is nothing to me, I am just not interested! I go to the theatre and to concerts instead.' Would this person go to exhibitions? These are certainly not as glamorous in the public mind as theatre, music, TV and films. So the Swedish government (Social Democrats, at the time) started, in 1965, a creation called Swedish Travelling Exhibitions, in Swedish Riksutställningar. Or, more specifically, a decree by the King in Council of 26 March 1965 empowered the head of the Ministry of Education to call a number of experts to carry out a survey regarding museums, travelling exhibitions and other matters. The committee of enquiry which was duly set up came to be known as MUS 65.

MUS 65 was a rather unusual committee of enquiry in that its business included not only fact-finding but also practical experiments with actual exhibitions. Thus Riksutställningar was part and parcel of the greater task allotted to MUS 65 to cover all aspects of museum activity in Sweden. The experts were given the interesting job of building up a brand new enterprise and providing a basic plan for the activities and policies to be pursued. A Secretariat was set up in the autumn of 1965: at this stage it consisted of three people. I was one of them. On this slender basis was to be developed a full-scale programme of exhibitions.

Riksutställningar expanded rapidly during its first few years. This was only to be expected, for, at the same time as it was purely experimental, it had to be conducted on a scale sufficient to allow for a definite conclusion by the experts and by all the parties whose opinions would have to be heard regarding state-sponsored travelling exhibitions on a permanent basis: museums, education authorities, popular educational associations, the communities and their cultural committees, art societies and, finally, the government and the parliament. On the other hand, there was at this experimental stage no call for a fully fledged organisation capable of meeting the entire national demand for exhibitions. (We are still not capable of that, and we do not want to be! We do not want to be dominant.)

Accordingly, the activities of Riksutställningar in the beginning would have to be limited to spot experiments. Every single project would (in theory!) have to make its own particular contribution to the general experiment. This principle was to apply to both the production and distribution of the experiments. This was perhaps bound to lead to occasional misunderstandings with organisations and individuals who, unaware of the limitations to which the experiment was subject, tried unsuccessfully to get their needs attended to.

Our first tour was an art exhibition. We were allowed to borrow one painting from each room in the prestigious Swedish National Art Gallery and to put this collection on tour all over the country – in the event, to twenty-two different places –'to celebrate an anniversary of the Gallery. Notice the policemen in the

Figure 7.1 Exhibitions are not as glamorous as theatre, music or TV

Figure 7.2 Riksutställningar's first tour

photo (Figure 7.2): we were fresh in the museum business, the paintings were valuable, we were quite frankly a bit scared, and the conservators were worried. More about that later.

In 1967 it was high time for our first information and PR folder. To sum up, perhaps I should quote the text in full (most of the leaflet consisted of pictures):

> The National Touring Theatre performs plays all over Sweden. The National Concert Tour Scheme travels round the country giving concerts.
>
> Should the State also organise tours of exhibitions? Riksutställningar was set up in the autumn of 1965, to look into this point.
>
> The exhibitions cover everything from Stone Age axes and stuffed birds to computers and Picasso. They deal with both topical problems and historical developments.
>
> The results of the experiments will be available in a few years' time. The question may then arise: Should there be a permanent governmental agency for travelling exhibitions? If so, what form should it take?
>
> Before we can answer these questions we shall have to know the following things:
>
> - Can we interest people from all categories of the population (i.e. achieve a full social coverage)?
> - Can we reach the public outside the big cities (i.e. achieve full geographical coverage)?
> - Can we make a useful contribution to the national education effort (primary schools, secondary schools, adult education, etc.)?
>
> We also want to investigate what co-ordinating functions can be performed in the sphere of travelling exhibitions by a central state agency. Since 1 July 1967, the activities previously undertaken in this sphere by the Society for Art in Schools and the Swedish Arts Council have been experimentally merged with those of the National Scheme for Travelling Exhibitions.
>
> The National Scheme for Travelling Exhibitions also wishes to attempt the following things:
>
> - Improve exhibition techniques (presentation and other pedagogical methods, transport systems, etc.).
> - Integrate exhibitions with theatrical and musical events.
> - Evolve sound economic principles for the production and presentation of exhibitions.
> - Make scientific studies of the effect of exhibitions.
> - Show objects in other ways than at exhibitions (e.g. film, television, etc.).

Amalgamation

The directives for MUS 65 envisaged the amalgamation of the activities of Riksutställningar with those long pursued by the Society for Art in Schools and the Swedish Arts Council. Subsidies were paid to these organisations for two years, with the proviso that they were to be used in consultation with MUS 65. This collaboration coupled with the general progress of the survey did a great deal to ease the way to an experimental amalgamation of all three bodies.

Identity

So, now we were united with two art organisations. And some of the largest projects carried out were conducted jointly with different art museums. As a consequence, a lot of people long thought us to be an art institution. This was beginning to be a problem. An early exhibition entitled 'Are We Poisoning Nature?' was created by the Swedish Museum of Natural History; Riksutställningar was mainly concerned with its distribution. A large exhibition called 'The Magic Cabinet', comprising objects and materials borrowed from as many different kinds of museums as we could find throughout the country, was produced by the County Custodian of Gävle. Work soon was in progress on an ethnological exhibition to be produced by the Norrbottens Museum in the far north of Sweden. Moreover 1970, being Nature Conservancy Year, was to be devoted to a large-scale joint project by the Central Office of National Antiquities, the Swedish Museum of Natural History and Riksutställningar.

People who realised that we were not simply an art institution regarded us as a *museum* institution. The museums *are* important partners of Riksutställningar, but other important co-producers and recipients of exhibitions are to be found in a variety of sectors: schools, popular education, libraries, public authorities and so on. Riksutställningar also co-operated closely from time to time with its heavenly twins, the National Touring Theatre and the National Concert Tour Scheme.

Consolidation

Travelling exhibitions were nothing new to museums. Rather, the novelty lay in the need for a new, multi-museum body specialising in travelling exhibitions and able to provide them on a larger scale than before, while at the same time not having any collections of its own.

Early experience had shown that Riksutställningar would have to develop its own productional organisation. Within a year or two, productional self-sufficiency had come to mean a permanent workshop and studio, partly for economic reasons and partly because existing workshops and studios proved to be lacking in experience of the technical requirements demanded by travelling exhibitions, namely toughness, ease of assembly, mobility and so on. Riksutställningar and its staff had themselves to acquire experience and knowledge if they were to be adequate partners to the museums, with their daily experience of the business of exhibiting. It was in the nature of things that the museums would be particularly exacting in their demands on Riksutställningar. As a result, Riksutställningar saw every reason during the early years to concentrate an appreciable proportion of its resources on production as well as distribution.

From the outset, a travelling exhibition has to be constructed with a view to travelling. This is not generally the case with exhibitions produced in Sweden, so that there is little chance of a ready-made exhibition being put into circulation. But it can happen, especially if Riksutställningar has been able to follow the original production period as observers and advisers. Great importance is attached by Riksutställningar to the development of better forms of collaboration regarding joint projects. Collaboration of this kind has to begin at the planning stage and must aim, among other things, at solving the technical problems involved in making an exhibition mobile.

A report on the trial period of national travelling exhibitions was ready for publication by the middle of 1974. This report included proposals by the experts regarding the tasks of a future permanent National Travelling Exhibitions Authority. The report was circulated for comment by the bodies concerned, and a bill on the subject was presented to the Swedish parliament. And so, in 1976, parliament decided on a permanent Riksutställningar. The altered status did not mean much change as far as working theory and practical matters were concerned. The show was supposed to go on, and it did, and does, up to this very day. There was nothing wrong with that: – the show had been approved, so why change it? The only real novelty in 1976 was the new film and video group (with broadcast standard) created within the production department.

Today

There are at present some 100 different exhibitions on show under the auspices of Riksutställningar. Some of these have been produced in several editions so as to bring them to a larger public. The original secretariat of three has evolved into a modern production and distribution enterprise, serving large areas of the country, and a cultural institution with a full-time staff of over fifty-five people.

What problems could an idea such as this encounter?

So far, I have described the Riksutställningar story as a success story. That's not the whole truth. Of course, Riksutställningar has encountered problems during its almost thirty years of existence. Personally, I love writing about problems. One can learn so much from negative experiences, so here goes.

The fear of strangers

It is common knowledge that a stranger from another village is regarded with suspicion or worse. In other words, most people are instinctively repelled by people different from themselves – different in colour, appearance, way of thinking, background and so on. Many handicapped people, for instance, are the victims of such attitudes. Now, for anybody who works in a museum, it is obvious that Riksutställningar is a little out of the ordinary, a little different. For Riksutställningar is *not a complete museum*. We have the exhibition side, we often use the same themes in these exhibitions, but we do not have our own collections of objects, we have no conservator, and we do not have any scientific research. Riksutställningar is simply not a museum! Those who work at Riksutställningar believe they are at least members of the 'museum' family, but many curators feel this is not so – at best we are in-laws, and at worst we are strange and repulsive aliens. This we did not expect. But the situation should not be exaggerated. Most of the time we get on extremely well, only to be the more shocked when the alien syndrome occasionally raises its ugly head!

Fear of competition

Riksutställningar is no bigger than one single, medium-sized museum, but some emotional turmoil took place in a few museum people's minds when we new-comers in the market turned up in the 1960s. Because of this state of emotion, the picture of Riksutställningar has grown and grown, and when people visit, the instinctive comment is 'How BIG you are!' This leads them to the thought that 'this Riksutställningar must cost some money – *our* money!' This is a mental somersault, as no museum would have had more money had Riksutställningar *not* existed, and no museum will get more money if we close down. What is important is that Riksutställningar *adds to the resources in the museum sector*, because we do quite a lot of service work for the museums each year, especially for the small and poor ones.

The fallacy about financial competition might be linked to a more general fear of *competition in the development of the exhibition as an artistic and pedagogical medium*. But in most cases the competition has instead spurred both parties to develop the medium. Some mean-spirited people have suggested that the success-ful development of the medium in Sweden during the last decades – on which everybody is in agreement – is the only benefit derived from the creation of Riksutställningar.

Are the objects in danger?

Part of our strength is that we are allowed to borrow objects from all state-owned museums. The question thus arises: is it safe to tour objects? Packing and unpacking, transportation in boxes, however cleverly constructed, showing objects in faraway places where thieves may prowl . . . is it wise? During the years we have built up a collection of letters from museums, where fears for the safety of different objects are voiced, letters that often end with a firm NO, you cannot borrow this or that.

In 1965 or 1966 we did have a bad start when one of our board members, quite an unusual and original colleague, made a speech at a big conference where all the important museum people from Stockholm were gathered. He said that he regarded collections as consumer goods, they existed for the general public, and if they stayed in storerooms they would, of course, be preserved for the next generation, and the next, and the next – but, in the end, no generation would ever see them. Better then to show them, tour them and risk them. If a few objects disappeared, or were damaged, there would still be objects enough left to satisfy everybody in the future. The audience at the conference interpreted this as if the man had said that museum objects were dispensable. They thought he spoke for us all.

It did not help much that he was the *only* one of us who took this fairly light view on objects, their preservation and their future destiny. He *was* at the conference as our official representative, it is true. Unfortunately, his speech gave a poor and inaccurate first impression of Riksutställningar, since during its thirty-odd years in existence, its record has certainly been no worse than any traditional museum in its handling of paintings, sculptures and other objects.

Failure to communicate the concept

I have already mentioned our art image. For the general public, too, in my part of the world, the word *exhibition* in an instinctive, unreflecting sort of way seems to mean 'art exhibition'. We are very proud that 30 per cent of what we do is in the art sector; when I tell a person I meet for the first time that my job is concerned with touring exhibitions, he or she automatically associates me with oil paintings, sculptures and so forth. So when our biggest tour for young people today (1992), in our exhibition railway train, turns out to be about how important it is that we all work hard to save the world from air and water pollution, it is not what everybody expects. The arts and crafts image has often caused us information problems. Colleagues in museums, on the other hand, tend to take it for granted that Riksutställningar is an enterprise wholly within their own cultural sector, namely *museums*. In fact, of the total time our exhibitions are shown to the public, only 20 per cent takes place in museum buildings. For the rest, our exhibitions visit libraries, schools and other localities.

The problem here is that a curator who firmly believes ('knows') that Riksutställningar is a *museum* service organisation may become furious when he or she notices that we devote ourselves to things outside the museum field. Thus, to their eyes, we seem to squander money earmarked for museums. Harsh words follow, sometimes in the press, which is bad PR for Riksutställningar, since we are to some extent dependent on the goodwill and backing of politicians and journalists, not to mention that of our museum colleagues.

Let the public make exhibitions!

It is a common observation that most visitors are initially reluctant to participate in exhibitions. However, so long as the active effort which is expected of them is not too complicated or demanding, there is generally no serious *opposition* to participation. To 'discover' by feeling objects and using movable parts is a useful first step for the reluctant visitor. However, to get the single adult visitor to take a more creative and constructive role is more difficult. To be creative in form and colour is considered very desirable, but it is mostly children and young people, and to some extent parents together with children, who make use of the facilities. The average visitor is not at all keen on taking part in activities which are time-consuming.

Readiness to act seems to be connected above all with age and earlier exhibition-visiting habits, as well as with an affiliation with a group, an organisation, an association, and the like. The most common reasons for inactivity are:

- The adult visitor looks on the activity as a form of play and therefore something which is mainly for children. The impression is reinforced by the fact that children often dominate in the activity rooms, at work tables, etc.
- The visitor does not dare to act because he or she is afraid that other visitors will pass judgements on the results. Visitors demand high-quality results from themselves.
- The visitor has been taught from childhood that exhibitions are only to be looked at.
- The visitor has the idea that participation in a certain activity is a right reserved for the 'establishment'.
- The visitor has little interest in the purpose of the activity.
- Those visitors who *took* an active role are, as a rule, more satisfied with the exhibition than those who were passive (Nylöf 1974).

Since 1972, however, Riksutställningar has collaborated with adult education associations with a view to encouraging study circles and other small groups to make their own exhibitions. The main object is to provide people with the requisite resources to express themselves through the medium of an exhibition. It is hoped thereby to remedy to some extent the defects of the one-way communication process from institutions to individuals, which is characteristic of so much of the present flow of information. It is a good thing if people who were earlier at the receiving end find a medium that can act as their mouthpiece. And costs for simple exhibitions are lower than most other media – an exhibition may cost anything from nil upwards, it may cost nothing if the material is second-hand or found at the local rubbish dump!

The members of the working groups usually consider it to be very stimulating to work together for a common aim with a practical and concrete nature. At a place where the participants have not known one another previously, there is a feeling of having been welded together, and of an enhanced sense of interdependence.

Knowledge of the exhibition medium

Some of the members of the working parties may never have been to an exhibition while many others may, for various reasons, have been infrequent visitors to such events. After such people have themselves worked on exhibitions, their views on the medium are changed. 'We have had our eyes opened,' said one member. 'I should never have driven to town to see the current exhibition were it not for my involvement in the working party. Now I am curious to see how it functions and how it was mounted. We have got into the process, as it were, we know how it works.' Another participant says that he now places greater demands on exhibitions. 'I want to know the purpose behind the exhibition.'

The art exhibition 'Art in the Village', and the art circle which was started as a consequence of this event, are also considered to have changed people's attitude to art. 'When we had the art exhibition, the atmosphere was relaxed, unlike exhibitions in town, which somehow seem so aloof and sterile. We saw the exhibition with entirely different eyes. It was the nature of our encounter with art which was different.' Participants said that they wanted the exhibition to take place in a setting 'where you can drink coffee and chat, for it is important to establish contact with people'. It was also considered essential to initiate a debate on what the exhibition had given to those who saw it. Many now realised the advantages of the exhibition over other media. 'Nothing can be more tangible and evident than an exhibition.' 'It is more alive, reaches more people and is less laborious to go through than a book.'

The pedagogical effects of exhibition work

These exhibitions mounted by amateurs in their spare time are not, of course, to be compared with professional productions. Training in exhibition techniques is not an end in itself. The fact of presenting something in practical terms has, however, had a stimulating effect on the study work. The representatives of the adult education organisations also pointed out that much could be gained from this form of work from a pedagogical point of view, not least where co-operation was concerned.

The exhibition as a medium, development through education?

Riksutställningar trains people in the art of producing and using exhibitions. Courses for amateurs have existed for a long time, but until recently there were no courses for professionals. Before the mid-1980s, Sweden had hardly any professional training in this subject at all. All this began to change, however, a few years ago when a study programme on the exhibition as a medium was established at university level. That programme began as an education project and also, above all, as a development project. Education, yes, but automatically

Figure 7.3 It is stimulating to work together for a common aim

this was to bring about a much-needed development: a development of the methods and theories of exhibition work, for the benefit of both Riksutställningar's exhibitions and those of other organisations. Apart from the very shortest course, priority for admissions is currently being given to people who are already professionally active in museums.

The courses have varied in duration between 3 and 20 weeks. They are intended to give exhibition professionals in the cultural sector a wider and more coherent knowledge of professional exhibition work from the viewpoints of, for example, artistic design, pedagogics, communication and technology. This is an important form of education for the praiseworthy purpose of combating something which the general public is sometimes affected by – exhibition abuse!

The aims of the study programme are:

- to give the participants a deeper knowledge of professionally conducted exhibition activities in the cultural sector, with regard to both the production and, not least, the use of exhibitions, and
- to provide a general introduction to various theories in the media sector which can form the basis of exhibition work.

I have made a list of topics for the training. Each item represents, in a way, a profession in its own right, with a couple of exceptions. A good (and fairly theoretical) question is: Do we need a group of twenty specialists to help the curator make an exhibition? Or: How many professions and crafts is the producer of an exhibition supposed to master? Our advice is to use as many specialists as you can afford, but at the same time try to learn as much as you can yourself about as many trades as you can.

Here is my list of training topics:

- Different types of exhibitions (basic exhibitions, temporary exhibitions, travelling exhibitions, fairs)
- The target group
- The project group. Planning
- The relation of form and content
- Spatial design
- Artistic design
- Exhibition pedagogics
- The pedagogics of work (or process work, learning by doing, user participation, audience participation)
- Journalistic working method
- Theory of learning. Psychology
- The art of mixing available media
- The exhibit
- Use of pictures
- Exhibition texts
- Graphic design
- Hanging
- Lighting

- Audio-visual media
- Printed matter
- The introductory screen
- The exhibition as a social meeting point
- Programme activities
- School activities
- Showing exhibitions
- Study material
- Help for intermediaries (between producer and public)
- Advance information and marketing
- The administration and economics of the exhibition
- Exhibition technology (i.e. technology in the studio and workshop)
- Literature for further reading on exhibition work
- Evaluation techniques for exhibitions

The fight between beauty and function

The making of exhibitions is a difficult thing. Architects like to think that the production of exhibitions is closely allied to their profession and professionalism. This was brought home to us in a curious way at Riksutställningar when, in 1986, we began expanding our experimental study programme in exhibition skills by adding a unit at post-secondary level. Our then associate, the National College of Art and Design, called in architects to serve as dedicated teachers. Several of them genuinely believed that architecture was the name of the game. We had lectures on how national pavilions (i.e. buildings) had been constructed at different world exhibitions, and how the Stockholm Exhibition of 1897 was spread out over Stockholm (landscape design). Parks also came into the picture. And Space with a capital 's'. Space indeed is a central issue in the making of exhibitions, but it is not the whole story. We were rather worried. Several of our exhibitions occupy 2 square metres. None of them exceeds 300 square metres!

During the study programme, discussions between the participants (teachers included) polarised in two directions. Putting it drastically but distinctly, the extremes were represented by 'dreamy, demanding aesthetes with religious features' on the one hand, and 'functionalist realists aspiring to be educators of the people and with a touch of sermonising, pretentious tedium', on the other. Imagine the quarrels we've had!

Many exhibitions have to convey both experience and knowledge and be capable of reaching the majority of visitors. The important thing is for exhibitions really to work. The exhibition-maker must be both creative and a down-to-earth realist. Exhibitions must be based both on artistic, architectural design and on the craftsmanship of education and journalism. This does not necessarily mean that I compromise on artistic standards. Instead, it means that I want to make the *same* high qualitative demands, e.g. on educational pedagogics and considerations for the visitor. The training should be designed accordingly.

The necessity of amalgamating practical function and beauty, and the problems which this involves, make producing and using exhibitions a speciality in its own right, calling for special training.

On the amateur side we are continuing our outreach activities with a series of fully subscribed exhibition courses for librarians. Last but not least, Riksutställningar's extramural seminars are still going strong. A recent one, held for two days in September 1991, was about the business of producing exhibition texts in museums, following on from our new book on the subject, entitled *Smaka på orden* [*Savour the Words*].

Waste of teachers?

The use of exhibitions is an important point to consider. Once the exhibition has been produced, we are still only at a half-way point. In a discussion at a seminar entitled 'Types of Exhibition', in the autumn of 1986, the Head of the Museum of Telecommunications pointed out: 'We must make our exhibitions so that they interact well with the visitors.' A museum educationalist at the National Museum of Science and Technology then remarked that not all museum people attached very much importance to what happened after the official opening. But that is just when the great task of bringing exhibitions to life has to begin. It is vital to make use of those who want to show the exhibitions. As one educationalist put it:

> Those of us who have to take over an exhibition and bring it to life when it is ready are educationalists who meet classes every day. But the problem then is that, in many people's eyes, we museum educationalists have a low status occupation – that's where you begin, and then you're expected to get on, to be promoted.

So, if someone becomes a good teacher, they stop teaching and move upstairs.

The educationalist who is in at the beginning, when an exhibition is built, also gradually builds up his or her own knowledge. But this is not usually the case with a travelling exhibition from outside. Perhaps one gets a bundle of literature a fortnight before the exhibition opens – here's your homework! Briefly then, we have to break this trend of museum educationalists not being in on the production from the very beginning.

Should exhibition work always be an art?

The 1986 course has been described as Sweden's first university course on the subject of the exhibition as a medium. That isn't true. But perhaps it is true to say that it was Sweden's first real study programme for exhibition makers in the cultural sector. But was it 'a real study programme'? This was, after all, a twenty-point course, untried and never previously operated.

Figure 7.4 Many exhibitions have to convey both experience and knowledge

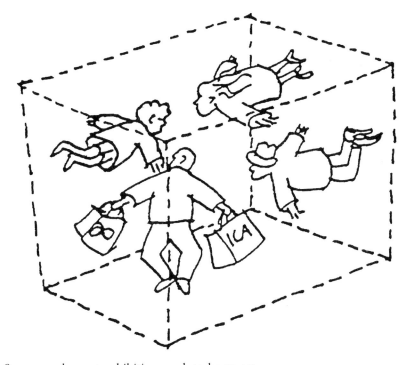

Figure 7.5 Some people want exhibition work to be an art

Only people count

At the beginning of the course I had the following to say about the exhibition as a medium, in a discussion with the participants. I reproduce it here because it illuminates Riksutställningar's (or at least my own) viewpoint when the course was about to begin.

> The prospects for this course are favourable. Because the exhibition, in Sweden, has a long way to go before its potentialities as a medium have been fully explored, *developed*, tested and utilised. There is a lot to be done. This is a rewarding starting point for the course, for you and for us. Exhibition work in Sweden today is not an art. Some of us think it would be a bad thing to give the exhibition the status of an art. A very bad thing! But some people *want* exhibition work to be an art. This is a fundamental conflict. Designers often take it for granted that everybody can decipher the language of form, of design. But the majority of people *do not* interpret the designer's language. We must also reach that majority!
>
> Normally a project group for an exhibition wants to get across to many people. To succeed, the group can benefit from a knowledge of design *and* pedagogics *and* other 'communication subjects' (journalism, for example). Faced with this, the designer has a choice. Many, for example, have studied and acquired first-hand experience of fields of knowledge outside design as such.
>
> Faced with the demand of getting across to many people, other designers go on the defensive, become evasive, make excuses and come up with counter-arguments, saying that 'If everybody were to know everything, the world would be a boring place! Regimented! Levelled down!' 'In any case, exhibition work is mostly a matter of design.' Or else they say: 'I detest rules and sermons.' The designer, equating sermons and pedagogics, thereby reveals great ignorance of the world outside art! People go on the defensive. At best they maintain that design is an 'overriding concept' which also incorporates communication subjects: 'If an exhibition has a high artistic standard of design, it will also be educational.'
>
> *Don't let exhibition work be proclaimed an art*! Year after year I have witnessed how helpless the public – like myself – is when confronted by artistically designed exhibitions which are projects for the initiated. True, they can convey an experience, but often not the experience intended. Conveying just *any* experience is not good enough. Often there is also a message which fails to get across. Perhaps there is knowledge and information to communicate which is distorted and misunderstood. That isn't good enough.
>
> It is the public – the majority of people – that matters most. Better exhibitions must cater to people's real needs.
>
> Artistic design is good for the public and therefore good for the exhibition.

Its benefit, perhaps its necessity, is obvious. But there are great perils in making the exhibition itself and the related exhibition work in itself an *art*. In the field of exhibition activities, a syndrome occurs which can aptly be termed *the tyranny of aesthetics* and which can lead to *exhibition abuse*.

Several course participants, and teachers, have emphasised that we must not make an antithesis of aesthetics and pedagogics. So there is one point which it is important to make. If I coin the phrase 'the tyranny of aesthetics', I haven't said a word against aesthetics, only against tyranny.

A colleague in Sweden, Sven Lidman, has expressed the situation as follows:

'Form is important in all information, but it has to be the form of the content, not of the surface. Form must sometimes be subordinated to the message and its insistence on getting across to the recipient. Cows, as we all know, have four stomachs. A consumer has at least two – the aesthetical stomach and the cognitive stomach. If the decorative form inspires cheerful sensations of repletion in our aesthetical stomach, perhaps we won't even notice that our cognitive stomach remains empty. A purely aesthetic form at the expense of content blocks the recipient and makes him passive. We must think in terms of both content and form: and a content and form which are adapted to the recipient's frame of reference and imagination – not the sender's. If I may use a metaphor: The sender walks along a road. A road is usually lined by two ditches. In the world of the informant, one of them is called 'Art for Art's Sake', and the other we might call 'By the Learned for the Learned', an excessively advanced presentation, inaccessible to the recipient. As a real-life road user, one can end up in either of the two ditches. But in the world of symbols, the informant–sender can actually end up in both of them at once.'

Acknowledgements

I am grateful for the help received from my colleagues Mr G. Nylöf, Mrs I. Hammer and Mrs U. Arnell over the sections of this paper on community-made exhibitions, and to Björn Ed and Benny Engman for the drawings.

Note

The Swedish government appointed an *ad hoc* Commission in 1993 to consider and make proposals for the Swedish museum sector and Riksutställningar.

References

Nylöf, G. (1974) 'Visits to museums and exhibitions seen in a sociological perspective', in U. Arnell, I. Hammer and G. Nylöf (eds), *Utställningar*, Stockholm: MUS 65.

115

8

'Why are you playing at washing up again?' Some reasons and methods for developing exhibitions for children

Gillian Thomas

Small children see little distinction between work and play. Activities which would be classified as one or the other by adults are used to an equal degree by young children as opportunities for learning, whether or not they are structured by an adult. What is studied is decided by the child in response to the opportunities offered by the environment. Every waking hour is an endless quest for information.

Contrast this with the learning experience for a child at the end of primary education; the motivation and enthusiasm for learning will have reduced, in many cases, to a spasmodic interest in some areas of study. The content, order and level is defined largely by regulations and by the adult who acts as a guide. Thirst for learning in the context of school remains in some individuals, but for many learning becomes equated with work, as a task imposed by others. On the other hand, adults acquire an interest in learning when the knowledge is of direct relevance to them, for example related to their jobs, hobbies or in response to changes in their personal situation, such as the arrival of children. A full cycle has been made; the programme is again established by the individual, in response to the environment, and again this is not always considered as learning.

Exhibitions developed and designed for children attempt to match this natural pattern of learning. Based on children's ideas, related to their styles of learning, not being perceived as 'work', such exhibitions aim to prolong and stimulate the natural curiosity of children and help them to develop a thirst for learning and a delight in the acquisition of knowledge. Information is selected for its relevance to the daily lives of children and is presented in the context of an environment. At the Inventorium in Paris and at Eureka!, the Children's Museum in Halifax, England, developers and designers have worked closely with children, both prior to exhibition opening and in the adaptation period afterwards. The procedures for developing exhibitions, their constraints and limitations as well as the unexpected advantages, are considered in this chapter. None of the methods described is necessarily relevant only to a public of children. Rather, having chosen children as a target public, the paucity of information concerning children's ideas of the themes under consideration and the discrepancy between their knowledge and interests and the proposed content make it inevitable that studies will have to be carried out. Nor should it be imagined that such work is ever completely satisfactory. Any one item suggested for an exhibition could be the subject of a thesis.

An attempt is made to indicate simple, low-cost techniques of developing exhibition content which can be used as extensively as timetables and budgets allow to ensure that the exhibitions are as well adapted as possible to the target public. Visionary pragmatism is the concept; how to achieve the impossible, with the minimum of time and money.

Why create exhibitions for children?

Children under 12 are one of the major groups of visitors for science centres and museums. For children's museums, the mixture of school and family visits ensures that the percentage of children approaches 50 per cent. At the City for Science and Industry at La Villette, Paris, children under 12 comprise 25 per cent of the total visitor numbers. In some months of the year, notably towards the end of the academic year, young people under 18 comprised almost 50 per cent of the visitors. Adolescents have traditionally been considered as a group showing little interest in independent visits to museums. However, the futuristic image of La Villette and youth-oriented marketing campaigns succeeded in establishing the centre as a place for young people to visit in their own free time, mainly in small groups of friends.

Most museums recognise the importance of children as a specific group among their visitors. However, activities for them are generally developed as an addition, an optional extra, rather than being an integrated aspect of exhibition design. Two strategies evolve: first, 'ghettoisation', keeping an area specifically reserved for extra activities, and largely containing children within these spaces; second, adding on exhibits, creating educational trails, or 'fun' exhibits designed to occupy and amuse. At worst, these can resemble the worthy Christmas gift, designed to keep the child quiet. The importance of a visit to a museum being an educational experience is no less valid for them than for adults, but their needs are specific, whether the content, educational level or approach, or the ergonomic constraints are considered.

Children under the age of 12 should be a priority as this is the period of their lives where maximum development occurs. It is also the period when attitudes are formed and habits established. If a child is disenchanted with education by adolescence, changes in attitude are difficult to achieve. A single visit that captures the imagination of a child can positively affect future interests and career orientations. Two vital areas need to be considered: how the maximum impact can be obtained and, second, the specific nature of exhibitions that ought to be developed for this age group.

Educational content

Some of the factors that influence decisions as to the content of an exhibition include the existence of specific collections at a museum; available funding related to particular themes; an externally organised cultural event (such as the Japan Year in the UK in 1991); influential trustees' particular interests or an expert body's opinion as to areas of study that are of importance or future relevance. A brief perusal of available information on the interests of the UK public indicates a considerable discrepancy between such themes and what interests the general public. The most popular topics of conversation between family and friends include TV programmes, bringing up children, sport, the present government, you and your family's health, and gardening.

Education is of more interest than the cost of living, and only of slightly less common occurrence as a topic of conversation than clothes and fashion. Sixty-eight per cent of adults were involved in some form of DIY in the last twelve months; 85 per cent have a garden. While romance and love for women, and crime for men, are the most popular types of books bought, car repair, sport, health, gardening, food and adventure stories all figure in the top ten. It would, perhaps, be inadvisable to take the existing interests of the public, which is the client, as the only criterion. On the other hand, it is inadvisable to ignore the real interests of the public.

For children, less research is available as to their current interests. However, any content which is proposed solely on the grounds that it is of educational importance, related to the National Curriculum, or important for future development, needs to be examined in terms of whether it is related to children's existing knowledge. Whether in a family or school group, the visit to a museum is not a coercive activity; children cannot be forced to learn, the information has to be relevant and attractive. Finding the appropriate educational level is essential. An exhibition designed intellectually for adults will not 'fit', any more than clothes would. Attempts to include children's corners, amusing exhibits and trails will, at best, give a child a very partial view of the educational message. The content must be defined by the educational needs of the visitor, both as to the interest of the subjects presented and to the range of learning styles that the exhibition can accommodate. Museums can offer a wider range of opportunity for learning than schools, and emphasise the autonomy of the individual to structure the visit. Information needs to be linked to a real experience in a context that can continue to be relevant and can be extended to outside the museum.

Visitors to a museum or science centre are, like day-trippers to an unknown town, trying to make sense of their surroundings. As well as requiring help to make sense of the visit, they need to be encouraged to become honorary citizens for a day, with a valuable part to play, rather than being simply non-participating spectators. All visitors, but in particular children, need to feel that they are individually involved in the exhibition, to have their emotions aroused and their imaginations stimulated. Creating a context that is relevant to the visitor, personalising a visit, taking home a souvenir, leaving a trace, all help visitors to feel that they have participated and to get to grips with the content. However, as with advertising, it is essential that the personality or device promoting a product has an image that is consonant with it, so any use of input from the visitor needs to be of relevance to the content and not simply a device to amuse.

Multi-sensory stimulation

Ask children to look at an object in your hands and they will automatically stretch out to touch. Depending on age and experience with similar objects, a child may also smell, suck, lick or bite the object. Training the eye is important, but children find it easier to concentrate on an object that can be touched, held or manipulated. The ideal object in a museum can thus be explored in a multi-sensory fashion and may also include physical movement. It is, however, important to ensure that the action proposed has some relevance to the learning experience. Crawling or climbing may well relieve the tension and will certainly be popular with children, but if it is dissociated from the educational content, it merely serves to excite. On the other hand, if the physical activity has relevance, it enhances the experience. This is the case for the Inventorium's ant farm, where visitors can crawl underneath the ant's feeding area and discover ants inside their nest, illuminated by red light. Here the action of crawling reinforces the message that the ants are underground. The physical activity is a means of encouraging observation. It enriches the experience and encourages a 'minds-on' experience.

Few adults and almost no children will pay attention to printed texts on plain panels. Interaction is important not only for objects, but for anything to which the visitor should be paying attention. While edible graphics would be of limited value, devices that require an activity before the text can be read serve to focus the visitor's attention.

Developmental level

The majority of children under 12 are not yet at a developmental stage that enables them to handle more than one variable at a time. Before the age of 6 or 7, even concrete experiences may not as yet be well established. At this age, counter-intuitive effects may produce little surprise; odd events are an everyday happening. Exhibitions thus need to emphasise the simple relationships between the visitor's action and its effect. More complex phenomena, with multiple variables, need to be limited and presented in a different way, so that simply acquiring the feel for the phenomenon, admiring its beauty, using it without an attempt at an explanation, may be sufficient. This must, however, be a conscious decision, rather than an overall justification for a high-play-level, low-understandability exhibit.

While the developmental level of exhibits obviously needs to be simplified for children, unsure adults also use a hands-on, concrete approach to solving problems in the unfamiliar world of exhibitions. Designing an exhibition for children can make it accessible for adults who would otherwise feel intimidated.

Role play

The use of role play in an exhibition can help children to explore both a situation and technical equipment. A happy equilibrium needs to be established between the realism of the situation and the technical complexity of the materials. Too real a simulation will limit the imagination; too simple and unstructured an experience and the exhibit will be enjoyable, but not communicate effectively. 'Playing' both sets the scene and creates the context for learning. In what way this play differs in a young child from that of an adult engaged in role play as a management training experience is difficult to define. The activity must be focused on the essential information to be communicated, and appropriate equipment integrated into the experience. The environment serves only to set the scene, the activity needs to be as realistic as possible.

Visitor interaction

Few children visit alone; coming to an exhibition is a social event. How children react with other members of their group, or with other unknown visitors, varies with their development and is dissimilar to adult behaviour. At a young age, children are still developing awareness of the others as individuals; characteristic play is alongside rather than with others. At the Inventorium, the 'Building Site' in the young children's section offers a structure sufficiently large for children to create their own corner for building and allows each child to develop an individual activity. At the same time, the size and weight of the high-density foam bricks and the crane to lift them to the upper floor of the structure encourage co-operation between the children. The exclusion of adults from the zone also encourages the child to develop a sense of autonomy, in an unfamiliar environment, with unknown people.

Once children are of school age, the importance of the peer group can become overwhelming. Children will often not attempt to investigate an activity until a group has been established. The first action is to occupy the exhibit, attract other members of the group to it, and only then does effective investigation occur. Exhibits that require the participation of several members of the group are necessary. Children will also adapt situations to conform to their current enthusiasms and interests. In this way, a coloured lights exhibit can be readily converted into a journey into space; exhibits on mechanics can be converted into a car race. However well the scene is set, the subversive spirit will appear. To some extent this also happens with adults; exhibits are used to further social contacts, to display knowledge or importance in a group. These would not be included in the exhibit developer's aims for the exhibition, and are less apparently subversive than creating a space setting in the coloured lights' exhibit. Children are perhaps simply more honest.

With the approach of adolescence, two conflicting types of behaviour emerge. Young people are still predominantly in groups, and tend first to make a whirlwind visit of the entire exhibition, apparently paying very little attention to individual exhibits, often using them simply to display to their peers. However, the interest in individual exploration is growing, and this initial tour is effectively used to pre-select items that are subsequently visited either alone or in smaller groups for more careful investigation.

The 'Television Studio' at the Inventorium was an exhibit which appealed to a very wide age range and offered a considerable variety in the types of activity offered. At a simple level, children can appear in front of a camera and present the news, the weather or any other programme of their invention. They can also be the camera man, use the zoom or focus, or, outside the studio, use the mixing table to manipulate the camera images. Without recording, groups of children will use the studio and need little supervision. As the number of controls are limited and all the equipment is protected, visitors find out how to use the equipment with little instruction, and frequently tell one another how to make it work. The emphasis is on demystifying television and on acquiring technical mastery of the equipment. The quality of the programme produced is low, but the pleasure and sense of achievement is high. With an enabler, more emphasis on the production can occur. At the Inventorium, a whole range of types of use of the TV Studio were developed, from the simple unassisted use of the material, through short 20-minute sessions with informal groups, to a series of sessions incorporating video material filmed by the group with hand-held material elsewhere in the science centre. This type of exhibit offers a wide range of types of use, and can both be adapted by the public for their particular interests and social needs and, at the same time, have structured activities proposed which encourage the public to pursue their nascent interests a little further.

The development process at the Inventorium and Eureka!

For the main exhibition areas at the City for Science and Industry, as in the majority of museums, little attempt was made in the period up to opening to target the younger visitor, either for the content or for social needs. Only the Inventorium was considered as having a specific function for the younger visitor. As a direct consequence of this specific aim, the team developing the Inventorium contained a wider variety of specialisations and the educational programme was defined in terms of the process of learning rather than of subject fields. None of the exhibitions was based on collections, but outside the Inventorium the exhibition policy was defined by broad definitions of essential areas of knowledge, rather than by reference to the public.

The educational aims and objectives of the Inventorium defined discovery learning as the approach to be encouraged, and content was chosen which was close to children's knowledge about themselves and their experience of the everyday world. Twelve themes spanning biology, physics and technology were included, with an emphasis on learning in a context. Largely inspired by the discovery rooms of American natural history museums, and considerably influenced by institutions such as the Boston Children's Museum and the Exploratorium, the development team of the Inventorium aimed to exploit existing good practice but was aware of cultural differences between the American and French publics.

Criteria for the selection of exhibits were not whether the content was essential scientific knowledge, but whether the phenomena or information were of intrinsic interest to children, and whether an appropriate hands-on activity could be developed. Giving intellectual coherence to the exhibitions and making the themes intelligible for adults were reasons behind the decision to group exhibits in themes, rather than leaving individual stand-alone exhibits to be explored as in many science centres. None the less, careful attention was paid to ensuring that the content of each exhibit was clear and could be explained and justified scientifically. High-play value alone was insufficient to guarantee inclusion. Nor were any exhibits constructed on a putative 'Stun the Visitor' factor. An equilibrium was sought between the intrinsic pleasurableness of a hands-on activity and an intellectually stimulating, minds-on challenge.

For all members of the development team, a perusal of available American research made it evident that considerable educational and cultural differences existed between the USA and France. There was little information available as to how these would affect visitor behaviour. Observable differences in the education system and in family attitudes could be ascertained. These include, for example, a carefully structured national education programme for the whole country in France, a lack of interest in experiential learning in the school context, more formal classes, little project or individual work in schools. Greater emphasis is placed on writing, observation and deduction in France. Attitudes as to the type of activities undertaken by families are also different.

French children are, on the whole, used to being part of a structured group from an early age. The majority of 3- and 4-year-olds are in state-funded nursery schools; parents register their children for residential holidays or all-day activities during the school vacations, whatever the social background. Less emphasis is placed on the child deciding on or defining an activity, or on the parent as sharing and participating in this. The child is seen more as a group member, whether of a class or a family, and less as an individual than in the American culture, with its emphasis on individual importance and expression. Such generalities can lead to unjustified assumptions, but with little hard fact available, the Inventorium team needed to develop methods that could identify potential problems and give easily accessible information about the likely behaviour of children and their accompanying adults, their interests and knowledge levels. Specialists from the USA, notably Alan Friedman, now Director of the New York Hall of Science, and Bernie Zubrowski of the Boston Children's Museum, came to advise on evaluation techniques and to help in the creative process. During the development, and in all subsequent work after opening, emphasis was placed on simple methods that could achieve results without expenditure on extra staff. By involving existing staff in the process of evaluation and by incorporating trainees, wide commitment to the process was established and increased general interest in visitor behaviour. This is one of the unanticipated advantages of having little or no budget available for evaluation studies.

The programme was developed over the four years prior to opening and was extended to include school programmes and educational activities after opening. It was restricted by the available time and budget, so that if results appear fragmented, this in many ways represents the reality. Emphasis was also placed on developing a variety of methods, rather than applying a consistent approach, in an attempt to discover the advantages and constraints of different techniques and their applicability to the situation. Even with these considerable reservations, the research carried out by the Inventorium team enabled the final exhibit programme to satisfy the target public, and to become one of the most successful spaces of the City for Science and Industry, with visitor numbers at double the level predicted and leading to the opening of an enlarged space, the City for Children in 1992.

Eureka!, the first children's museum to be built in the UK, opened in 1992. It offers hands-on interactive exhibitions, emphasising learning in a context and encouraging the autonomy of the individual. The exhibition content and approach are based on children's interests and ideas, but materials will be available to enable teachers to use these resources in relation to the National Curriculum. At Eureka!, a characteristic aspect of the development has been the emphasis on ascertaining children's ideas for all the proposed themes, and developing the techniques used at the Inventorium. For one of the themes, 'Me and My Body', a substantial amount of knowledge already existed on children's concepts.

Carried out as part of the Health Education Authority's Primary School Project, currently directed by Noreen Wetton of Southampton University, extensive testing of children using write-and-draw techniques proved an invaluable resource. Specific areas where additional knowledge was required were identified and research is being carried out in local schools. For other themes, such as 'Living and Working Together', which looks at the exchanges that occur in everyday life and the influence of design and technology, some information was available from the Primary Enterprise Pack, educational material designed to help primary teachers develop children's awareness of their economic and industrial environment. There was, however, little precise information available as to the specific content of the planned exhibits. An extensive programme of working with schools to identify areas of interest and children's ideas has been set up by Dr Tim Caulton, Head of Education and Interpretation, with the collaboration of the Calderdale Education Authority and incorporating a variety of techniques.

Some examples of how these techniques have been used at both the Inventorium and Eureka! help to indicate their advantages and shortcomings. Most of the evidence is anecdotal; it tells something of children's thoughts at a particular time, in a specific place. The influence of the cultural context for each subject under study makes a rich terrain for cross-cultural comparisons, but reduces the scope for generalisations. The techniques are reproducible, the results are not. Three different approaches that have proved of use are considered.

Visits and discussions

An initial feel for an exhibition area or theme can in some cases be established by visits with children. This technique is also used by toy manufacturers such as Fisher Price to establish initial interest for proposed toys where a relevant visit can be proposed, for example in developing a model fire station or garage. This technique is particularly appropriate at Eureka! in the 'Living and Working Together' theme, which relies on role play and learning in a context to interest children in the hidden aspects of the everyday world and, in particular, in design and technology. A set established around a town square will present a house, a shop, a factory, a bank, a garage, and a recycle centre for exploration. To gauge the interests of particular areas, visits and discussions were carried out with different school groups. Some unexpected interests have been revealed, such as enquiries as to relative pay levels of different staff members in the shop, or questions as to whether the manager had ever been sued. Simple discussions of this sort often reveal unexpected knowledge, and also areas of knowledge short-falls. Some 8-year-olds have been unable to offer any concept of what a factory might be or do; the word had no meaning for them. In general, the range from lack of knowledge to detailed information is wider than would have been anticipated without such visits and discussions. This has implications for the activities to be developed; there is a need to start from very simple questions ('What happens in a factory?') and yet offer in-depth information and games for those children who already have considerable knowledge.

Information on concepts underlying a theme can also be gathered from discussions. Questions such as 'Do you do any work?', 'Why do people work?' and 'Is all work paid?' are among questions discussed with children. Initial information had been taken from the Primary Enterprise Pack. Similar studies in Halifax revealed that while a majority of children had identified 'you get paid for it' as a reason for going to work, overcoming boredom, learning to do things, or making people happy were also given. Work is distinguished from play in being hard, requiring thought, and not being voluntary.

Children's enthusiasm for finding out more and having an opportunity for role play in areas such as the bank was also greater than had been anticipated. Some conflict between children's interests and perceptions and the potential sponsors' image can also be revealed. This is again of relevance for the bank, where the image backed by the industry is to promote the use of plastic cards as the medium of exchange and to emphasise all other aspects of banking rather than coin-handling. Children, on the other hand, are particularly interested in coin-handling, and concepts such as units of currency, interest and foreign exchange would be difficult to develop without a hands-on experience of handling coinage. On the other hand, simple studies and anecdotal evidence from children can also be of use in persuading sponsors of the appropriateness of the educational approach proposed.

Some stereotypes need to be challenged. On being asked 'What does a bank manager do?' half of one group of 9-year-olds folded their hands behind their heads and put their feet on the desk. Similarly, drawings of a bank manager following a discussion revealed everyone with a bowler hat, which cannot be the result of personal experience in Halifax. In discussions concerning the garage, one 7-year-old thought his mother could not mend the car because she was 'too small'. Such information enables the exhibits to fit in closely with children's interests, indicates ideas to be challenged, and gives some guidelines as to the level of information to be presented.

Write and draw

One of the difficulties in ascertaining children's knowledge is that techniques applicable to adults are generally unsatisfactory when applied to young children, either because their reading and writing skills are insufficiently developed or because the techniques such as questionnaires and interviews have no relation to their habitual learning styles or social activities. Peer-group pressure is also very strong, and the school context often makes children unwilling to express their ideas. It is essential to develop techniques that will encourage all children to express their ideas individually, by a method that is familiar and reassuring.

Write-and-draw techniques encourage children in the security of their class or in a quiet museum space to respond either to questions or situations. Both writing and drawing may need assistance from a friendly adult, to help label an unclear picture, or to help spell words. It is the child who decides on the content and asks for assistance only when necessary. The activity can be presented as a game, a secret, so that each child gives an individual response. Children with a limited mastery of English can take part fully, provided an adult who understands what the child wishes to say is available. Initial ideas as to the questions or scenarios to be presented often develop after a few small trials. These can vary from simple word definitions, to continuing a story which sets a scene.

This technique was used extensively at the Inventorium, in particular for areas where there seemed to be little existing information about children's ideas. In some cases, preliminary research by this method caused a shift of emphasis of the content. In the 'Techniques for Communicating' theme, a variety of different technical appliances was available for children to explore, with games designed to encourage investigation of the advantages and disadvantages of each. Consideration of an appropriate choice of technique for a particular use was an educational objective. To achieve this, and to encourage an analysis of the techniques offered, a simple schema for communications needs to be established.

The necessity of both sending and receiving signals was considered as the basis.

Children were invited to write a sentence with the word signal or to draw a picture involving a signal, in order to identify how children perceived and would use the word. It was not, of course, anticipated that 7- and 8-year-olds would use it in the conventional communications theory sense, but before it can be used as the basis for explaining how communications work, it is essential to find out what is the common usage. The predominant image was of an ambulance or a police car with a flashing light, and the word was used almost exclusively in the context of 'signal d'alarme', a fire or other siren. Here the discrepancy between the children's idea of the word's meaning and the intended use of it in explanations was so great that it was decided to substitute 'message', which may be less accurate in terms of information theory, but does have relevant meaning for children. The same technique was used to select subjects for short video sequences on concepts such as nutrition, disease and cell development, in some cases leading to a topic being rejected, when the difference between the child's concept and that of the scientific knowledge to be proposed proved too great.

Setting the scene for the children to write and draw is important, particularly in a context where they may feel inhibited or embarrassed. One area of the 'Me and My Body' exhibition at Eureka! is called 'Growing and Changing', and aims to present child development in the context of answering questions such as 'Where did I come from?' and 'What will happen to me as I grow up?' Gail Richards, of the Calderdale Health Education Unit, with advice from Noreen Wetton of Southampton University, has been working with the Eureka! team and is carrying out a research project aimed at clarifying children's ideas about adolescence and their worries associated with this period of their lives. Asking children directly may reveal little; creating a scene that allows children to project their feelings and thoughts on others gives richer results. The scene is set by inviting children to participate in helping with the writing of a book – the story of a boy and a girl who are teenagers, starting to change into young adults, and both of whom are about to go out on their own, for the first time. Children are asked to draw and write about one or both of them, ready to go out. Speech bubbles can be included to indicate how they feel about growing up. Children are also asked to indicate how the picture shows that they are growing up. A second chance to draw invites children to draw either the boy or the girl coming out of a shower and to write how it can be seen that they are growing up. In some cases, children can also be invited to say how they feel about their bodies changing and growing up.

Positive feelings about growing up have, on the whole, predominated, a pleasure in increased responsibility and independence. The importance of accessories, such as hairstyles, make-up or clothes, as signalling the grown-up state was evident. Any worries, namely about being 'different' from others, were expressed as being those of the character, rather than for themselves. One did however, 'wish it wasn't noticeable', and another did not 'want to grow any older than 49'. Security lies in the fact that it happens to everyone: 'I'm growing out like my Mum', 'It's going to happen anyway', and 'I am not too embarrassed, 'cause everyone else is going through it', being typical comments.

This project was carried out in local schools. Considerable sensitivity has

127

to be shown when carrying out the exercises. Moreover the teacher or researcher needs to be very sure of the children and the parents, and to have the full backing of the school. The information gathered can also be of considerable use to the school, in evaluating the results of their educational programmes and in signalling misunderstandings. It would be extremely difficult to obtain this information in the museum context. On the other hand, an exhibition which did not have this information available risks being irrelevant to children's real interests and questions. By carrying out such tests in a wide variety of schools, any important cultural sensibilities can be gauged and appropriate content developed.

Prototype testing

One of the more accepted ways of developing exhibits involves the use of simple prototype construction and testing. Different aspects such as the intrinsic interest of specific exhibits, technical viability, and visitor behaviour and learning can be investigated. The process is time-consuming, expensive and often essential, particularly where phenomena-based exhibits are concerned. Care has to be taken to ensure that the conditions of use approximate as closely as possible the final feel of the planned location, particularly as regards free access to the exhibits. A well-taught class, carefully controlled by their teacher, will not interact with the exhibit in the same way as children on an unsupervised visit. This can be difficult for museums and science centres that have not as yet opened. With testing in schools, it is important to ensure that simulated free access is available and to mix, if possible, the ages of the children in the groups. In France, the widespread existence of holiday and after-school play schemes provides a rich resource. More organised groups are useful when finer detail, such as the content of graphics, is being considered.

This process can have unanticipated outcomes. Prior to the opening of the Inventorium, the 'Water Machine' exhibit was constructed in prototype by Bernie Zubrowski and tested in a Parisian school. The exhibit presents a choice of different techniques as a range of solutions to the problem of raising water. Constructed out of wood and plastic, the machines were intended to have a short life and to elucidate any technical problems, as well as discover how children would interact with them. The educational aims focused on increasing children's understanding of the mechanics of the process. Children very quickly became engrossed in the different machines, and tried to fill containers, all of an identical size, and lively discussions ensued. Some of the machines broke down rapidly, but their home-made nature, which did not look like a finished product, encouraged children to have a go at mending them, or suggesting what was wrong. After repair, groups of children established optimum rhythms for operating them. An activity which had been planned as an investigation into mechanics was thus transformed into a consideration of work, both in the physical and economic sense. This technological approach reflects the steps in the increasing interest of the children.

Beginning with pure delight in simply operating a machine, they were drawn to a consideration of determining the conditions for optimum use. How the machine works was a relevant piece of information, rather than a question which was posed in isolation. This leads to learning in a context, which enables the visitor to make sense of the information offered.

This prototype testing with children also revealed one of the intrinsic difficulties with this approach. While the machines provided an excellent morning for several groups of children, their inherent flimsiness meant that final construction of the exhibit for the Inventorium used different materials. This, of necessity, eliminates the problem of breakage as a stimulus to enquiry as to how the exhibit works.

Few free-access exhibits can have as open-ended an exploration available as can be integrated into a prototype. However, the prototype testing does reveal the range of interactions probable to allow a judicious selection to be made. The change of materials, the different space, the use of lighting and graphics, all alter visitors' behaviour to such an extent that testing gives only a faint foreshadowing of final results. It is, however, in many cases the only available tool. For a phenomenon or experience that is outside the everyday lives of children, little can be gained by asking them to imagine, write or draw. Trying out the exploration to develop the final exhibit is the only solution.

Adaption and educational aids

However carefully the exhibit has been researched and tested, some elements of the public's behaviour will be unexpected. The addition of simple graphics can significantly improve both visitors' attention and the learning that occurs. This is of particular relevance for children's museums, where adults may tire or feel uncomfortable for reasons quite different from the children's and unconsciously inhibit the learning process.

In early versions of the Inventorium exhibits, a limited use of graphics and written information was made. It was felt that since children start school at age 6 in France, many of the younger visitors would be unable to read. It was thus essential that the way of using the exhibits should be evident without written instruction. For the initial 'Techniques for Communicating' exhibition, all supplementary information was contained in a small brochure. While this in no way inhibited the younger visitors from actively investigating the exhibits, discussing and arguing about how they worked and what you could do, parents, and in particular fathers, appeared worried and confused. Hands firmly clasped behind their backs, leaning forwards to look but not touch, few parents were willing to participate, and only some read the available information. A similar result was seen in the 'Time and Rhythm' exhibit, where a collection of mechanisms from gear wheels to sand clocks invited visitors to experiment with ways of measuring intervals of time. Adults in this space, which contained only one conventional clock, did not want to stay and were often to be found dragging children away.

Simple cartoon-style graphics were added, illustrating some of the things that could happen in the timespan of a visit to the Inventorium, from the number of babies born to how far a snail could crawl across a football field. On entering the space, adults were attracted by the images, while the children happily began to manipulate. Understanding what the previously inexplicable content was, adults were now more at their ease and could initiate discussion as well as join in the activity.

Exhibits in a children's space must fulfil the needs of children at widely different developmental stages and also at different intensities of interest. The activity of children in a well-prepared class may be more goal-directed and organised than a group of friends on a birthday treat. None of the needs can be ignored. The wide range of possible interactions needs to be complemented by educational support material that is adapted for each group of users. Some of this can be available integrated into the exhibition, the remainder has to be available on demand. The needs of the adult are of considerable importance. Unless they feel able to cope with the proposed content, adults will tend to draw children to other activities. On the other hand, graphics designed for children are perceived by adults as potentially easy to understand: adults have a positive attitude to such information. Specific information, informing adults what the children in their charge may be investigating and learning, can change a bored parent into an interested observer.

Visitor comfort

If visitors are feeling uncomfortable, whether adults or children, the visit will be rapidly curtailed. This is of particular importance for parents in a children's space, where adults' enthusiasm is generally more ephemeral than that of the children. Simple measures such as providing adequate seating, additional reading material, and crawling areas for the younger family members can significantly increase the time a child will spend on an individual exhibit. The provision of drinks and cloakroom facilities are similarly important. Not all visitors' desires can be granted, however. On visiting the new Eureka! building with school groups, Dr Caulton asked the children what they would most like to get rid of as soon as they arrived. The unexpected answer was not coats and bags, but the teachers!

Conclusion

Developing exhibitions adapted to a public of children and the adults accompanying them remains a skill rather than a science. Techniques for identifying children's ideas offer largely anecdotal evidence, relevant to a particular time and place, but guaranteeing no certainty if they were to be applied in another context. Nevertheless, a body of skills is being acquired, a methodology of development. Echoing visitors' experience of the exhibitions: the wider the range of exploratory techniques used, the richer the information gained. As children, asked about the difference between work and play, commented:

'Work is hard – sometimes it's long and you don't know what to do.'
'Working – you have to think a lot.'
'Playing is fun, but work is interesting, and you get things done – work improves what you're doing – you're actually improving.'

This is also our aim when developing exhibitions, but also, like playing: 'It makes a mess and is much more fun.'

9

Museum education: past, present and future

Eilean Hooper-Greenhill

Changing roles for museums today

Museums and galleries today are striving to develop new relationships with their audiences. New ways of working, and new ways of thinking, are being negotiated in order to modify museums to appeal to people who would not normally visit them. At the same time, museums and galleries are endeavouring to increase their market share in both the leisure and the educational industry.

These moves are underpinned by a new perception of the possible roles for museums. Many museum workers have a vision of museums as much more closely linked to their communities, and much more directly useful to their publics, than has been the case for a large part of this century (Hooper-Greenhill 1991a: 9–15). It is also true that in some cases this new role has been forced on to museums by government and other purse-holders, who have become impatient with claims for social relevance based on little except scholarly expertise, which in itself has sometimes been rather tenuously related to the functions of the museum.

In Britain, it is increasingly necessary for museum managers to have detailed information at their fingertips. Much of this information relates to the nature of the museum audience, their level of satisfaction with the experience the museum offers, how much the provision of this experience costs, and what percentage of the overall budgets of the institution these costs represent.

The national museums are being encouraged to carry out visitor surveys twice a year and to use these surveys to measure visitor enjoyment and understanding of displays (Office of Arts and Libraries 1991). Local authority museums are being urged to carry out market research and to alter the balance and focus of their collections to bring them into line with the priorities of the service and the needs of target audiences (Audit Commission 1991).

The exhortations to research the needs of the public, and to deliver services that are relevant to these needs, are made in the context of increasing competition for scarce resources. Museums have been forcefully alerted to the stark facts of being in competition for visitors with both other museums, and other leisure venues (Middleton 1990).

The need for effective and well-managed communication is underlined: 'Without effective communication (in the language of the audience) museums have no purpose.' (Middleton 1990: 13). This statement was made in relation to a particular type of museum, the independent museum, which has always been largely dependent on visitor income for survival, and which has therefore concentrated efforts on the development of successful communicative strategies. Today, though, this statement has relevance to all museums. In Britain, as public funds become scarcer and therefore more liable to be called to account, museums will become more and more dependent on their services being of real and demonstrable value. Research into the effectiveness of communication processes will become critical. This shift can be observed elsewhere; in North America, for example, detailed performance indicators are being developed that will measure the accessibility of museums to those with low incomes, the level of service take-up by minority groups, the institutional commitment to the evaluation of its services, and similarly its commitment to education (Ames 1991: 62–7).

Increased accountability and increased competition have been brought about by marketplace economics, and have sometimes been insisted upon by those outside museums that do not appreciate their value or potential. Alongside this can be found genuine moves from within museums to become more open and democratic. The Open Museum at Kelvingrove Museum, Glasgow, for example, is a radical new venture which is experimenting with and evolving methods of using objects from the museum's stores with small community groups. In some instances, groups are able to select artefacts from the museum's collections to display in exhibitions held outside the museum in community venues. To take a second example, the new museum being developed in Croydon will take account of the findings of a specially commissioned market research group who have talked to people who answered 'yes' to the suggestion that they wouldn't be seen dead in a museum (The Susie Fisher Group 1990).

The educational role of the museum is expanding as new methods of collaboration and communication with audiences are tried. In the past, museums were collection driven: that is, exhibitions were mounted to assemble and display collections; publications were produced to disseminate research about objects; museum professionals were curators appointed to care for different sections of the collections, classified generally in relation to academic disciplines. Now, museums are becoming more audience driven: that is, exhibitions are mounted to appeal to the researched interests of specific target groups; publications are produced to relate to particular audience segments and research itself now includes research about visitors as well as about collections (Harvey 1987; The Susie Fisher Group 1990; Merriman 1991; Trevelyan 1991); and new museum professionals such as marketing officers, museum development officers, caterers and shop managers have made their appearance.

We seem to be at a time of apparently unprecedented change in museums.

However, looking back into the past, it is clear that museums have always been subject to change, although the pace has varied from abrupt violent dislocations caused by wars or revolution, to longer periods of slower change. Different elements have not always changed at the same time; perceptions of what counts as rationality in museums have sometimes remained static while display methods have modified. Sometimes what counts as knowledge in museums has radically altered, while collections have remained intact, which has meant a complete reconstitution of the meaning of those collections (Hooper-Greenhill 1992a).

What is clear at the present time is that fairly rapid change is upon us. This situation of change has been resented and resisted in some institutions, others have had change violently forced upon them, while some few museums have been able to negotiate change in a planned and purposeful way. In all situations of change, it is of vital importance to be very clear about the philosophy and objectives of the museum, and to be able to articulate with informed precision exactly why one course of action is more desirable than another. A time of change is also a time of opportunity. Those who are not prepared will find themselves at the mercy of those who are. Those who have researched the logical economic and philosphical arguments may well be able to win the day, and will at least be able to mount a coherent stand.

In museums, this clarity is required at the most basic level of all. What is a museum, and who is it for? Many museum professionals cannot answer these questions. Almost everyone who is not a museum professional cannot answer them either. These are slim grounds for the continued existence of museums and galleries.

What is a museum and who is it for?

If there is one basic common function for museums, it is the acquisition, care and use of artefacts and specimens. This relationship to objects distinguishes museums from other kinds of institution, although within this basic paradigm can be found an immense range of positions in relation to communicative strategies.

Some museums, like many art galleries, for example, are almost completely object centred; that is, the objects *per se* have a prime role in displays. In other museums, like some science museums, the objects are used to illustrate and communicate ideas. Some museums exploit both these positions rather well; in the Kodak Museum, part of the National Museum of Film Photography and Television in Bradford, a narrative is told using objects but also using other means of communicating such as interactive exhibits, paintings, models and reconstructed rooms. Objects are only included where they fit the narrative, and where they are included, the method of display contextualises the meaning of the object: thus a 'waistcoat' camera is displayed in a perspex case attached to the stomach of a life-size figure of a waistcoated Edwardian gentleman. These narrative displays occupy the centre of the galleries. Nearer the periphery are object-rich displays, cases filled with varieties of specific types of camera, for example, laid out in serried ranks demonstrating small technological and physical changes to the basic camera concept.

It is important to cling on to this basic object-centred function of museums, but also to recognise that there are many different ways of interpreting it. There are many ways of being a museum, and the ways are modifying all the time.

Who are museums for? This, at the present time, is perhaps a more vital question. On the whole, museum visitors still have the characteristics that have been familiar for many years: there is a slightly greater proportion of men than women visiting museums; students and socio-economic groups ABC1 are over-represented in proportion to their numbers in the population, while the retired, the unemployed and groups C2, D and E are under-represented (Merriman 1991: 43). There are, however, great varieties between museums, with art museums generally attracting the most highly educated and elite group, and multi-disciplinary and historical museums, especially those with outdoor sites, attracting a more democratic audience. The audience for museums is, on the whole, more democratic than that for theatres or concerts, and some museums, such as the National Museums on Merseyside, have been very successful in attracting those who are often excluded (Myerscough 1989).

Current demographic trends can be seen to play themselves out in museums as elsewhere in society (Henley Centre 1989). It is noticeable that families, and particularly families with small children, are a fast-growing segment of the audience; 45 to 59-year-olds are increasingly looking to museums for leisure, education and shopping; and all of the museum's consumers are more discerning and more demanding. The general shift away from blue-collar industrial work to the white-collar service industries means that the potential (and traditional) audience for museums, the ABC1 group, is itself growing. At the same time, many people working in museums want to broaden the audience, and are finding ways of working with the groups that have not in the past been frequent visitors. These ways include new modes of display, more aggressive marketing, making personal links with specific groups, and a variety of outreach projects.

Children have generally not been included in the measurement of museum visitors. Where they have been included, they have often formed the largest group of visitors (Merriman 1991: 43). These include children in organised school parties and children in family/peer groups. There is some evidence to suggest that children might, in some museums, form about one-third of the museum's audience (Hooper-Greenhill 1992b: 670–89). With the development of the National Curriculum, quite specific links can be made to the requirements of schools, and with the recognition that families are an important audience segment, greater attention is being paid to provision of experiences that children will enjoy.

The audience for museums is beginning to shift away from traditional patterns, and without doubt it is now firmly recognised by the museum profession that the audience matters, and that delivering a product that is valued by the audience is of vital importance in the present struggle for relevance and survival.

The museum as educator

Since their foundation, museums have been linked with education, but the way in which this has been understood has changed enormously. In the late nineteenth century, museums were seen as the universities of the people, places to learn for adults who had had few opportunities. Museums were also visited by school children, and on the introduction of compulsory schooling were accepted as appropriate learning environments (Smythe 1966: 11).

These two thrusts continued into the twentieth century, although different types of museum tended to offer different educational opportunities. On the whole, national museums provided for adults through lectures and guided tours, and local authority museums developed provision for schools through teaching sessions in the museums themselves and through loan services which took objects into schools.

In both instances, education was seen as an activity separate from the main role of the museum, which was to collect and conserve. Education was an adjunct function, an additional extra, subservient to the processes of collection, which were seen as ends in themselves. This perception of the functions of museums was reproduced in its staffing patterns: curators held permanent senior posts and defined policy, while education staff were often seconded from other institutions (mainly schools), and worked at a temporary, generally low level. It is not surprising to find that education staff had minimal input into policy-making and management.

Education as a process has not been well understood in museums. At the end of the nineteenth century, museums and schools worked relatively well together, and it seems that as museums opened, schools began to use them (Frostick 1985; Stephens and Roderick 1983). Many schools at this time were using the 'object-teaching' method, developed by the Victorians, as a way of instruction. Initially innovative, this method soon declined into a form of rote-learning (Calkins 1880; Busse 1880; Smythe 1966: 7; Lawson and Silver 1973).

Museums were well placed to help in the supply and use of objects. Loan services took objects into schools, and curators used objects to teach in museums. Methods were somewhat crude, on the whole. The development of progressive educational methods, based on the work of Dewey, Pestalozzi and Montessori, with its emphasis on the use of experience and real things, should have opened up the museum as an ideal learning environment. Sadly, these developments in educational methods coincided with the move in museums to develop as a distinct and discrete profession (Hooper-Greenhill 1991a: 25–35).

The establishment of this distinction meant the separation of museums from too much identification with education, or at least with school-based education. (There was no problem regarding links with that higher-status site for learning, the university.) Even the opportunity after the First World War for local authority museums to become a mandatory service, administered through the local education authority, was rejected in favour of remaining a discretionary service administered by anybody who felt inclined (Kavanagh 1988). This move to isolation was exacerbated by the disruptive effects of the Second World War and the consequent restructuring that followed.

The separation of museums from the world of education meant a separation from the development of educational theory in relation to both children and adults. The progressive educational movement, which focused on a learning process that centred the child as learner, and which introduced the open classroom into primary schools, passed museums by. During the 1960s and 1970s, pedagogy shifted from the learning of standard operations tied to specific contexts to learning as an exploration of principles. The teacher was reconceptualised as a problem-poser rather than as a solution-giver (Bernstein 1975). This change in pedagogy altered the authority relationship between teacher and taught. A more democratic and equal relationship became possible.

At much the same time, theories of andragogy (adult education) began to be elaborated that celebrated the possibility of life-long learning (Collins 1981). Learning was understood as a way of life, as the possession and use of an enquiring mind, and as an active outlook on the world. Learning ceased to be limited to those opportunities offered by formal educational institutions, and moved out into the community, becoming capable of being sustained throughout life, methodologically diverse, calling on a range of sites, experiences and individuals as sources.

The educational world celebrated diversity, democracy, equality and openness. But the museum world remained in an older mould, where relationships continued to be hierarchical and unequal, where processes were closed, and where power was preserved and defended. In some instances, the methods of the open classroom were carried into museums by museum educationalists. Examples can be found in the work of Molly Harrison at the Geffrye Museum, Rene Marcouse at the Victoria and Albert Museum (Hooper-Greenhill 1991a: 51–3), and in the work of the Cockpit Arts Workshop Curriculum Unit with some of the large London museums and galleries (Measham 1974; Heath 1976).

However, the unequal relationships between curators and museum educators meant that on the whole these approaches were not understood by curators, and the lessons that could have been learnt remained in the museum classroom and were not applied to museum displays or to other forms of communication in museums.

Educational theory in museums

One form of educational theory *has* made its appearance in museums, and this is educational psychology. During the 1970s and early 1980s in Britain, educational psychology was applied to exhibition design. Similar moves can be discovered at a much earlier date in the United States (Lawrence 1991). Proposals were made for the systematic application of a body of organised objective knowledge to the mounting of didactic exhibitions (Miles and Tout

1979). A museum technology was proposed based on lessons from educational technology and observations of the behaviour of museum visitors. The approach to educational psychology which was employed was underpinned by the paradigm of behaviourism, with its emphasis on stimulus and response, and on the structure of the learning environment (Lawrence 1991).

The emphasis on the learning environment appeared particularly appropriate in museums, and was applied to the structure of exhibitions. This led to a focus on the spatial design of exhibitions, with recommendations being made to divide the space into cells or chambers, to have a clear organisational plan for the exhibitions, and to make this clear to the visitor. In relation to the exhibition content, recommendations based on educational technology suggested having clear learning objectives, dividing the material to be learnt into appropriately sized steps, making provision for a range of abilities, and providing feedback (Miles and Tout 1979).

Once exhibitions had been designed that followed these principles, visitors were observed and their behaviour in the exhibitions was measured (Griggs 1984). Variables that could be observed and measured, such as the stopping power and holding power of exhibits, were identified. Attention was paid in detail to the exhibition as an environment for processing visitors. The underlying assumption was that if the environment was correctly designed, then the visitors would respond and learn.

The opening up of the idea of exhibitions as learning environments, with the focus on the design and the pacing of both space and content, was in many ways a big step forward for museums. However, this approach, drawn from educational technology and behaviourist psychology, focused on the environment for learning rather than on the learner him/herself. This approach takes its epistemological model from the physical, quantitative, laboratory-based sciences, where social data is treated in much the same way as data drawn from the natural world (Hein 1982). These positivist and empiricist methods can still be found underpinning many of the accounts of the 'evaluation' of museums and their visitors (Screven 1986), in spite of the inadequacy of these methods that has been demonstrated in the fields of social theory (Fay 1975) and the philosophy of science (Chalmers 1982).

If ideas drawn from educational psychology have been applied to museums and galleries, other forms of educational theory have been less influential. By the 1970s the work of Bruner and Piaget and other educational psychologists, who had rejected the mechanistic implications of behaviourism, was well known and was proving useful in school-based learning situations (Bruner, Jolly and Sylva 1976; Richardson and Sheldon 1988). Cognitive psychology, which focused on the meanings made of the learning situation by the learner, offered another way forward which was influential in the interpretation movement in North America, but had little effect in Britain (Ham 1983).

Insights from other educational disciplines were totally unfamiliar to museums. Educational sociology, for example, might have led to a focus in museums on the social rather than the behavioural elements that related to learning. The sociology of education led to a new awareness in schools of the effects of middle-class values on non-middle-class children, exposed the existence of the hidden curriculum, and analysed the power-effects of the classification and framing of the educational experience (Bernstein 1971, 1975). All of these ideas would still have relevance if applied to museums (Hooper-Greenhill 1980, 1982). Educational philosophy calls into question the objectives of education in relation to the needs of society, the understanding of what it is to be educated, and the development of mind. These ideas, too, have important lessons for us in museums, but have barely been examined (Hooper-Greenhill 1983).

However, the pressure on museums to change, to develop closer relationships with their audiences, and to find new ways of communicating effectively, have led to a moment in which it is at last seen as appropriate to use ideas from the world of education in the museum as a whole. There is a pressing need for a broad re-reading of educational theory in relation to the potential of museums and galleries.

The emergence of common objectives

During the 1980s, museums began to develop a new awareness of their audiences. It became important to try to attract greater numbers, and a greater range of audiences. New museum professionals – marketing or development officers – were appointed, and efforts were made to persuade people to visit museums which, on the whole, were largely unreconstructed. The old hierarchical, undemocratic, closed patterns were still very much in evidence in many museums (Hooper-Greenhill 1988b), and it became clear that the efforts of marketing officers, appointed to develop methods of selling the museum, would be a waste of time and money if the product itself, the museum experience, did not change. The ever-increasing shortage of funds, with its consequent emphasis on accountability, sharpened this perception as the deep recession of the early 1990s approached.

The move in museums towards audience relevance coincided with the large-scale introduction into schools of curricula based on learning from sites, primary evidence and experience. Museums were seen as places that were pre-eminently suited to deliver the new educational requirements. Although initially there were (and in some places still are) conflicts between education and marketing staff, some museum education staff found that the objectives of the museum were beginning to run in parallel with their own. Where previously the educational objectives of education staff had often been in conflict with the conservation ethic of the curators, there was now the possibility of developing common institutional aims. This has coincided with the emphasis by government on the development of institutional aims and objectives, and of corporate and forward plans.

During the 1980s, curatorial staff became more and more aware of a variety of ways in which they could work comfortably and profitably with visitors (Greenwood *et al.* 1989; Nicholson 1985), and education staff became more and more confident in relating the demands of the new curricula to the possibilities inherent in museums. Both curators and educators offered lively, practical, object-based workshops and events, which employed a broad range of active learning techniques. These practices, sometimes in operation in the same institution but in separate corners and with different staff, were united by the underpinning understanding of what education could and should be in museums. It is fascinating to see how those working mainly in the realm of informal education (curators) and those working mainly in the realm of formal education (educators) arrived simultaneously at very similar conclusions. 'Discovery rooms', for example, were developed by the curatorial staff in Liverpool and by education staff in Edinburgh (Hooper-Greenhill 1991a: 181–6). Exhibitions that collaborated closely with their target audiences were evolved by curators in Leicester and education staff in Southampton (Nicholson 1985; Jones and Major 1986).

Education, which has been understood so narrowly in museums for so long, is now understood much more broadly. This, in turn, relates to the way in which the process of education is understood generally. In schools and equally in relation to adults, the best practice emerges when education is conceptualised, first, as *based in experience* – with objects, sites, people and places all providing learning opportunities; and, second, as *active* – involving students in thinking skills such as comparing and classifying, and in negotiating their own learning to some degree; and, third, as *structured* – through careful planning which allows for flexibility in the process.

Learning happens through the interrogation and analysis of experience, which can happen in classrooms, but equally at home, out shopping or in museums. Sometimes the classroom is taken into the community (or museum); sometimes the community, in the shape of people perhaps (or museums, in the shape of people or objects) is taken into the classroom. This notion of learning sees the process of education as open and accessible, as integrated into everyday life, and as potentially enjoyable and exciting.

These ideas offer new opportunities for museums. A new definition is possible for the educational role of the museum. Intelligences of all sorts can be brought into play (Gardner 1985, 1990). Making and listening to music, sorting objects, spinning, pond-dipping, role-playing, mapping spaces, interviewing people, assessing evidence – all these are 'educational' activities at school, in adult life and in the museum. As the activities that museums can and do offer are now seen as congruent with the best educational theory, the potential educational role of the museum expands.

The educational role of the museum or gallery can now be understood very broadly indeed. It encompasses the entire public face of the museum. The educational function of museums is delivered by a combination of events, exhibitions and publications which may take place in-house or offsite. This can include a vast array of phenomena, including structured or informal activities, practical workshops, lectures, films, concerts, fashion shows, exhibitions, displays, publications, videos, theatre, mobile buses or trains, and so on. One of the greatest strengths of the museum is exactly this variety. Given that the audience for museums can potentially include children of all ages, families of all types, individuals, and social, educational, neighbourhood or religious groups, the range of specific events for specific target groups is literally endless.

It is important at this stage to recognise that very few museums, at least in Britain, have fully developed either the theory or the practice of museum education. In some museums, much older ideas of museum education can be found. In others, the enormous range is understood, but shortage of resources prevents implementation and development. In many museums, a good range of both understanding and practice exists, but in disparate pockets within the museum, with poor connections between them. In many museums, too, the audience remains limited to the traditional museum-goers, and this needs to be addressed. It is time now for museums to develop the theory and the practice of the full potential of the educational role of museums.

Policies for museum education

The development of museum education is the responsibility of the management of the museum. It will concern the deployment of financial and staff resources, and will require training for new and existing staff. It requires careful forward planning and is dependent on good staff relationships and effective communication. Above all, it requires vision and the power to implement that vision.

Looking at museums in Britain, a number of dilemmas can be identified. The first is how museum education is understood. Is it understood holistically, as the major mission of the institution, and if so, is there evidence that this objective is enabled through adequate resource provision?

The second question concerns the achievement of the educational role. Is this to be delivered through exhibitions, through events, through educational materials, or through outreach work? And who are the target audiences – families, schools, students or specialists?

The third dilemma is over the funding of educational posts, and their structuring into the museum. This is critical in Britain, especially in local authority museums, where local education authorities have in the past funded the majority of school service staff. In these museums and in independent museums, these funds have always been tenuous, and are now more vulnerable than ever. In the past, very few staff have been charged with developing adult education.

A further, perhaps more fundamental, point is the percentage of staff charged with the educational work. As the educational role expands, so staff provision must expand. Models of good practice exist: in Canada, at the Museum of Civilization in Quebec, the educational staff make up roughly 25 per cent of the staff of the institution overall. This includes those staff who work with exhibitions, with events and with educational programmes.

The fundamental nature of these dilemmas throws into relief the depth of the changes that museums are now experiencing. Many aspects of museum practice that were taken for granted in the past must now be reconceptualised and renegotiated.

The development of an educational policy is a useful way in which to rethink the educational responsibility of the museum or gallery. In the process of writing the policy, many matters will have to be debated, and hard decisions will have to be taken.

Currently in Britain there is an assumption that museums and galleries will have an educational policy (Museums and Galleries Commission 1991a; Audit Commission 1991; Museums Association 1991). Indeed, the Office of Arts and Libraries (now the Department of National Heritage) stated in 1991 that the museum policy itself should be an education policy (Pittman 1991).

The process of writing an educational policy will necessarily involve the museum management team and the staff charged with working to achieve the educational role, however this is defined. It will also probably involve a number of advisors. In order to develop the Victoria and Albert Museum Education Development Plan, the Education Department worked with an Education Advisory Committee drawn from outside the museum which represented the main sectors of education. The Committee was chaired by the Director of the museum and included several trustees and senior members of museum staff (Hooper-Greenhill 1991b: 19).

The process of development of the educational policy is a long one, which may require a complete review of the mission of the museum. The resulting policy will require the ratification of trustees or the museum governing body, as the implementation of the document will require the commitment of resources.

There are a number of areas within which decisions will have to be made. These include the following: the roles and functions of education in the museum; target audiences; types of provision; resources and budget; networks outside the museum; marketing; evaluation; training (Hooper-Greenhill 1991b: 8–15). Experience has clearly demonstrated that although each institution should consider each of these areas, the resulting policies will be totally unique in each case. The educational policy must be informed by the mission of the museum, and this, combined with the geographical location, the type of the museum, the size of museum, the nature of its collections and resources, and its potential audience, will serve to produce a unique policy, even though the analytical process covers the same areas.

We live in interesting times. There *are* opportunities for museums and galleries in today's fast-moving and often difficult world. At the end of the twentieth century, postmodernism emphasises fragmentation and reintegration, pluralities and renegotiations. The postmodern museum is one that has thrown off the constraining yoke of outdated practices, and which has successfully used the best elements of the past and the most useful ideas of the present to forge a way towards the future. This is not achieved without a struggle in the present climate of decreasing world resources, of war, of the need for a new vision for the future of humankind. At such times, however, perhaps a faith in the radical liberating power of the material evidence of the past can offer present strategies towards the future.

References

Ames, P. (1991) 'Measuring museums' merits', in G. Kavanagh (ed.), *The Museums Profession: Internal and External Relations*, Leicester: Leicester University Press, pp. 57–68.

Audit Commission (1991) *The Road to Wigan Pier? Managing Local Authority Museums and Art Galleries*, London: HMSO.

Bernstein, B. (1971) *Class, Codes and Control: volume 1. Theoretical Studies Towards a Sociology of Language*, London: Routledge and Kegan Paul.

—— (1975) *Class, Codes and Control: volume 3. Towards a Theory of Educational Transmissions*, London: Routledge and Kegan Paul.

Bruner, J.S., Jolly, A. and Sylva, K. (1976) *Play – Its Role in Development and Evolution*, Harmondsworth: Penguin.

Busse, F. (1880) 'Object teaching: principles and methods', *American Journal of Education*, vol. 30, pp. 417–50.

Calkins, N.A. (1880) 'Object-teaching: its purpose and province', *Education*, vol. 1, pp. 165–72 (Boston, Mass.).

Chalmers, A.F. (1982) *What is This Thing Called Science?*, Milton Keynes: Open University Press.

Collins, Z. (1981) *Museums, Adults and the Humanities*, Washington, DC: Association of American Museums.

Fay, B. (1975) *Social Theory and Political Practice*, London: Allen & Unwin.

Frostick, E. (1985) 'Museums in education, a neglected role', *Museums Journal*, vol. 85, no. 2, pp. 67–74.

Gardner, H. (1985) *Frames of Mind: the Theory of Multiple Intelligences*, London: Paladin, Granada.

—— (1990) 'Developing the spectrum of human intelligences', in C. Hedley, J. Houtz and A. Baratta (eds), *Cognition, Curriculum and Literacy*, New Jersey: Ablex Publishing Corp., pp. 11–19.

Goodhew, E. (1988) *Museums and Primary Science*, London: Area Museum Service for South Eastern England.

Greenwood, E.F., Phillips, P.W. and Wallace, I.D. (1989) 'The Natural History Centre at the Liverpool Museum', *The International Journal of Museum Management and Curatorship*, vol. 8, pp. 215–25.

Griggs, S.A. (1984) 'Evaluating exhibitions', in J.M.A. Thompson (ed.), *Manual of Curatorship*, 1st edition, London: Butterworth.

Ham, S. (1983) 'Cognitive psychology and interpretation', *Journal of Interpretation*, vol. 8, no. 1, pp. 11–28.

Harvey, B. (1987) *Visiting the National Portrait Gallery*, London: OPCS/HMSO.

Heath, A. (1976) 'Civil war co-operation', *ILEA Contact*, vol. 4, no. 32, pp. 16–20.

Hein, G. (1982) 'Evaluation of museum programs and exhibits', in T.H. Hanson (ed.), *Museums and Education*, Copenhagen: Danish ICOM/CECA.

Henley Centre (1989) 'The discerning consumer', *Leisure Management*, vol. 9, no. 5, pp. 34–6.

Hooper-Greenhill, E. (1980) 'The National Portrait Gallery: a case-study in cultural reproduction', MA thesis, Institute of Education, University of London.

—— (1982) 'Some aspects of a sociology of museums', *Museums Journal*, vol. 82, no. 2, pp. 69–70.

—— (1983) 'Some basic principles and issues relating to museum education', *Museums Journal*, vol. 82, no. 2, pp. 69–70.

—— (1987) 'Museums in education: Towards the twenty-first century', in T. Ambrose (ed.), *Museums in Education: Education in Museums*, Edinburgh: Scottish Museums Council, HMSO, pp. 39–52.

—— (1988a) 'Museums in education: working with other organisations', in T. Ambrose (ed.), *Working with Museums*, Edinburgh: Scottish Museums Council, HMSO, pp. 41–8.

—— (1988b) 'Counting visitors or vistors who count', in R. Lumley (ed.), *The Museum Time-Machine*, London: Methuen/Routledge, pp. 213–32.

—— (ed.) (1989) *Initiatives in Museum Education*, Leicester: Department of Museum Studies, University of Leicester.

—— (1991a) *Museum and Gallery Education*, Leicester: Leicester University Press.

—— (ed.) (1991b) *Writing a Museum Education Policy*, Leicester: Department of Museum Studies, University of Leicester.

—— (1992a) *Museums and the Shaping of Knowledge*, London: Routledge.

—— (1992b) 'Museum education', in J.M.A. Thompson (ed.), *Manual of Curatorship*, 2nd edition, London: Butterworth.

Jones, S. and Major, C. (1986) 'Reaching the public: oral history as a survival strategy for museums', *Oral History Journal*, vol. 14, no. 2, pp. 31–8.

Kavanagh, G. (1988) 'The First World War and its implications for education in British museums', *History of Education*, vol. 17, no. 2, pp. 163–76.

Korn, R. (1989) 'Introduction to evaluation: theory and methodology', in S. Berry and S. Mayer (eds), *Museum Education, Theory and Practice*, Reston, Virginia: The National Art Association, USA, pp. 219–38.

Lawrence, G. (1991) 'Rats, street gangs and culture: evaluation in museums', in G. Kavanagh (ed.), *Museum Languages: Objects and Texts*, Leicester: Leicester University Press, pp. 11–32.

Lawson, J. and Silver, S. (1973) *A Social History of Education in England*, London: Methuen.

Measham, T. (1974) 'Kidsplay 11, 1974, at the Tate Gallery, London', *Museums Annual*, vol. 6, Paris: Education Cultural Action, ICOM, pp. 43–5.

Merriman, N. (1991) *Beyond the Glass Case: The Past, the Heritage and the Public in Britain*, Leicester: Leicester University Press.

Middleton, V.T.C. (1990) *New Visions for Independent Museums in the UK*, West Sussex: Association of Independent Museums.

Miles, R.S. and Tout, A.F. (1979) 'Outline of a technology for effective science exhibits', *Special Papers in Palaeontology*, vol. 22, pp. 209–24.

Miles, R.S., Alt, M.B., Gosling, D.C., Lewis, B.N. and Tout, A.F. (1988) *The Design of Educational Exhibits*, London: Allen & Unwin.

Museums Association (1991) *A National Strategy for Museums*, London: The Museums Association.

Museums and Galleries Commission (1991a) *Local Authorities and Museums: Report by a Working Party 1991.* (The Last Report), London: HMSO.

—— (1991b) *Report 1990–91. Specially Featuring the National Museums*, London: Museums and Galleries Commission.

Myerscough, J. (1989) *The Economic Importance of the Arts in Britain*, London: Policy Studies Institute.

Nicholson, J. (1985) 'The museum and the Indian community: findings and orientation of the Leicestershire Museums Service', *Museum Ethnographers Newsletter*, no. 19, pp. 3–14.

Office of Arts and Libraries (1991) *Report on the Development of Performance Indicators for the National Museums and Galleries*, London: Office of Arts and Libraries.

Pittman, N. (1991) 'Writing a museum education policy. Introductory remarks to a workshop', Museums Association Annual Conference, 24 July 1991, Newcastle-upon-Tyne.

Richardson, K. and Sheldon, S. (eds) (1988) *Cognitive Development to Adolescence*, East Sussex: Lawrence Erlbaum Associates.

Screven, C.G. (1986) 'Exhibitions and information centres: some principles and approaches', *Curator*, vol. 29, no. 2, pp. 109–37.

Smythe, J.E. (1966) 'The educational role of the museums and field centres in England from 1884', MA thesis, University of Sheffield.

Stephens, F. and Roderick, G.W. (1983) 'Middle-class nineteenth century self-help – the literary and philosophical societies', in F. Stephens and G.W. Roderick (eds), *Samuel Smiles and Nineteenth-Century Self-help in Education*, Nottingham: Department of Adult Education, University of Nottingham, pp. 16–46.

The Susie Fisher Group (1990) *Bringing History and the Arts to a New Audience: Qualitative Research for the London Borough of Croydon*, London: The Susie Fisher Group.

Trevelyan, V. (ed.) (1991) *Dingy Places with Different Kinds of Bits – an Attitudes Survey of London Museums Amongst Non Visitors*, London: London Museums Service.

Part 3
New analyses

The term 'new museology' has two current meanings in European museum studies. It is used, particularly in connection with the French ecomuseum movement, to embrace the development of museums out of the interests and efforts of local communities, as distinct from their imposition by specialists from the outside. It is also used quite differently to signal a young, theoretical discipline which is concerned with the purposes of museums rather than with their methods, and which has called, particularly through the efforts of Peter Vergo, for a more reflective approach toward the making and studying of exhibitions. All four articles in Part 3 (also Robert Lumley's in Part 1) echo this call.

Brown Goode's much-quoted, one-hundred-year-old definition of an efficient educational exhibition as 'a collection of instructive labels, each illustrated by a well-selected object' recognises that traditional museum objects are not, and cannot be, the unaided conveyors of messages in exhibitions. As Peter Vergo and Roger Silverstone (also Eilean Hooper-Greenhill in Chapter 9) show, objects carry with them different meanings depending on their context; meanings which vary from time to time, from place to place, and from person to person. Peter Vergo argues that a better understanding of the rhetorical strategies by which such meanings may be manipulated is one of the first tasks of the new museology. This is one of the tasks taken up by Bernard Schiele and Louise Boucher in Chapter 12.

Exhibition-making has moved on since Brown Goode coined his definition of an efficient exhibition. El Lissitzky's 1928 Pressa exhibition in Cologne broke with the idea that a gallery must be a visually static cube with flat images applied to vertical walls. He paved the way for Herbert Bayer, in the 1930 Deutscher Werkbund exhibition in Paris and the 1931 Building Workers' Union exhibition in Berlin, to create a much more dynamic form of exhibition, comprising a total environment of communication.

Science and natural history museums, with their relatively unproblematic, democratic sense of purpose, have on the whole found it easier than other museums to accept the changes introduced by El Lissitzky and Herbert Bayer.

So it is not surprising to find science and natural history museums at the centre of the contributions from Roger Silverstone (Chapter 11), Bernard Schiele and Louise Boucher (Chapter 12), and Pere Alberch (Chapter 13). Roger Silverstone draws out the particular character of a modern exhibition's relationship to time and space, which is related to the use of all the modern – including electronic – media of communication. Here, surely, lie the defining characteristics of the science exhibition, as an agent of communication, in comparison with the mass media; and, it might be added, with the heritage attractions described by Robert Lumley in Chapter 4, which base their claim to authenticity on the presentation of the real. Roger Silverstone points out that communication within an exhibition is not simply the presentation of pre-existing subject matter, as found, but is the product of creative work undertaken by the various members of the design team (as well as by the visitors). He argues for a greater understanding of this work, as an important step in trying to understand museums as a medium of communication.

Bernard Schiele and Louise Boucher in Chapter 12 have much to say about this creative work from another angle, as they explore in detail the way in which the physical form of an exhibition, as it stands in the space of a gallery, interacts with the objects and other media of communication to give the characteristic language of science exhibitions. Like Roger Silverstone, Bernard Schiele and Louise Boucher note that visitors characteristically experience an exhibition as a text, through which they walk, and with whose enforced meanings they interact. The contribution of these last two authors shows how exhibition designers attempt to generate these enforced meanings through the action of a limited set of rules.

Pere Alberch argues in Chapter 13 that most natural history museums have yet to speak in the language of science exhibitions that Bernard Schiele and Louise Boucher describe. As a consequence, these museums present an outdated view of nature and science: displays of preserved animals, plants and minerals in glass cases reflecting nature as orderly and amenable to classification. They present, in other words, a pre-Darwinian, nineteenth-century view of the world. In arguing for the development of exhibits that convey the dynamic aspects of nature, for processes over objects, Pere Alberch's message is relevant beyond the bounds of natural history museums, if museums aspire to speak to more than a small band of scholars. All museums that would engage with the modern world, and come to terms with its views of the past as well as of the present, need to ponder its implications.

10

The rhetoric of display

Peter Vergo

This article has not one but two starting points. The first is a volume of essays about various aspects of museums which I edited, and to which I contributed, published in 1989 under the title *The New Museology*. One aim of that book was to induce a more reflective and critical attitude towards the wide range of activities in which museums engage. While this aim remained largely unfulfilled, the book instead provoking a good deal of annoyance and even hostility in certain quarters,[1] the questions it raises have not simply gone away but continue to be debated and refined, not least among the younger generation of museum professionals.

My own contribution to *The New Museology*, an essay entitled 'The reticent object' (Vergo 1989: 41–59), had a more specific, even limited objective. My concern was, and is, with the making of various kinds of exhibitions, not necessarily in museums. My disquiet was, and is, that there continues to be (in Great Britain, at least) a tradition of what I would call unreflective exhibition-making. This seems, at worst, to have no more sophisticated purpose than to draw in the crowds and to make money. At best, it amounts to little more than what I would call exhibition-making for the sake of it, doing almost nothing to define its goals or justify (other than in terms of pure entertainment value) the immense expenditure of time and money and intellectual and physical effort which go into the making of large – or even medium-sized – exhibitions.

No doubt, one could adduce numerous counter-examples which might be used to undermine my thesis – exhibitions carefully thought out in terms not only of what is being displayed but also of the different publics that are being addressed. However, the fact that shows of this kind do happen, and happen in increasing number, does not wholly allay my fear that a significant proportion of exhibitions still simply bring together objects for no very good reason – in order to create the opportunity of seeing examples of different phases of an artist's work all at the same time (the hallowed 'retrospective exhibition'), or to give (usually spurious) expression to a nation's cultural or political aspirations, or to celebrate some meaningless anniversary or historical event[2] – all of which seem to me relatively unsophisticated aims.

My second starting point was an article by Susan Pearce published in the first issue of the journal *New Research in Museum Studies*, under the title 'Objects as meaning'. In this important, absorbing essay, the author draws both on the discipline of material culture studies and on linguistic theory in order to engage in a 'case study' of a single object: an officer's jacket, bullet-holed and lovingly preserved, worn at the battle of Waterloo, an item now part of the collection of the National Army Museum in London. She discusses in some detail the wide range of meanings implicit in this apparently simple garment, with its countless personal and social and historical associations, and how those meanings are part of a complex web of relations in which the perceptions of the individual (determined in part not merely by the tastes and preferences, education and upbringing of the viewer, but also by factors such as ethnic origin or social class), the memory or consciousness of the group, even the passage of time, all play a part.

Pearce's aim, first and foremost, is to examine the dynamics of viewing such an object when, for example, as in the case of the Waterloo jacket, it is exposed for public inspection as part of a permanent museum display. She seeks to uncover the various layers of signification with which we as viewers invest it, depending on our associative relationship both with it and with the event which it, in a sense, symbolises. She also touches on the vexed question of the standpoint of the curator or other person responsible for devising the manner of display, stressing that every presentation of an object, far from being neutral, is in fact 'part of the dialectical process . . . a rhetorical act of persuasion' (Pearce 1990: 138). Most important of all, she emphasises that the *context* (personal, social, historical) of which the jacket is part not only confers various 'meanings' upon the object itself, but also allows it to function as a 'sign' or 'symbol' in its own right (an item of military as opposed to civilian dress, bearing insignia which identify it as the jacket of a lieutenant rather than a colonel, and so on).

The notion that context and meaning are inextricably linked is, of course, by now something of a commonplace in the study of language. The particular interest of Pearce's account is that she seeks to transfer this underlying linguistic model to the realm of objects, examining the various ways in which different possible contexts will bear upon the interpretation of objects on display. These different contexts are, however, not to be envisaged as antithetical, or as mutually exclusive. Rather, the viewer will choose, consciously or unconsciously, from among a number of *equally valid* contexts, while the object itself remains intractably multi-layered – multi-valent, one might say – in the almost infinite number of ways in which it is capable of being understood and interpreted.

Of course, various kinds of museums in a sense create their own contexts. Our reaction to a jacket encountered in a museum of military history will inevitably be different from that provoked by seeing a similar object in a museum of theatrical costume. In the case of special (usually temporary) exhibitions, the nature of our interest in any particular object will also be partly determined not only by the identity or ethos of the venue, but also by the overall subject or topic of the show itself. To pursue for a moment longer our Napoleonic theme: a gold fob watch once worn by the Duke of Wellington will acquire a quite different significance in the context of an exhibition entitled 'Napoleon – his Rise and Fall' from any it might have if displayed as part of an exhibition which had as its subject the evolution of the goldsmith's art. These various kinds of significance that all objects potentially have – or, more correctly, with which they may be invested – will be reinforced or largely suppressed, depending upon the relative importance of all these factors: the character of the museum or other organising institution, the theme and purpose of the exhibition or display, the physical context created by the exhibition maker or exhibition designer, the juxtaposition of objects on display with other kinds of related or unrelated material.

Perhaps the most important achievement of Pearce's article is to make clear the complexity of the different kinds of possible relationships between things. The intellectual argument which lies at the heart of her account also has, however, serious implications for any consideration of the strategies employed by curators or museum professionals in the display of exhibitions or collections. In the most banal terms, one might even visualise a kind of exhibition layout or floor plan which physically mimicked this conceptual model – the 'web of relations' referred to above.

Imagine, for example, an exhibition which revolved around a single, centrepiece object of special rarity and value – a portrait, say, by a celebrated artist. Go in one direction, and you might encounter other paintings by the same artist, showing the evolution of his or her work over a period of time – the path of style. Go in another, and you will see preparatory drawings and related studies pertaining to the portrait in question – the path of creation. Another direction again, and displayed in showcases are documents, letters, memorabilia relating to the family and social life, the interests and calling of the sitter – the path of personal and social history. A fourth, and one might find pigment samples, the artist's palette or brushes, x-ray photographs revealing underdrawing beneath the visible paint layer, or spectroscopic analyses of the materials employed – the path of technique.

At this juncture, it seems advisable to sound a note of caution. I have referred to a physical layout or exhibition design of this kind as 'banal', and so it is, in more than one sense. 'Social history on your right, artist's life and works turn left' can by no stretch of the imagination be regarded as a highly sophisticated conception of exhibition-making. Not only that; it also leaves out of account all aesthetic considerations. There is no escaping the fact that the physical arrangement and juxtaposition of objects along the lines suggested here might, from a visual standpoint, simply look horrible. Among the delights and torments experienced by every exhibition-maker – by everyone who does it 'for real' – are the tricks that objects (not only works of art but other kinds of objects as well) can play: how they can look grandiose and striking from one vantage point but mean and diminutive from another; how they can be visually effective, tell their part of a story in certain physical contexts and juxapositions while remaining taciturn and intractable in others.

In choosing as my 'centrepiece' object a portrait – a painting, in other words – I have deliberately embarked on perilous seas, since the display of works of art (as opposed to other kinds of objects) raises aesthetic questions in a peculiarly acute form. Paintings, in particular, are especially problematic, because they are frequently discussed in terms that suggest that they are genuinely considered to be artefacts different in kind from any others in the real world. One reason for this is that a painting – unlike a chair, a teapot, or even a tapestry – is held for the most part to have little or no practical use. Paintings, so the argument goes, are unique in that they were in most cases conceived and executed purely as objects of aesthetic contemplation.

This notion of an objectless art – an 'art for art's sake' – is a distinctively modern one: one, moreover, which conveniently ignores history. The essentially traditional, post-Renaissance view of the dignity and seriousness of painting derived to a large extent from the fact that painting was perceived as dealing by its very nature in moral lessons, capable of inculcating virtues such as piety or self-sacrifice or patriotism. In other words, far from being purposeless, traditional history painting – which prior to the middle of the nineteenth century was regarded as the most elevated form of painting – was conceived with precise moral or political or didactic messages in mind. Even an artist such as Hogarth, whose art was for the most part deeply rooted in contemporary life, wrote explicitly of his ambition to paint modern moral subjects, and made several attempts at various stages in his career – though more by example than through precepts – to estabish an English school of history painting.

From our standpoint *vis-à-vis* such kinds of older art, decoding these messages is an essential part of deciphering or reconstructing the intentions which originally lay behind the creation of the work of art – an activity which involves knowledge, sometimes even quite extensive knowledge, of the history of the times, of the events depicted, of the literary sources on which the artist drew, or the iconographic conventions to which he had recourse. Yet it is still the case that, in the minds of many exhibition-makers, demonstrating or explaining such things via the medium of the exhibition is simply anathema, because any such didactic aims are held to be incompatible with that silent, purely private dialogue between artist and spectator in which the work itself functions solely as vehicle for the communication of emotional states – a dialogue which it is the role of the exhibition to facilitate.

My own standpoint is, as I have perhaps implied, diametrically opposed to such a view. In my opinion, the primary function of any exhibition must be to enable the visitor not merely to enjoy or appreciate, but also to understand the objects (including works of art) on display; indeed, I do not really think it is possible to draw any clear-cut or meaningful distinction between 'enjoyment', 'appreciation' and 'understanding'. In the case of works of art, 'understanding' entails unravelling and explaining – to oneself or to others – the various meanings which the artist has purposely encoded in them; and the particular excitement of exhibitions, it seems to me, is that they offer the perfect vehicle for doing precisely this in a variety of ways, many of them purely visual.

Consider, for example, the famous painting of the dying Marat by Jacques Louis

David, now in the Royal Museum in Brussels.[3] The story of the event depicted in the painting is well known, and can easily be told in words – by means of a lecture, in a book or exhibition catalogue, or by whatever means. But the meaning of the painting is by no means identical with the story on which it is based. What did the artist intend – and how, in particular, did he ensure that the public (which was, of course, in his mind the public of his own day) got the 'right' message? On the face of it, the picture is susceptible to various interpretations. Marat was by any standards a monster, physically repulsive, morally indefensible, capable of sending innocent men, women and children to imprisonment and death on little more than a whim or a pretext.[4] How do we know that David is not saying to us: 'Here I show you the image of a tyrant, justly despatched by one of those innocent victims he sought to oppress'? Or is he in fact saying: 'Ecce Homo; here you see a great a good man, slain in cowardly manner by his treacherous opponents'?

In reality, the intended message of the painting is relatively easy to decipher and to appreciate on the basis of purely visual evidence. Not merely that it has the mood, the appearance of an altarpiece, the packing case that served Marat as makeshift writing desk evoking a tombstone, while the sombre greenish light which pervades the picture calls to mind the dim interior of the Church of the Cordeliers in Paris in which his putrefying body was (briefly) exposed for public veneration (Brookner 1980: 114). More important is the fact that subtly, and purely visually, but quite explicitly, David has identified Marat with the most revered of all great and good men to have been unjustly murdered by their enemies, with Christ himself. The corpse is deliberately placed in the conventional pose of a Pietà as employed by Raphael, Michelangelo and innumerable artists from the Renaissance onwards, with slumped, twisted torso and dangling arm. If only on a subliminal level, this association would certainly have struck a chord even in the minds of an illiterate or irreligious Parisian audience who had, none the less, to a man (and to a woman) been brought up in a still essentially religious age, with holy pictures derived ultimately from the imagery of Renaissance art constantly before their eyes.

Of course, the irony of all this is that it has taken several hundred words of text to describe; yet, in the context of an exhibition, the salient points could have been made very quickly and very effectively, without much recourse to words, mainly by the simple juxtaposition of images. Yet I must confess that I have never seen an exhibition in which works of art have been used to explain each other in quite the manner suggested here – partly, I think, because of an entrenched resistance to the idea of works of art serving as tokens of other things, other meanings – of anything other than themselves.[5]

The still widespread notion of the work of art as an autonomous, indeed sacrosanct icon of contemplation has brought in its train any number of (to my mind) unfortunate consequences. These are, however, often difficult to counter, since the arguments employed against the kind of didactic exhibition-making I have been advocating here are constantly shifting, and in any case are by no means wholly consistent. For example, the aesthetic standpoint in many cases proscribes the printed word, which supposedly intrudes on that purely private process of aesthetic communication already referred to; thus, any form of verbal elucidation, at least in the gallery itself (caption, label, text panel) is more or less taboo, or is reduced to a minimum. It should, however, be noted that this obsession with excluding words from the gallery is clearly all about not intruding on the purely *visual* process, the act of seeing, since the ban on verbal material does not apparently extend to the *spoken* word. On the contrary, the far more intrusive adjunct of the audio-guide is now actively marketed in most large-scale exhibitions, while any exhibition with serious pretensions to grandeur will also include a variety of audio-visual programmes, though these are often (usually to one's relief) banished to some remote corner of the building.

This notion of the sanctity of the purely visual experience which the viewer, confronted with the object on display, supposedly undergoes, might be more persuasive were it not for the extraordinary lack of visual sensitivity shown – one might almost say flaunted – by so many exhibition designers. One museum experience that will live in my mind for ever – though it is perhaps better not to say in which museum it occurred – involved a relatively small-scale, extraordinarily beautiful drawing by Charles Rennie Mackintosh. In fact a decorative design for a piece of furniture, the drawing – mainly in pencil – also showed delicate touches of that fugitive colour which is not quite mauve and not quite lilac, for which Mackintosh and the designers of the Glasgow school had a particular predilection. In the 'modern' manner, it was displayed quite bereft of any accompanying explanations as to the circumstances of its creation, the purpose for which it was intended – no documents, no photographs of the interior in which the piece of furniture in question belonged. The reason for this was, of course, so as not to disturb one's purely ocular experience of the drawing itself. It was, on the other hand, placed immediately next to a bright red and, as far as I could see, newly painted fire hydrant.

Even more unfortunate is the fact that this obsession with avoiding any form of visual intrusion that might come between the viewer and the object of his or her contemplation should have led to the exclusion, not merely of words, but of other kinds of explicative material as well, even when that material is itself of a purely visual character. In the recent exhibition 'The Fauve Landscape', at least in the version shown at the Royal Academy of Arts in London, even though each section of the exhibition was preceded by well-written and informative, if brief, text panels, there was displayed in the gallery not one single photograph of any of the locations depicted. This was despite the fact that the catalogue stressed how crucial these particular localities – the suburban region of Paris bordering on the river Seine, small towns on the Mediterranean such as Collioure and L'Estaque – were to the evolution of this particular genre of Fauve painting. Any fear that the paintings might have been overshadowed, or their effect in any way diminished, by the juxtaposition of photographs, might surely have been dispelled, not merely by the quality of the works themselves, but also by sensitive decisions regarding the layout and design, and especially the scale of such adjunct material. This material could, of course, perfectly well have been reproduced as part of the text panels already mentioned, thus diminishing still further any possibility of intruding upon the visual effect produced by the actual paintings.

Photographs are merely one example of a category of adjunct material capable of being used either for the sake of their historical significance, or for explicative purposes, or as objects of aesthetic contemplation in their own right; indeed, it is perfectly possible to conceive of the kind of display in which all three purposes would be fulfilled at the same time. Many other kinds of purely visual material might be used in similar ways: rich in explicative potential, of sufficient visual interest in themselves to hold the viewer's attention, requiring little or nothing by way of verbal elucidation. Among these other kinds of material are maps, diagrams, architectural designs, genealogical tables, manuscripts, personal diaries and letters, printed ephemera (tram tickets, theatre programmes), costume and jewellery, furniture, items of decor, coins, medals and seals.

Another argument against educative or contextual exhibitions is that shows of this kind amount to little more than putting a book on the walls. According to those who adhere to such views, elucidation of a theme or topic in the manner I have described is the business of the book, the illustrated lecture, the learned article, and not of an exhibition. In reality, the essential difference between them has nothing whatever to do with didactic purpose, but resides rather in the physical three-dimensionality of an exhibition. At best, a book or article will allow, by means of illustrations, the comparison of two or more photographic images, while the accompanying verbal argument, no matter how discursive, is in essence linear, in the sense that only one chain of thought or sequence of arguments can be traced at any one time.

An exhibition of original material – documents, photographs, objects, art works – is radically different in almost every important respect. First, there is the physical, tangible reality of the objects themselves, even if one is not permitted to touch them: their real colours and shapes and textures, the sense of weight and mass, those qualities which are invariably diminished or lost altogether in reproduction. Capable of being viewed in any sequence and – allowing for a limited degree of visual memory – being held in one's mind's eye and compared all at the same time, the fact that each object potentially carries not one but a number of non-verbal meanings adds still further to the variety of levels on which the exhibition can be experienced, even in purely visual terms. Add to this the various ways in which space itself can be exploited, the manner in which objects may be placed side by side on the wall, juxtaposed within the showcase, seen from a distance or close to, dimly perceived in the periphery of one's vision, glimpsed high up or viewed from above, and it will be seen that in truth the exhibition has little in common with the book; rather, it resembles far more closely a work of music, which depends for its effect precisely upon the ability of the listener to trace various strands of melody and counterpoint at the same time, as well as recognising inversions or transformations of a particular musical motif, the component parts of a canon or fugue, the extended musical paragraphs of a sonata-form movement, and so on.

In one of the most perceptive and sensitive pieces of writing about music ever

155

penned by a dramatist, Peter Shaffer in his play *Amadeus* puts into the young Mozart's mouth words which might, if adapted, well serve to illustrate the particular non-sequential, non-linear, simultaneously perceived character of the didactic exhibition which, in my own more halting way, I have been trying to describe. What Mozart – or Shaffer – has in mind is the extraordinary finale of Act II of the *Marriage of Figaro*, 'a quartet becoming a quintet becoming a sextet'. In this finale, Count Almaviva and his Countess and Figaro and Susanna and Cherubino all voice at the same time, though more to themselves than to each other, their hopes and fears and secret intentions; but in order to convey the utter realism of the situation he wishes to portray on the stage, Mozart takes the particular moment of embarrassment in which he finds himself as an example of how differently such a dilemma would be represented by a poet or playwright, by comparison with a musician:

> Look at us! Four gaping mouths. What a perfect quartet! I'd love to write it
> – just this second of time, this *now* . . . Herr Chamberlain thinking
> 'Impertinent Mozart: I must speak to the Emperor at once!' Herr Prefect
> thinking 'Ignorant Mozart: debasing opera with his vulgarity!' Herr Court
> Composer thinking 'German Mozart: what can he finally know about
> music?' And Herr Mozart himself, in the middle, thinking 'I'm just a good
> fellow. Why do they all disapprove of me?' That's why opera is important
> . . . because it's realer than any play! A dramatic poet would have to put all
> those thoughts down one after another to represent this second of time. The
> composer can put them all down at once – and still make us hear each one
> of them. . . . I bet you that's how God hears the world. Millions of sounds
> ascending at once and mixing in His ear to become an unending music,
> unimaginable to us!
>
> (Shaffer 1981: 69–70)

Should not the sensitive exhibition designer be able to mimic to a large degree this peculiar character of music, as well as its ability to evoke, to suggest, to imply? No need to prescribe for the visitor a physical route around the exhibition by simple-minded devices such as arrows, or signs saying 'start of exhibition', when it is surely possible to engage the viewer's attention, to cajole, to beckon by more subtle means. An object invisible from one standpoint is suddenly espied from another. A splash of colour captures one's eye. A carved capital stands in a metonymic relationship to the building from which it was taken, while set against a wall on to which is projected an image of the building itself. Shapes and forms echo one another like the various voices in a church antiphon, calling to one another across the exhibition space just as in sixteenth-century Venetian music the widely separated instruments called to one another from the opposing galleries and choir lofts of St Mark's Basilica. Or, to take an up-to-the-minute example: one of the most breathtaking effects achieved in the display of early and high Renaissance paintings in the new Sainsbury Wing of the National Gallery in London is the way in which the real architecture of the galleries mimics the fictive architecture of the Cima da Conegliano altarpiece seen in the distance at the far end of the gallery.[6] The purpose of this piece of virtuoso display is evidently to create by purely visual means a kind of ostinato effect which entices the visitor, willy-nilly, along what turns out to be the central aisle of the new gallery, while further spaces, new vistas, no less intriguing juxtapositions open up on either side, like the counter-subjects of a fugue.

Thus far, we have been considering the role of the exhibition-maker or designer in creating those kinds of exhibitions which, in a sense, open up a given subject by revealing the wealth of possibilities for interpretation implicit in various kinds of material. Didactic purposes of this kind are, however, sometimes overshadowed by other, more specific, on occasion even sinister propaganda aims.

The notion of art as propaganda is, of course, a very old one. An extreme view, though not an entirely ridiculous one, might hold that in fact the vast majority of works of art have some covert if not overt propagandist aim: to retail a particular religious narrative, to uphold a moral or political idea, to glorify a certain individual or a given ideology, to support or subvert the social or political status quo. The individual artist, working in a specific social or political or historical context, may deliberately use a work of art as a vehicle for the communication of such ideas; and one purpose of the art historian must surely be to unravel these threads, to decode these messages, as in the case of David's *Marat* painting cited earlier – a task which is especially crucial when, as so often, the original context or the imagery employed is remote or unfamiliar to us now.

But it is not only individual works of art that may embody such aims; exhibitions, too, are often made with an unashamedly propagandist purpose in mind. Under totalitarian regimes, exhibitions as propaganda are a frequently occurring phenomenon in which not only works of art but artefacts and even specimens taken from the natural world are used to exemplify a particular political idea or reinforce a certain ideology, while the products of earlier periods or epochs are often held up to public ridicule or used to demonstrate the inadequacy or degeneration of a now discredited ideology or political order. The Nazis, in particular, were past masters at the latter kind of exhibition, the notorious 'Degenerate Art' exhibition shown in Munich and other German and Austrian cities from 1937 to 1941, in which virtually all avant-garde artists from Expressionism onwards were vilified and their works exposed to scorn, being merely the largest and most famous of a number of similar propaganda manifestations.[7]

Apart from one's disquiet at the notion of artists and their works being abused and exploited in this manner, what is almost equally unsettling about the notion of exhibitions as propaganda is the realisation that precisely the *same* object can be used in different contexts and exposed in different ways in order to tell radically opposite stories. This, it should be said, has nothing to do with the problems of decoding the complex messages encoded in works of art, since the argument is in fact not about works of art at all: any product, any artefact, any object taken from the real world can be subjected to this kind of process. An exhibition of petrol pumps might be part of a campaign to enhance the image of

157

the petro-chemical industry by pointing to the benefits it has conferred on technologically advanced societies; or those self-same petrol pumps might be displayed in the context of an exhibition all about pollution, global warming and the importance of environmental issues. Or they might simply be part of a more neutral kind of historically conceived display which simply traced the evolution of certain technologies and the development of certain products and machines. Putting the 'right' message across will be a function not merely of the manner of display, but of the use of adjunct material, the content of captions and information panels as well as all the paraphernalia of marketing and publicity, including, of course, the ubiquitous catalogue.

I referred briefly in passing to the possibility of a more 'neutral' – by which I meant not overtly critical or political or propagandist – kind of display. But in reality, no exhibition is entirely free from social or political or economic concerns. As already pointed out in the context of Pearce's discussion, the very act of selecting objects and putting them on public display is not neutral. What is most disquieting of all about our present modes of exhibition-making is their underlying dishonesty in that we pretend, tacitly or explicitly, to an objective standpoint, steadfastly averting our minds from the knowledge that our approach is nothing if not partial. When will we 'come clean' about our purposes in exhibition-making? When, instead of (or as well as) writing in the catalogue about the artist, the historical period, the techniques by which objects were made, the uses to which objects were put, will the exhibition-maker or 'guest curator' write about the underlying aim of the exhibition itself, about the choices made in selecting those same objects of display, the criteria that governed those choices, even – dare one say it – about objects *not* selected for the exhibition? And when, no less crucial, will the exhibition catalogue be found to contain an essay by the designer, explaining how the transition from idea to reality was achieved, how the design decisions and design strategy were arrived at, and what the purpose behind those decisions and that strategy might have been?

All this, of course, if it is ever put into practice, will be the result not of more efficient training nor of improved curatorial methods; rather, it depends upon the cultivation of an entirely new sensibility. Upon curators or makers of exhibitions will fall the task of developing an increased sensitivity to objects themselves, to their multifarious meanings and to the contexts that confer those meanings upon them. It would also be laudable if those same curators were also to cultivate a much greater sensitivity to the many audiences who flock to contemplate the objects on display, and to their different levels of education and understanding, in order to educate without patronising, to entertain without cheapening. To the designer, meanwhile, falls the task of cultivating humility, a capacity for self-effacement, a sense of reverence confronted with the reality of objects – and, at the same time, a heightened visual awareness, an apprehension of the 'modifications supposedly inanimate objects impose on one another' (Gleizes and Metzinger 1912). Tact, humility, sensitivity, a sense of propriety – these are strengths that are often mistaken for weaknesses; but the greatest of these is sensitivity, so that if the particular notion of exhibition-making that I have here been advocating ever gains wider currency, I should like to christen it 'the new sensitivity'.

Notes

1 See, for example, the review by Anna Somers Cocks in *Crafts* magazine, March–April 1990, p. 58.
2 Much the same points are made, with refreshing brevity and force, in an editorial published in response to the British Association of Art Historians' one-day conference 'Why Exhibitions?', held at the Victoria and Albert Museum, London, in November 1987: see 'Still too many exhibitions', *Burlington Magazine*, CXXX: 1018 (January 1988), p. 3.
3 Brussels, Musées Royaux des Beaux-Arts, inv. no. 3261: see the catalogue *Jacques-Louis David 1748–1825*, Paris (Réunion des musées nationaux) 1989, cat. no. 118 and pp. 282–5.
4 On Marat himself, see Gottschalk (1967), also the probing article by Hampson (1981: 11).
5 The nearest thing to an exhibition of this kind was the highly unusual show organised by the *Burlington Magazine* and held at Sotheby's, London, in September 1971 under the title 'Art into Art. Works of Art as a Source of Inspiration'.
6 Cima da Conegliano, *Altarpiece, The Incredulity of S. Thomas*: London, National Gallery, inv. no. 816; see Davies (1961: pp. 144–5).
7 There is an extensive literature on the subject of 'degenerate' art. The fiftieth anniversary, in 1987, of the Munich showing of the exhibition 'Entartete Kunst' occasioned a spate of publications, of which one of the most useful is the anthology edited by Schuster (1987). For a more recent survey, see now the catalogue by Barron (1991).

References

Barron, S. (1991) *Degenerate Art. The Fate of the Avant-Garde in Nazi Germany*, Los Angeles: County Museum of Art.
Brookner, A. (1980) *Jacques-Louis David*, London: Chatto & Windus.
Davies, M. (1961) *The Earlier Italian Schools*, 2nd edition, London: National Gallery Catalogues.
Gleizes, A. and Metzinger, J. (1912) 'Du Cubisme', in R.L. Herbert (ed.), *Modern Artists on Art. Ten Unabridged Essays*, Englewood Cliffs, NJ: Prentice-Hall, pp. 2–18.
Gottschalk, L.R. (1967) *Jean-Paul Marat. A Study in Radicalism*, Chicago and London: Chicago University Press.
Hampson, N. (1981) 'A power hungry patriot', *Times Higher Education Supplement*, 11 December.
Pearce, S. (1990) 'Objects as meaning; or narrating the past', *New Research in Museum Studies. An International Series*, vol. 1, pp. 125–40.
Schuster, P.-K. (1987) *Die 'Kunststadt' München: Nationalsozialismus und 'Entartete Kunst'*, Munich: Prestel.
Shaffer, P. (1981) *Amadeus*, Harmondsworth: Penguin.
Vergo, P. (1987) 'The reticent object', in P. Vergo (ed.), *The New Museology*, London: Reaktion, pp. 41–59.

11

The medium is the museum: on objects and logics in times and spaces[1]

Roger Silverstone

I would like in this chapter to offer some thoughts on the particular character of the museum as a medium of communication, and to provide a framework for its analysis. In doing so, I will draw on recently completed research, based at the Science Museum, London, which examined the processes through which a new gallery in the museum was created and which undertook visitor research in the light of that examination (Macdonald and Silverstone 1990a, 1990b, 1992). I will also seek to refine and develop ideas that I have already expressed on this subject in previous essays (Silverstone 1988, 1989a).

The New Museology (Vergo 1989), among other things, recommends that the study of museums, as well as professional work within museums, should adopt a greater reflexivity in relation to its activities, a reflexivity which enquires not just into methods, but into purpose, context and consequence. The museum is no longer, if ever it was, an institution which can be understood in its own terms as innocently engaged in the processes of the collection, conservation, classification and display of objects. On the contrary, it is one among many components in a complex array of cultural and leisure industries (Lumley 1988; Hewison 1987), no longer certain of its role, no longer secure in its identity, no longer isolated from political and economic pressures or from the explosion of images and meanings which are, arguably, transforming our relationships in contemporary society to time, space and reality (Giddens 1990).

One possible route into the kind of reflexivity called for is through a consideration of the museum, and those institutions that we might see as providing variations on the theme of the museum, as medium. Such a proposition, of course, implies both that there is something distinctive about the museum's mediation of the world, and that that distinctiveness has particular consequences for our understanding of the museum's significance. So what kind of medium is the museum? How do museums relate to, and participate in, the wider, intensely mass and electronically mediated culture of the late twentieth century? What can we learn about museums by drawing on that body of research and writing that has taken the study of contemporary media, most significantly television, as its focus?

A consideration of the museum as a medium will involve a consideration of all aspects of the process by which the communications involved in display are conceived, created, implemented and received. Museums are in many respects like other contemporary media. They entertain and inform; they tell stories and construct arguments; they aim to please and to educate; they define, consciously or unconsciously, effectively or ineffectively, an agenda; they translate the otherwise unfamiliar and inaccessible into the familiar and accessible. And in the construction of their texts, their displays, their technologies, they offer an ideologically inflected account of the world.

But equally, of course, there are obvious differences between museums and other media such as newspapers, radio or television. Museums are not broadcast media: they occupy physical spaces; they contain objects; they encourage inter-activity; they allow the visitor, literally, to wander (and wonder) through their texts; and they have an uncharacteristic permanence – even a temporary exhibition has a kind of permanence not granted to the television programme or the newspaper.

Indeed, the relationship that museums have to media goes beyond their own status as a medium as such, for museums increasingly have to compete with other media for attention and for visitors; they increasingly come to depend on other media, particularly video and interactive computer-based technologies, within their own exhibitions; and they increasingly have to rely on other media both as a source of information (this was true, for example, when the gallery which was the subject of our research found itself dealing with a matter of public and scientific controversy (Macdonald and Silverstone 1992)) and as a mediator of its own product – its own exhibitions are marketed and reviewed in the same way as other cultural products.[2]

I have subtitled this chapter 'Objects and logics in times and spaces'. Increasingly, it is being recognised that the distinctive character of modern media lies in their capacity to articulate and to transform relations to time and space. Their mediation not only consists in a set of complex relations to various presents, pasts and futures (the contrary temporalities of production and reception, as well as of the texts themselves), but also results in shifts in society's own relationship to time and space. Television news, for example – always present – brings a sense of instant contact, irrespective of both geographical and temporal distance. The televising of national events provides the basis for the invention or imagination of new, or the resurrection of old, communities. Studies of the media, too, have focused on the particular logics of their texts: the narrative structures of programmes, the rhetoric of their discourses, the structures of argument, and of course the role of the viewer/reader in constructing or reconstructing all of these. Likewise, studies of the media attend to the processes by which, through sound and image or written text, verisimilitude is created: a sense of realism without which no trust in the medium could be sustained.

In focusing on the museum, therefore, it is these neo-Kantian categories – logic, time and space – that will provide the framework, though the starting point is of a different order. Perhaps the single most obvious, and most determining characteristic of the museum is the necesssary presence within it of objects: of objects that have been collected, conserved, classified and displayed; of objects that have, by their presence in the museum, to claim a particular status – unique, significant, representative.

The object

Objects have biographies. They move through a world of public and private arenas, and in and out of the world of goods and commodities. Born in a factory, an artist's studio or a craftsman's workshop, they may end up on a scrap-heap, on a mantelpiece, or in the glass case of a museum: now on display, now hidden in the bowels of our or others' domesticity. As Igor Kopytoff (1986) suggests, material objects, like people, have not one biography but many. For example, a car will have an economic biography ('its initial worth, its sale and resale price, the rate of decline in its value, its response to the recession, the patterning over several years of its maintenance costs')

> but it will also have several social biographies: . . . one biography may concentrate on its place in the owner-family's economy, another may relate the history of its ownership to the society's class structure, and a third may focus on its role in the sociology of the family's kin relations, such as loosening family ties in America or strengthening them in Africa.
>
> (Kopytoff 1986: 68)

The point, of course, is that the biography of an object is not just a matter of an individual life. That life gains its meaning through the various social, economic, political and cultural environments through which it passes, and its passage can in turn illuminate those environments in the way that a flare or a tracer can illuminate the night sky.

As Charles Saumarez-Smith (1989) suggests, the biography of an object and the museum's own contribution to that biography, are neither of them straightforward. It is a commonplace to observe that objects in museums are more often than not divorced from the world which bore them and in which they gained their various meanings. It is also a commonplace to observe that objects in museums are fixed in their meaning, now that they have reached their final resting place and been included in a collection and placed (or not) on display. However, there is, as Saumarez-Smith argues, life after death, even in a museum – or, at least, a life of a sort. A sculpture of a Saxon god still pock-marked and lichened from its life in various English country gardens, a late-seventeenth-century doorway and a late-seventeenth-century interior, all have been transformed by their passage through the Victoria and Albert Museum: the statue is uncomfortably displayed alongside elegantly restored and polished sculptures of different origin and aesthetic intention; the door has become a shop fitting and a company logo; and the room is wrapped in polythene awaiting a decision as to its ultimate fate.

In the gallery which was the focus of our research, Food for Thought: the Sainsbury Gallery (Macdonald and Silverstone 1990a), a permanent exhibition which opened in the Science Museum, London in October 1989, objects of various kinds (though none of them part of a permanent food science or technology collection in the Science Museum) were displayed. Some of them would be entirely familiar to the visitor, but at the same time would require a kind of reorientation by the shock of the unfamiliarity of their display in the museum. A McDonald's interior, a supermarket check-out, would provide a firm link between the everyday world of the consumer/visitor and the exhibition in the museum. Other objects, less familiar perhaps, and which include various food production technologies, make other claims. They offer an account of the production process that says little of those who operated the machines or the conditions under which they worked. Similarly, and perhaps more conventionally, the exhibition includes 'historical' objects: models of kitchen interiors with original artefacts, examples of early packaging – the cans and packets of half or recently remembered pasts – each with their own biographies, each 'rescued' by their inclusion in the gallery and their mute appeals to the visitor to complete their meaning.

The museum's work in relation to the objects it has on display and in relation to the meanings it defines, or attempts to define for them – in other words, the particular biography it constructs for these objects as justification for their inclusion in the collection or display – results in an abstraction. The ensuing meanings are of necessity partial but, more importantly, they are an essential part of the particular claims for authority and legitimacy on which the museum's whole status depends. It is after all through the object, and through the object's membership of a collection, that the distinct character of the museum is achieved.

However, two things complicate matters even further, particularly in the contemporary exhibition. The first complication lies in the recognition that the meaning of an object, its communication, does not stop with its display, nor is it determined either by its place in the display or the description offered of it in the adjoining label. The meaning of an object continues in the imaginative work of the visitor who brings to it his or her own agenda, experiences and feelings. As Ludmilla Jordanova (1989) points out, the object in the museum becomes a kind of fetish, an object of exaggerated attention, frozen in time and space, an expression of the claims of mastery that are inscribed within the very fabric of the museum. It has a magic potency. The object invites a kind of identification with the Other, at once distanced and close at hand. This dialectic of distance and accessibility, of course, is a commonplace in accounts of the workings of the contemporary media. Indeed, it is possible to see it as a central defining characteristic of them: the familiar made strange; the strange made familiar. Yet both the attention and identification claimed rhetorically by the display of objects cannot be guaranteed merely by their display and classification. Visitors are actively engaged in what they see. This is an issue to which I shall return later in this chapter.

The second complication, and one dramatically revealed in the Food for Thought Gallery, is provided by the inclusion in the exhibition of non-objects:

mock-ups, audio-visual technologies, interactive computer information points, and panels of text and pictures/illustrations which make another, but quite different, claim to be providing an experience of the real. Alan Morton (1988) argues that the increasing trend to appropriate new technologies and media by the museum, and to include examples of them as part of a multi-media interactive experience, has turned museums into commodities. The commodification of the museum echoes and reinforces the commodification of the objects that the museum displays. The reality that is being claimed through these media-objects is a reality grounded in the experience of everyday life, and of the domination of the mass media in that experience. So alongside the claims of objects grounded in the authority of the past and in the authority of the curator, these technologies make their claims through the familiarity, security and seductions of what Umberto Eco (1987) and Jean Baudrillard (1981) would see as the 'hyper-real' – the over-mediated world of simulation and self-referentiality which we seem in our daily lives to take entirely for granted.

The final point I want to make about the status of the object in the museum is eloquently made by Eugene Donato (1980). It concerns the importance of understanding the object in the museum not in isolation, but as an element in a collection, a collection that itself has inevitably something of the arbitrary about it, but which nevertheless is 'the fiction' upon which, once again, much of the authority of the museum as medium is sustained:

> The set of objects the Museum displays is sustained only by the fiction that they somehow constitute a coherent representational universe. . . . Should the fiction disappear, there is nothing left of the *Museum* but 'bric-a-brac', a heap of meaningless and valueless fragments of objects which are incapable of substituting themselves either metonymically for the original objects or metaphorically for their representations.
>
> (Donato 1980: 223)

An object is nothing unless it is part of a collection. A collection is nothing unless it can successfully lay claim to a logic of classification which removes it from the arbitrary or the occasional (cf. Stewart 1984). In its work of collection, the museum provides both a model for, and an echo of, the work of consumption in which we all engage, extracting from a world of use or commercial values objects which, in our appropriation of them, gain their meaning by their inclusion in our own symbolic universe (Douglas and Isherwood 1979; Miller 1987).[3]

However, there is clearly more to the museum than the work of classification, and while objects may well gain their authority from their place in a classificatory system, they gain their meaning from their place in a display. Once again, of course, as I have argued elsewhere (Macdonald and Silverstone 1990a, 1990b), the meaning of an object or of an exhibition is significantly dependent on the 'curatorial' work of the visitor in which objects are reinscribed into a personal culture of memory and experience. But even the possibility of this reconstruction is premised on the prior existence of a display which may or may not be ordered (and, in contemporary museum practice, is increasingly *not* so ordered) by the logic which informed the collection. It is to the question of logic – the logics of display – that I now turn.

Logics

Museums are communicating environments in which complex meanings are negotiated. Those meanings are only partly dependent on the meanings ascribed to individual objects by their place in a historical, an archaeological or an aesthetic classificatory system. As Tony Bennett (1989) suggests in his comparison of three different museums, objects which on the face of it seem remarkably similar are displayed in very different ways in each – with potentially significant ideological consequences.

Donna Haraway describes the representational activities in which museums engage in terms of the deployment of 'technologies of enforced meaning' (Haraway 1984–5: 30; cf. Jordanova 1989). At the heart of these activities is an attempt to create a realist text, in which the aim is a kind of transparency: this is how it was; this is how it is; this is how it will be. But, in this, museums are not alone. For all texts, all attempts to communicate in a coherent fashion, are 'technologies of enforced meaning', even those that are self-evidently dealing in fantasy. What is at issue, as Haraway herself demonstrates, is the particular character and claim of the museum as a textual phenomenon, and the relative degree of openness and closure that it desires or appears to offer the visitor/ reader in his or her involvement with it.

Museums, galleries, exhibitions are texts. And, as texts, they are constructed according to a variety of logics. They have emerged as a result of a complex interplay of institutional and individual forces (Bud 1988). They are consumed in a multitude of different ways by visitors. But they appear as anything but arbitrary. They are structured according to their own rhetoric, a rhetoric which seeks, as all rhetorics seek, to persuade the visitor that what is being seen and read is important, beautiful, and/or true. They are also structured narratively, by principles of classification and representation that create stories or arguments, or perhaps a more open logic, and which provide a framework or a route through which the visitors pass and in relation to which they make sense of what is seen.

It is, of course, the case that individual galleries or exhibitions, never mind museums as wholes, may express multiple logics.[4] A classificatory logic may overlap and be arranged in historical sequence, as it often is in classical museums of science and technology, where the grand narrative of progress is inscribed in the arrangements of, and reflections in, the ubiquitous glass cases. A historical narrative may be grounded in a number of different and overlapping histories, as it is for example in the Museum of the Moving Image (MOMI) in London, where histories of the technologies of moving images (from the camera obscura to the cartoon and the computer) overlap with a more dominant, extensive and intensive history of their products and the production process. As it happens, MOMI is a particularly significant example of a narrative structure – historical but selective – which is very tight in its material and symbolic closure. The constraints imposed by the site (but not only those constraints) appeared to have encouraged those who created the museum to impose a relatively inflexible linear structure on the exhibition. A single route through it is marked intermittently by labels indicating how much has been seen and how much is still to go.

Narratives, historical or otherwise, do provide a framework for the display of objects in the museum. The stories that are told about them, and the larger stories in which they are the actors, provide a particular form of closure, that may or not be followed or re-created by the visitor. Visitors literally walk, or are propelled, through the stories which museums provide for them in their display. But in so doing, and given the varying degrees of freedom so to do, they create their own versions of the narratives on offer (de Certeau 1984).

Somewhere embedded in these narratives is, as Robert Bud argues, a version of myth:

> a specially authentic, intense, or direct contact with the 'sacred' subject, be it historical event or current development, in a sphere with the power, danger and distance of science. . . . The museum acts to reduce fear and provide 'understanding' of the special phenomenon. . . . The museum as a religious centre is an established phenomenon.
>
> (Bud 1988: 135)

Bud's account of the making of the Chemical Industry Gallery at London's Science Museum is, of course, another museological narrative. It tells of the inevitable compromises in gallery design under pressure of what he calls 'the machine': the machine of organisational, political and economic forces; the machine of the often arbitrary and haphazard processes of gallery production.

Yet what emerges, compromised or not, is presented as neither arbitrary nor haphazard. Something of the myth remains, structured into the stories of the achievements of science and technology and in the containing metaphors and metonymies of the display of the objects themselves.[5] What also emerges, of course, is a particular inflection of that myth, of necessity ideological, and in one way or another expressing a world view which excludes or relegates to insignificance other versions of reality.

The Food for Thought Gallery also did not emerge fully formed. The story of its creation and of the emergence of its dominating logic is a story that will be easily recognisable to those who have experience of such work (Macdonald and Silverstone 1990a, 1990b). Early decisions, for example, not to tell a single story about food – either grounded historically or in terms of a narrative of production and consumption – were sustained. But the preferred logic of themes and topics took some time to become fixed, and the final structure of a pyramidal logic in which wider messages subsumed smaller ones had a number of consequences for the later inclusion of specific ideas and materials (for a detailed discussion of these aspects of the gallery, see Macdonald and Silverstone 1992). In particular, this had consequences for the representation of

167

controversy. But such a logic, in its relative openness, also apparently had consequences for the visitor.

The decision to present the science and technology of food and nutrition in this relatively open way was informed by a desire to create a gallery informed by a commitment to the public understanding of science and, as a result, to grounding the science of food and nutrition in the experience of the everyday. As it happens, the gallery also had a number of different points of physical, and therefore logical, entry, so a single narrative would have been difficult to impose. Visitors therefore were presented with an open structure whose logic was perhaps clear to the curators but not fully declared. In the event, visitors' retrospective accounts of their visit provided little evidence of their capacity either to reproduce 'the logic' of the exhibition or indeed to produce a narrative of their own, except perhaps in a fragmented version. Their accounts of the gallery, informed by their own progress through it but also by prior expectations and experiences, were often disjointed and presented in ways which suggested that they recognised that they had not 'done the gallery properly' (Macdonald, 1993). Buried in these fragmented accounts of their visit, however, was a sense of the gallery as providing either a history of food and nutrition or a structured exercise in health education.

Central to an understanding of the museum as medium, therefore, are the logics which underpin the arrangement of the objects on display. Such logics are not determined by the principles by which the objects in the collection have been classified (though they might be), and even those principles are not consistent (compare, for example, the ethnographic collections of the Pitt-Rivers Museum in Oxford to the Museum of Mankind in London or to Paolozzi's *Lost Magic Kingdoms* (Paolozzi 1985). Histories of discrete areas of science or technology, biographies of artists expressed in the arrangements of their work, pedagogically oriented structures or arguments in favour of one interpretation of a slice of material culture over another, all in their various ways can provide, singly or multiply, a framework for the museum's textuality. It can be relatively open or it can aim for closure. In either event, the framework is not ideologically neutral, nor is it unconstrained or inconsequential in its effects. Especially significant for the present argument and especially important for understanding, once again, the particularity of the museum as medium are the exhibition's relationships to time and space. These will be the subject of the next two sections of the chapter.

Times

Time is itself a medium. I have already referred to aspects of the museum's relationship to time, in its production, in its articulation of myth, history and memory, and in the work of visitors. The museum, perhaps most supremely in contemporary culture, is seen as an institution for the mediation of time. In its representation of the Other, that Other is, as often as not, the Other removed in time: a historical Other. But this truism masks much diversity and complexity in the temporality of the museum, both in its various referents and in its own internal structuring. I can barely do justice to this complexity here, so once again I will try and focus on those aspects of the museum's temporality that bear centrally on its status as a medium of communication.

There is a strand in media research and criticism which finds in the explosion of electronic communication in the late twentieth century a fundamental challenge to our customary experience of both space and time. The following quotation from Patricia Mellencamp (1990) is not atypical of those discussions of media and technology which see them as having a fundamental effect on the infrastructures of society, culture and consciousness (McLuhan 1964; Ong 1982; Goody 1977; Eisenstein 1979; Meyrowitz 1985):

> US network television is a disciplinary time machine, a metronome rigorously apportioning the present, rerunning TV history, and anxiously awaiting the future. The hours, days, and television seasons are seriated, scheduled and traded in ten-second increments modelled on the modern work week – day time, prime time, late night or weekend. Time itself is a gendered, hierarchized commodity capitalizing on leisure.
>
> (Mellencamp 1990: 240)

The power of television is, among other things, grounded in its ubiquity. No such power can be accorded the museum. Yet both experientially and phenomenologically, the museum does offer a distinct kind of temporality, and one that is arguably changing both in response to changes in the dominating media environment of contemporary society and by its incorporation of those media technologies into its own displays. But before we run away with the idea that mediation is all powerful, and that the times of the museum (the representation of the past, the immediacy of the present, the extrapolations into the future), and of the exhibition, are overwhelming in their effects, we must remember (cf. Ferguson 1991) that at the very least there are two significant temporalities involved in the experience of the museum: that of the museum itself and that of the visitor.

One way of approaching these difficult issues is to borrow a conceptualisation of the social construction of time developed in some of the literature in family therapy (Kantor and Lehr 1975; Reiss 1981). Here a distinction is made between orienting and clocking. Orienting refers to the selection, direction and maintenance of attitudes and behaviours towards the past, present and future, and to non-temporal realms of experience, by emphasising one or more of these realms or of the particular relationships among them (Kantor and Lehr 1975: 78–9). Museums, like families, it can be argued, define for themselves a dominating orientation to time which provides a framework for the culture of the institution and for the representations of science, art or culture which they contain. Orientation does not refer only to the representational activities of the museum, however. It also refers to its organisational activities, for example, whether the museum as an organisation defines its activities principally in relation to the past (a kind of atavism in which old collections are preserved and displays protected); or to the present (a kind of entrepreneurialism in which the museum constantly adjusts its priorities and designs its galleries in response to immediately felt needs and pressures); or to the future (a kind of conservationism in which emphasis might be placed on collection and conservation at the expense of display).

Orienting can also refer to the particular character of a gallery in which the same kinds of decisions, embodied in the texts of the exhibition, are expressed. The Food for Thought Gallery is, relative to those galleries that surround it in the museum, significantly oriented to the present. The communications that it contains are locked into the present, grounded as they are in an appeal to the visitor's own daily life. Of course, this is not exclusively the case, but it could be argued that even those parts of the exhibition that are distinctively historical in orientation are structured as subordinate to those parts that relate to the present. This is, of course, reinforced by the 'presence' of so much in the way of contemporary media and other technologies.

Clocking refers to 'the regulation of the sequence, frequency, duration and pace of immediately experienced events from moment to moment, hour to hour, and day to day' (Kantor and Lehr 1975:82). Whereas orientation is, in the context of the museum or the gallery, a relatively undynamic quality, relatively non-negotiable, relatively invisible, clocking is both dynamic and visible, and it is also open to negotiation.

From the point of view of the gallery itself, as a text structured through the activities of curators and designers, clocking consists in the efforts to define the dynamics of its internal logic. Narrative, a logic of theme and topic; the particular arrangement of exhibits in space and the physical, intellectual or aesthetic links between them; the assessment of concentration span in relation to specific exhibits and the estimation of average length of visit as a whole; the attempts to control a visitor's movement through the gallery – these are all aspects of clocking strategies, manifestations of which can be observed in each and every museum gallery, both old and new. The order in which things appear, the frequency with which they appear, the intensity of objects, and the duration of the visit are all therefore material to this aspect of the museum's mediation of time (and, of course, space – see below).

Clocking, in the context of such activities, is a bid for control, for control over a particular environment – the environment created for the display – but more especially for control over the visitor's progress through that environment. And it is here, of course, that the problems arise. Patricia Mellencamp's description of the particular temporality of US television is a description of a deeply engrained rhetorical bid for the medium's articulation of the times of daily life, both orientational and in terms of our clocking schedules. Such a bid may be visible in the texts, in the programme schedules, the fragmentation of programmes, and their narrative structure; just as such bids may be visible in the structure of the museum's texts. But the museum presents a different kind of temporality, more physical and grounded in a face-to-face present, less compelling in its exclusion of other realities, other forms of mediation. The result is, even at its most extreme, a multiply open text, in which visitors will bring to bear their own orientations (do they match those defined for them in the exhibition?) and clocking (choosing a route through the gallery and according a particular time and times to the visit as a whole and to individual exhibits). Pace, sequence, duration and scheduling are all aspects of the visitors' clocking mechanism and their times are not necessarily those anticipated by the designers, or structured into the texts, of the gallery through which they pass.

Yet some matching of the orientation and clocking of both exhibition and visitor will have to take place if the communication in which the gallery engages can be considered successful. Indeed, the range of meaningful freedoms that the visitor has is inevitably constrained, both as a result of a kind of prior enculturation into the temporality of the museum which most visitors will have and a preparedness to be directed through the gallery, more or less, in the terms implicitly or explicitly stated in its design and construction (cf. de Certeau 1984; Silverstone 1989b).

Spaces

Time in the museum remains, in all its manifestations, intangible. Less so space. The museum, unique among contemporary media, provides a physical – a material – embodiment of space: a geographical, an architectural environment which once again, though for different reasons, masks the complexity of the various spatially-related relationships that characterise the museum's mode of communication.

Of course, in a literal sense, space provides one of the key constraints on gallery design. The shape of it, the amount of it, its quality, accessibility, all are crucial material factors at every stage of the creation of a new exhibition (Macdonald and Silverstone 1990a). The dimensions of a visit, the likely route a visitor might take through a gallery, the need to structure the exhibits so that a variety of different routes can be catered for, are all well-known problems for museum designers (e.g. Miles *et al.* 1988). Yet the spatial dimensions of the museum's communication extend well beyond these albeit vital, practical considerations.

In what ways? What kind of space is museum space? How important is an understanding of space in the museum for an understanding of its distinctive character as a communicating medium?

I want to approach these questions by considering museum space both materially and phenomenologically, and I will do so with reference to the Food for Thought Gallery. The gallery occupies space previously devoted to the astronomy collection. It occupies 810 m^2 in the National Museum of Science and Industry. Within those 810 m^2 are exhibited 166 interactives, working demonstrations, videos, computer information points, objects and replica sets. The average number of objects per square metre is 0.1 (compared to 0.6 in the museum as a whole). These individual exhibits are incorporated in a gallery that has been carefully designed and structured in accordance with a logic built around questions and answers, themes and topics, to which I have already referred. No overall narrative structure was imposed on the gallery. No arrows mark a preferred progress, a preferred reading. Multiple points of entry and exit (a constraint imposed by the given space) make it almost impossible to control a visitor's route through it. Within the gallery, various subsections, though not always clearly identified as such, focus on food consumption and food production, with sub-themes, for example, on diet, additives and food safety. At many stages of the design and production process, planned exhibits were withdrawn because of lack of space (cf. Bud 1988).

Space in the museum, then, is a finite resource. It is also a territory, more or less jealously guarded and colonised. It is the object of considerable emotional attachment, as a result of which, for those who are responsible for it, the space becomes place, an intensely meaningful location which excites a whole series of proprietorial feelings and close identifications. And it is also, of course, a phenomenological reality, a set of perceptions subject to constant structuring and restructuring in the imagination and experiences of all those involved in the museum's mediation of the world.

Anthony Giddens (1990) writes of the quality of space and time in modern societies in terms of space–time distanciation. Electronic media have, he suggested, removed us from the close-knit networks of face-to-face communication and attachment to place which were the norm for those living in pre-modern societies. Watching television, making a telephone call, receiving instantaneous financial information on a global computer network, are activities which have fundamentally affected our relationships to, our perceptions of, space and time. Space, in particular, has become dematerialised. The museum is both part of this world and not part of it. I have already noted that it increasingly incorporates (and maybe even relies on) those very technologies which Giddens is claiming have altered our senses of space, and our own position in space. Yet, quite obviously, at least for the time being,[6] museums remain traditional spatial environments requiring a physical journey and physical movement through an exhibition.

Increasingly, new galleries – especially in science and technology – are becoming media hybrids. They are grafting two kinds of spatial orientation together. The first is one in which objects are both displayed in a structured space and at the same time refer to a space outside the walls of the museum in which they have another, distant significance. This is how the 'traditonal' museum might be described. The objects act as media, metonymically related in their displacement to other places. The second kind of spatial orientation is provided by the secondary mediation of those objects by their recontextualisation through the images and sounds of electronic media on the one hand, and the interactive experience on the other. Videos provide an immediacy and a realism, often at the expense of the objects themselves. They become metaphors of the real, no longer imagined, but trusted as accurate representations of other places and other times. Interactives have a different, but correlative, spatial significance, offering the opportunity for the visitor to transcend the otherwise unbridgeable distance between his or her individual space and the world of the Other: mythically and metaphorically extending reach and control. Both these media, once incorporated into the museum, blur the boundaries between the museum's private space and the public world, a boundary which was pretty well held when both objects and visitors had to cross the same threshold. But they also blur the boundaries between the individual's private space and the public space of the museum, in this case reinforcing the familiar elision of domestic and public which the consumption of television, in particular, tends to produce (Silverstone 1991).[7]

Yet visitors do still have to come to the museum. When they come, they are faced with a physical arrangement of objects, images and texts through which they will pass and of which they might make some sense. That space is in a number of senses a *potential* space (Winnicott 1974). It is a space in which visitors are offered, and of necessity accept, an invitation to create and to complete the experience of being in the museum. This idea of the potential space which is occupied by the receiver of a communication requires us to understand our involvement with media technologies as an extension of our early childhood involvement with other objects that provided us with a sense of security and that enabled us to engage safely in cultural activity – in imagining, in creating, and in playing.

Museums, of course, literally do provide such a potential space and such objects. Visitors are offered a more or less containing and structured environment through which they move and within which they can, in every sense of the word, play. In the face of the rhetorics and narratives of the gallery or exhibition, they construct their own 'perambulatory' rhetorics and narratives (de Certeau 1984). And they do so more or less creatively, more or less securely, in the space physically provided for them in the arrangement of the gallery, and metaphorically provided for them in the extension of that space to include their own experience. This potential space, which surrounds and contains any act of communication, is an essential part of the museum's communication. The objects that are displayed within it gain their meaning and their power both from their significance as items in a collection and their claims for authenticity, but also from the imaginative work that visitors can and must do in relation to them. Their aura and their magic, the aura and magic of the exhibition or museum as a whole, are products of the joint creative work undertaken in this potential space.

Conclusion: the consuming visitor

It may seem perverse to lay so much emphasis on the visitor in these discussions of the museum as a medium. And it would be wrong to read into my account a sense of the visitor's exclusive priority. Communication is, after all, a process that involves a complex set of actions in different contexts and under different constraints: politically, economically and culturally determined and determining. The museum is no exception to this, and I hope I have not been seen to suggest otherwise. Yet, perhaps now more than ever before, the visitor – the consuming visitor – has become increasingly important not only in any theoretical consideration of the medium, but increasingly also in the process of gallery and exhibition creation itself. Again, perhaps, this has been particularly true in the United Kingdom where, since the early 1980s, a market-based ideology has permeated all aspects of society, leaving few areas of public service and cultural provision untouched. Within this ideology, consumers have become the kings and queens of the marketplace. In the museum the hypostatisation of 'public understanding', especially in relation to science and technology, has provided an increasingly insistent framework for gallery design. The visitor is encoded in the texts of the museum in a way that can scarcely have been the case in earlier years.

Maybe the current preoccupation, in the literature, with the receivers of mass media (the audiences, viewers, readers of their various texts) is part of the same ideological shift. It probably is. Yet the two are necessarily interconnected. And it is self-evidently the case that any understanding of the process and dynamics of the media in contemporary society cannot exclude a concern with reception. The status of the object in the museum; the plausibility, persuasiveness and the offered pleasures of the museum's texts; the representation and articulation of space and time, all are ultimately dependent on the involvement and competence of the receivers of the communication. The enormous amount of evaluative research in the museum is testimony, of course, to the acceptance of this view – however, much of that evaluative work is premised on, at best, an inadequate view of the museum as a medium, and also on an inadequate view of the role of the visitor in contributing to, rather than simply receiving, the communications on offer. I hope that some of the discussions offered in this chapter will go some way towards changing that.

Notes

1 This essay arises from work undertaken as a result of a grant from the Economic and Social Research Council under its Public Understanding of Science programme. The field-work for the research was conducted by Dr Sharon Macdonald of Keele University. I would like to thank Dr Macdonald for her generous and challenging comments on an earlier draft of this paper.
2 Of course, the media are not the only source of information for the museum, and as Sharon Macdonald and I have suggested (Macdonald and Silverstone 1992) the Food for Thought Gallery was still powerfully dependent on science's own representation of itself, however contradictory this might be in individual cases.
3 The links between the parallel emergence of the museum and the emergence of the department store have often been made (see, for example, Bayley 1989).
4 The sense of the multiple logics of the museum is given material form in the existence of galleries constructed at different times within the same museum, or the existence of different museums within an identifiable genre of collection and representation (ethnographic, science, art). There is ample scope for a kind of archaeology (in Michel Foucault's sense of the term) in these simultaneous displays of historically specific discourses, though this has yet, as far as I am aware, to be undertaken in the literature.
5 cf. Jean Szenec, *Flaubert à l'exposition de 1851*, pp. 16–17, quoted by Donato (1980: 225): 'I am inclined to believe that an object is chosen on account of its special power of evocation. This knick-knack, that accessory, is the fragment of a civilisation which, by itself, it is capable of suggesting. Is not *all of China* contained in a Chinese woman's slipper decorated with damask roses and having embroidered cats on its vamp? In basing

itself on objects, the imagination reconstructs that universe whose quintessence they express.'

6 For the time being . . . Museums are now in the business of providing computer-catalogued images of all objects or art-works in their collections, which can be transmitted anywhere for instant scholarly attention. I understand that such a scheme is being considered in the Science Museum itself.

7 I am aware in making these generalisations that they mask differences between electronic media, both in terms of their relative degrees of involvement of the viewer/visitor in their workings, but also in the different claims that are being made by them in their mediation of reality and in their definition of the boundary between the familiar and the unfamiliar. I am indebted to Sharon Macdonald for once again pointing out the dangers in such generalisations.

References

Baudrillard, J. (1981) *For a Critique of the Political Economy of the Sign*, St Louis: Telos Press.

Bayley, S. (ed.) (1989) *Commerce and Culture: from Pre-industrial Art to Post-industrial Value*, Tunbridge Wells: Penshurst Press.

Bennett, A. (1989) 'Museums and the "people" ', in R. Lumley *The Museum Time Machine*, London: Routledge, pp. 63–85.

Bud, R. (1988) 'The myth and the machine: seeing science through museum eyes', in G. Fyfe and J. Law (eds), *Picturing Power: Visual Depiction and Social Relations*, London: Routledge.

De Certeau, M. (1984) *The Practice of Everyday Life*, Berkeley: California University Press.

Donato, E. (1980) 'The museum's furnace: notes toward a contextual reading of Bouvard and Pécuchet', in J. Harari (ed.), *Textual Strategies: Perspectives in Post-structuralist Criticism*, London: Methuen.

Douglas, M. and Isherwood, B. (1979) *The World of Goods*, Harmondsworth: Penguin.

Eco, U. (1987) *Travels in Hyper-Reality*, London: Picador.

Eisenstein, E. (1979) *The Printing Press in an Age of Social Change*, Cambridge: Cambridge University Press.

Ferguson, M. (1991) 'Electronic media and the redefining of time and space', in M. Ferguson (ed.), *Public Communication: the New Imperatives*, London and Newbury Park: Sage, pp. 152–71.

Giddens, A. (1990) *The Consequences of Modernity*, Cambridge: Polity Press.

Goody, J. (1977) *The Domestication of the Savage Mind*, Cambridge: Cambridge University Press.

Haraway, D. (1984–5) 'Teddy bear patriarchy: taxidermy in the garden of Eden, New York City, 1908–1936', *Social Text*, vol. 11, pp. 20–64.

Hewison, R. (1987) *The Heritage Industry: Britain in a Climate of Decline*, London: Methuen.

Jordanova, L. (1989) 'Objects of knowledge: an historical perspective on museums', in P. Vergo (ed.) *The New Museology*, London: Reaktion Books, pp. 22–40.

Kantor, D. and Lehr, W. (1975) *Inside the Family*, San Francisco: Jossey-Bass.

Kopytoff, I. (1986) 'The cultural biography of things: commoditisation as process', in A. Appadurai (ed.), *The Social Life of Things: Commodities in Cultural Perspective*, Cambridge: Cambridge University Press, pp. 64–91.

Lumley, R. (ed.) (1988) *The Museum Time Machine*, London: Routledge.

Macdonald, S. (1993) 'Museum visiting', working papers, Department of Sociology and Social Anthropology, University of Keele, Kent.

Macdonald, S. and Silverstone, R. (1990a) *Food for Thought: The Sainsbury Gallery. Some Issues Raised by the Making of an Exhibition in the Science Museum, London*, Report to the Science Museum, Uxbridge: Brunel University CRICT.

Macdonald, S. and Silverstone, R. (1990b) 'Rewriting the museums' fictions: taxonomies, stories and readers', *Cultural Studies*, vol. 4, no. 2, pp. 176–91.

Macdonald, S. and Silverstone, R. (1992) 'Science on display: the representation of scientific controversy in museum exhibitions', *Public Understanding of Science*, vol. 1, pp. 69–87.

McLuhan, O. (1964) *Understanding Media*, London: Routledge.

Mellencamp, P. (1990) 'TV time and catastrophe: or beyond the pleasure principle of television', in P. Mellencamp (ed.) *Logics of Television*, Bloomington: Indiana University Press, pp. 240–66.

Meyrowitz, J. (1985) *No Sense of Place: The Impact of the Electronic Media on Social Behaviour*, New York and Oxford: Oxford University Press.

Miles, R.S., Alt, M.B., Gosling, D.C., Lewis, B.N. and Tout, A.F. (1988) *The Design of Educational Exhibits*, 2nd edition, London: Unwin Hyman.

Miller, D. (1987) *Material Culture and Mass Consumption*, Oxford: Blackwell.

Morton, A. (1988) 'Tomorrow's yesterdays: science museums and the future', in R. Lumley, *The Museum Time Machine*, London: Routledge, pp. 128–43.

Ong, W. (1982) *Orality and Literacy: The Technologizing of the Word*, London: Methuen.

Paolozzi, E. (1985) *Lost Magic Kingdoms*, London: British Museum.

Reiss, D. (1981) *The Family's Construction of Reality*, Cambridge, Mass.: Harvard University Press.

Saumarez-Smith, C. (1989) 'Museums, artefacts, and meanings', in P. Vergo (ed.), *The New Museology*, London: Reaktion Books, pp. 6–21.

Silverstone, R. (1988) 'Museums and the media: A theoretical and methodological exploration', *International Journal of Museum Management and Curatorship*, vol. 7, no. 3, pp. 231–42.

—— (1989a) 'Heritage as media: Some implications for research', in D. Uzell (ed.) *Heritage Interpretation Volume 2. The Visitor Experience*, London: Frances Pinter.

—— (1989b) 'Let us then return to the murmurings of everyday practices: a note on Michel de Certeau, television and everyday life', *Theory, Culture and Society*, vol. 6, no. 1, pp. 77–94.

—— (1991) 'From audiences to consumers: The household and the consumption of communication and information technologies', *European Journal of Communication*, vol. 6, no. 2, pp. 135–54.

Stewart, S. (1984) *On Longing: Narratives of the Miniature, the Gigantic, the Souvenir, the Collection*, Baltimore and London: Johns Hopkins University Press.

Vergo, P. (ed.) (1989), *The New Museology*, London: Reaktion Books.

Winnicott, D.W. (1974) *From Playing to Reality*, Harmondsworth: Penguin.

176

12

Some processes particular to the scientific exhibition

Bernard Schiele and Louise Boucher

We start by noting,[1] by way of information, that the scientific exhibition involves the invention of a 'language'. The scientific exhibition is a particular type of documentary exhibition which, like the exhibition halls and major exhibitions from which it originates (e.g. in science museums), has progressively transformed the format and spatial presentation of discourse, while concurrently developing rules of reformulation which now make it a textual system and media form in its own right. The description of the principal elements of this 'language' proceeds from a synchronic approach to media; this represents the objective of this article. An integrated description would require consideration of the three co-present systems which characterise it – communication, dissemination, and socialisation of knowledge, directly interwoven and articulated one with the other. However, given our limited framework, we will confine our examination to the medium and its language: classifying the principal dimensions of the exhibition system and describing the processes.

Preliminary theoretical comments

The scientific exhibition falls into the category of 'message-exhibition'[2] whose explicit aim is to transmit information. As such, it is the vehicle of a communication strategy and the anchoring point of a communications practice. We can define it using this dual central dimension. We note, first, that the communication strategies pertain to the overall selection and format device of the exhibition's textual system; the textual system designates the exhibition's overall message, in its iconic, sound and linguistic components as well as its media components; and, second, that the scientific exhibition is a correlative communication practice, since it mediates a relationship between the public and science. It entails using the exchange set up between the producer elements as a whole (directors, curators, designers, etc.) and the visitors (Perraton 1987: 15). To analyse the exhibition as medium therefore demands that both its form as a medium and its textual form be taken into account, since its communicational strategies derive from the articulation of these forms.[3]

The form as a medium

The exhibition's form as a medium designates the material and spatial modalities for formatting its statements. First, these modalities serve to modulate the reception. They orient the observation, define a space, mobilise certain socio-cognitive processes, and especially invite use. The modalities express the condition of access to the exhibition. Second, they differentiate the exhibition from other media. It is the spatialisation of the content which makes it stand out, and this correlates with the physical presence of the visitors to guide their progression through the exhibition.

The textual form

The exhibition's textual form refers first to the significance of the object and its status. The exhibition is created from a discourse being attributed to an object (Davallon 1986: 14). None the less, two types of objects are featured in the exhibition: the exhibited objects (referents) and the exhibition tools (devices and supports). They respectively actualise the two operations of selection and recontextualisation by which the world comes to be exhibited and is constituted as text[4] (Schiele and Boucher 1987: 175).

The textual form, then, refers to the content's dialectic and to the relationship that forms the basis for the communication link set up. We know, in fact, that all communication is a paradoxical excursion which takes place at two levels simultaneously, since it specifies the content and the way it should be interpreted. All communication situations involve:

> a dual self-determination in a single and sole act which applies to itself: it reduces the self-determination of the propositional content by defining its mode of use or its meaning; it denotes an interpersonal relationship by actualising one of the socially instituted role-plays.
>
> (Quéré 1982: 32)

The textual form thus covers two dimensions: the axis of representation which sets up the referents, and the axis of communication which integrates the registration of the respective positions of the participants in the exchange and the relational interplay which accompanies them (Schiele and Boucher 1988: 24).

Syntagmatics of the textual system

Assembling the textual system reveals the intention of the exhibition. The two complementary levels of syntagmatics involve gathering the different components into syntagmas (word groups) and reorganising these into sequences.

The levels of analysis

From this first point we garner the fact that the exhibition, as a textual system, expresses itself by means of two main parameters: the medium and textual forms. Both involve various levels of analysis, in themselves defined by a group of precise indicators. For the media form we distinguish: (a) the specificity of the exhibition and of its reception system (theme, place, space, devices); and (b) the oppositions generated by the overall spatio-thematic organisation of the exhibition (spatial distribution of devices and media, conditions of lighting, colours, sound, etc.). For the textual form we have: (a) analysis of the axis of representation (the referents used, types of illustrations, iconic and linguistic codes); (b) analysis of the communication axis (declaration and language actions); and (c) analysis of the syntagmatics (types of syntagmas and their arrangement in sequences).

Some processes of the scientific exhibition

The exhibition is a whole which the analysis progressively deciphers. To clarify further, the main processes described are presented in the order adopted for describing the levels of analysis.

Axis of representation

First process *The thematic delineation, a true zoning of the exhibition, fosters an ideal trajectory by means of the modules which break the space into segments . . .*

The spatial distribution of themes is generally accentuated by the intentional zoning of the route, delineated by separate devices. This delineation frequently reduces to a dual dynamic of 'seeing' and 'doing'.[5]

These subdivisions – more or less marked out within a specific space of an exhibition, modulated and accentuated by lighting, the play of colours, placement of boundaries – serve to attract, guide and inform. These spatio-temporal operators, utilising contrastability, stimulate and reinforce the visitor's attention through partial but systematic masking–demasking of the elements of the content. The addition of an arrow induces visitors to follow a route. A progressively increasing darkness leads visitors from the entrance to the exit of 'The Solar System' hall of the Palais de la Découverte in Paris. An extensive segmentation of the space, like that of the '*Immatériaux*' (Ethereal) obliges the visitor to move, in all senses, through the labyrinth to be sure to see everything.[6] In this regard, it should be emphasised that formal orientation systems, such as arrows, the numbering of the panels or the use of an introduction at the beginning of the exhibition, are sometimes less effective than a more diffuse series of subtle signs, since the visitor spontaneously participates in the skill of 'reading' an exhibition

179

and will use the other devices only as a final recourse, thereby expressing a temporary inability to orient himself or herself in the exhibition.[7]

Finally, the spatial segmentation supports the ordering of the exhibition's constituent elements: in a general way, the distribution of sub-themes is emphasised by the modulation of the walls or the delineation of the space. While this set-up does not ensure that the visitor has a clear understanding of the conceptual organisation,[8] it increases the distinctive signs to facilitate understanding. The 'Leonardo da Vinci: Engineer and Architect' exhibition presented by the Montreal Museum of Fine Arts was an exemplary illustration of this process since the exhibition's subthemes (engineering and architecture) were set forth on two separate floors.

Second process *This spatio-thematic delineation develops, in terms of the signified, a system of structuring oppositions which enables an initial reading and an initial integration of content.*

A system of opposites ensues from this spatio-thematic organisation. These opposites are established from dialectic relations established between the different parts of the exhibition and between the devices ('large/small', 'dark/bright', 'black–white/colour'), to note just a few possibilities. The system of opposites ensures the conjunction of a theme, of a time, place and space which designate an exhibition. For example, the 'Solar System' room of the Palais de la Découverte, structured by the 'clear/obscure' opposition, produced by the distribution of the lighting, encourages a route which is also that of the progression of knowledge continuously advancing: 'the distant reality becomes clear as the acquired knowledge enables us to apprehend it' (Schiele and Boucher 1987: 104). On the other hand, the 'Computers' hall contrasts 'knowledge' and 'use' by reserving a space for conceptual development, as witness the contribution of mathematicians and logicians grouped together at the exhibition entrance, and another space for technological applications. Various systems of secondary oppositions, a larger space and a less uniform treatment, generate a contrastive torsion which shifts the dynamic of the main opposition in favour of the technological results (Boucher 1987: 98).

Third process *But the treatment of themes displayed by the scientific exhibition is done mainly through recourse to the world of the specialist.*

The scientific exhibition invites three realms of reference: 'everyone's world', the 'world of class' and, often to the detriment of the other two, the 'world of the specialist'[9] (Jacquinot 1977: 59–74). In comparison with televisual forms of popularisation (Schiele 1986) or again the didactic film (Jacquinot 1977), in which the 'world of the specialist' co-exists with the other two world-referents, the exhibition displays the 'world of the specialist' as the principal assigned universe of reference, the others being confined to the role of justifying. This real dominance derives in part from the necessary reference to the source-discourse in any initiating effort. And it is emphasised by the rejection of the educational explanation linked to the constraint of generating interest and motivating a public whose very presence is the gauge of an exhibition's success. But the maintenance of a necessary relationship of communication overdetermines the recourse to the 'world of the specialist'. Hence the exhibition depends readily on the most familiar representations by inviting, like so many recognition signs, the most socialised forms of knowledge. However, there is nothing to indicate that this recognition contributes to the desired reduction of the gap between science and the public (Roqueplo 1974). Perhaps it is even the condition for perpetuating the myth of science (Jurdant 1973; Decrosse, Landry and Natali 1987).

The insertion of 'everyone's world' into the exhibition's grid emphasises, by contrast, the distancing produced by the displaying of the referents of the 'world of the specialist'; it proposes a parallel framework of reception which makes it possible for the visitor to integrate science or its results into the immediate context of everyday activities. The function of the referents of 'everyone's world' is to appeal to the everyday reality of visitors, and thereby assure a temporal and partial adhesion during their visit. Their discreet or explicit recall, materialised, among other things, by the insertion of illustrations (references to business, cultural, artistic worlds, etc., present or past, depending on the needs) or the graphic treatment (colour, texture, matter, form, etc.), opposes the elements of content of 'everyone's world' against those of the 'world of the specialist'.[10]

As for the 'world of class', it never appears alone: it superimposes over the other two world-referents. With the help of a multitude of means, it orients the relationship of approval of contents in terms of a desired objective (training, information, sensitisation, etc.). Because one overshadows the other, it is the assimilation of the 'world of class' to the 'world of the specialist' which:

> leads to an improper definition of the scientific exhibition as the set-up of a didactic relationship of communication. . . . While the world of class necessarily introduces itself into the world of the specialist, the reverse is not true.
>
> (Schiele and Boucher, 1987: 108)

Fourth process   *In any case, the world of the specialist is apparent to the visitor through the object or its image, thus reinforcing the illusion of transparence between what is seen and what is known.*

The iconic level of the scientific exhibition is limited: photography[11] is favoured over all other possible forms of illustration.[12] Moreover, it is further limited by being restricted to a quasi-exclusive use of the photo-witness.[13] This provides an implacable proof: it is witness to the real, seen or observed, just like the real object or its reconstitution when it is absent: two ways of doing–being but a single function. To reveal the real without having to construct it, that is, without recourse to a whole notional or conceptual arsenal, the scientific exhibition has no other choice within its context of reception than to use the processes of visualisation whose use is the most socialised, and which immediately sets up a relationship of transparence.[14] While the universe of the 'world of the specialist' appears spontaneously to draw upon the use of more abstract visual forms or ones that are simply more familiar, it is only through the means of representation that the scientific discourse is developed, the constraints of mass-media communication exercised on the exhibition promoting the use of visualisation procedures which reveal the concrete reality, that which is evident by observation. In the scientific exhibition, nothing astounds, everything exists to be recognised.

Fifth process *While it even seems to disappear behind the expressive power of the image, the scientific discourse controls the attribution of the meaning.*

The world-referents, if they are 'seen', are above all 'read'. The traditional support panel for the text–image relationship resembles a page in a book like the window of the board, which yields the inevitable nearing of the book-type discourse with that of the exhibition (Jacobi and Jacobi 1985). It should be added that no matter what type of articulation of text and image is used, the exhibition spontaneously opts for a uniform mode of presentation. It thereby satisfies two imperatives: the standardisation of the 'format of the panels favours the mobilisation of a single scheme of reading for the entire exhibition' and thus facilitates the work of 'labyrinthic reconstruction' (Davallon 1986: 250); the set-up of the fixed reference points indicates, by default, whatever 'else' there is to see or to do (Boucher 1987: 107). Jacobi and Jacobi (1985) stress the role of 'basic canvas' played by the panels. Little noticed most of the time, and possibly even assimilated with the materiality of the walls, they none the less contribute to ensuring the discursive grid of the exhibition: their potential is then re-affirmed at another level (see below). Studies on visitor behaviour clearly indicate that their use of museum orientation tools serves, among other things, to determine those halls they wish to avoid (Cohen *et al.* 1977). And everything leads to the belief that this discrimination also operates for an exhibition hall and that the set-up of the devices can play this same role.

The syntax of the text–image relationship designates the same economy of means[15] as that reserved for the visualisation processes. The role of the text consists primarily in anchoring[16] the image which accompanies it: this reduction of the polysemy redoubles the effect of transparence provoked by the recourse to the photo-witness. Moreover, this effect is further accentuated when the signi-fied of the exhibition organises itself further in terms of the space rather than as a function of duration, which we observed in the textual systems of the exhibitions analysed.[17] Even in unmasking the designation, it is the discourse's unmitigated hold on the construction of the scientific 'fact' which resurges. And the more the image is to be coded, as with diagrams or graphics, the more abstract it is, and the more the discourse and image call upon each other and are integrated with each other to produce a meaning. This recourse and this reference to the source-discourse is at once a condition and a limit of the scientific exhibition, since it is the reason for the target discourse. Even the interactive devices, which purport to innovate in terms of the presentation of information and to liberate the individual from the traditional procedure of having a panel to read, fall back on the dominant linguistic and iconic juxtapositions and, a technological paradox, the image becomes even more subject to the verbal, when it is not completely eclipsed. One reservation however: when there is adjustment of the articulation of the text to image, a less frequent procedure, as in the case of the substitution of a sound track[18] to the written text, for example, the anchoring relationship is reversed and the iconic prevails over the verbal.[19] It is perhaps at this moment that one of the paradoxes of the exhibition is pointed up: to be able to inform but without renouncing myth.

Sixth process   *To conclude in terms of the axis of representation: the exhibition naturalises the 'reality' that it constructs and displays; it disappears as the textual system which produces meaning.*

Axis of communication

Seventh process   *Science presents itself as if those comprising it or its purpose were non-existent.*

All messages contain a representation of the receiver to whom they are addressed. The statements[20] that comprise them assign positions to the participants and activate communication strategies. The characteristic of the communication relationship instituted by the textual system of exhibitions analysed is the elision of the producer elements. This strategic erasing, as demonstrated by the preponderance of 'the non-oppositional' for the person signs, opens on to a situation of communication in which the object, visual or linguistic, can be seen or presents itself without any address notation:[21] the textual system of the exhibition thus adopts the narrative mode.[22] This produces a distancing effect, since the narrative directs an attitude of communication (a way of presenting the content) which favours relaxed detachment in relation to the 'speaker'. Its statement strategy, centred on the context,[23] presents the facts, situations and events without the intervention of the speaker. 'The events are presented as if they are produced as they appear on the horizon of history' (Carontini 1986: 15). All this confines the visitors to a role of witness to, or spectator of, science; he or she follows with detachment and at a distance.[24] This conclusion should be qualified because both the sender and receiver of the message[25] are actively involved in the discourse. However, the dominant strategy of the scientific exhibition remains that of the narrative.

Eighth process   *The scientific exhibition ensures the maintenance of an authoritarian and linear knowledge–learner relationship.*

The analysis of the acts of language[26] informs us on the relational interplay in which the participants become involved when confronted by such statements. The analysis of the actions of language completes that of the positions of communication conferred on participants by the person signs and time, by indicating, mainly with the help of the mode signs, the relational interplay instigated. In fact, the study of the actions of language shows that beyond the actual capacities of individuals, the success of a communication situation depends on a certain number of criteria and conditions that define the pragmatic skill, itself instituted and supported in and by a determined social structure (Carontini and Perraton 1987).

The content, qualified by its nature, either genuine or false, is highly valued by the scientific exhibition. The recurrence of 'assertives'[27] guarantees a consistent textuality (Wienrich 1973: 204). But as these 'assertives' accommodate themselves to the discreet presence of 'directives'[28] and 'expressives',[29] homogeneity is assured. By these traits the exhibition shows another basic characteristic: it establishes a linear relational interplay between the 'knowledge-sender' and the 'receiver-learner'. The recourse to assertives results in the production of denotative statements (Lyotard 1979, 1980) whose practical effectiveness is to maintain for the producer elements the position of authority conferred by knowledge; the visitors, on the other hand, in a complementary position, can only express their agreement or disagreement. Visitors can observe only what is presented to them.

The few directive and expressive acts[30] in the scientific exhibition, a feature which distinguishes it from other documentary exhibitions, runs counter to its much sought-after objectives of dissemination: these depend on the bringing together of scientists and the public. The physical, media-type and textual distance which we have highlighted in terms of the axis of representation (use of vitrines, protective barriers; modalities of staging of the 'world of the specialist', reduced use of sound codes which contribute to an effect of abstraction by stripping down the events or items from their concrete connections), is found to be amplified in terms of the relational interplay of the communication.

Ninth process *Specific case of relational interplay, the interactivity associates the visitor with the production of the message without, however, transforming the exchange relationship.*

Interactive devices purport to introduce a new link with objects; they propose to create occasions to act, to experiment and to decide: they therefore merit being used in their role of instrument of communication.[31] The interactivity proceeds from the persuasive strategy: the involvement of the visitor is sought by the generalised use of 'us-inclusive' pedagogy, or further of the convivial 'I', such as the messages that the computer conveys to its users. Articulated to prescriptive statements, it confers on visitors the role of sender and receiver at the same time. This double relational interplay characterises the interactivity. The interactive message mobilises the persuasive and poetic functions[32] to make the visitor, whose participation is obligatorily required, an element of its device and, beyond that, an element of the overall system of the exhibition. This is how interactivity is distinguished from the other modes of presentation.[33] But interactivity confronts two limitations. The first is set by the already existing implacable aspect of knowledge, whose structural anteriority is the condition of the exhibition. The second entails the modalities of exchange: whatever the form of the interaction and the complexity of the relations of the visitor to the interactive system, the communication remains unilateral and the forbidding of a reciprocal exchange remains just as definitive, if this is only in the instrumental relationship anticipated by the producer group. But a deeper dynamic, which substitutes the 'loisir du dedans' ('inside recreation') for the 'loisir du dehors' ('outside recreation'),[34] seems to be operating, something which transforms the intrinsically multiform character of the exhibition with, as alibi, the promises of new communication technologies.

Tenth process   *To conclude in terms of the axis of communication: the apparently objective presentation of science conceals a discreet but firm taking charge of the visitor.*

Like the axis of representation, the correspondence of the participants' positions by the statement signs, the relational interplay by the actions of language and the types of devices reveal the internal co-ordinating rules of the axis of communication of the textual system of the exhibition. The obscuring of the declarative element produces two simultaneous effects of objective communication and distancing. But an analysis of the declaration signs indicates the activation of two strategies, which are more buried, and oriented to the context or the receiver.[35] Depending on the predominance of one over the other, the receiver's role differs. With the referential strategy, observers are passive; with the persuasive strategy, which applies from the point of involving them in a process of interaction, they fulfil an assigned function in a preregulated exchange.

Syntagmatics

Eleventh process   *The exhibition chooses to show rather than demonstrate since it can't tell all, nor can the visitor choose all.*

The scientific exhibition can avail itself of two possibilities: to put forth the work of the researchers or to appeal to truth. But to achieve its objective, the exhibition only has at its disposal elements which it brings together. Hence, the analysis of their regroupings makes it possible to know what is the established relationship of dissemination. The scientific exhibition shows more frequently than it demonstrates.[36] The textual system of the exhibition depends almost exclusively on the use of show-oriented syntagmas.[37] The content elements undertake relationships of accumulation, enumeration and inclusion of the part to the whole, synecdoches, etc. Basically, they are thus adjoined one to the other. The exhibition performs a task of bringing together through omission of information and it is more rare that elements of information would be subordinated to each other. This is why it is correct to maintain with Decrosse, Landry and Natali (1987: 179) that the visitor can embark on each exhibition location

> by accepting the individual significance of each object encountered. Visitors know that each of them participates in the overall knowledge, but there is no necessity to understand the intermediary structures. This being done, and in responding to the thematic organisation proposed, they completely avoid the rigour (and the difficulty) of disciplinary frameworks. Each object encountered thus contains its own significance, being linked to its environment more by holistic types of associations than by the very well-defined structural relationships.

Certain textual modalities (anchoring text) and particular categories of illustrations (referents whose iconicity is maximal) appear to correspond naturally to these syntagmas. This leads us to believe that their special type of use is due both to the properties of the media and to mass-media constraints, a solution which, overall, responds to the enclosing of the discourse of sciences (as if, since it is not possible to say everything or show everything, a choice must be made) to the imperatives of capturing and holding the constantly solicited attention of a visitor, whose presence is the very reason for the event.

Twelfth process   *To accommodate visitors' expectations and behaviours, the exhibition provides several levels of reading which are also levels of deepening the content.*

Grouped into sequences,[38] the syntagmas define and structure the exhibition's subthemes. Or, inserted in the sequences, they punctuate the textual system to mark a transition, make an allusion or strive for a synthesis. It is these isolated syntagmas, as pointed up by the address signs which they bear, which reveal all the tension of the scientific exhibition:[40] to treat science without teaching, but to guide the visitor through the labyrinth of discourses. The exhibition is mandated to speak and to be understood. As well, its entire effort consists of proposing different fixed points and different itineraries which are as much delineation as levels of articulation and integration of the thematic and content. The specificity of the scientific exhibition resides in this forced co-existence of two opposing aspects, which it denies and constantly seeks to obviate; a co-existence which, when all is said and done, makes the articulation of the problematic of demonstration that of showing the regulating system of its textual system.

Notes

1   This text is part of a larger series entitled 'La mise en exposition de la science: contexte, langage et évaluation', to appear as part of a work devoted to the museology of sciences.

2   The two other categories of exhibition proposed are the 'encounter situation' exhibition between visitors and objects, as the art museum exhibitions can be, and the 'witness-exhibition', which aims for social impact, e.g. ecomuseums. As far as we are concerned, we would state that all exhibitions contain a minimal aspect of these different aspects but that the emphasis on one or other dimension enables us to promote a specific type of approach (Davallon 1986: 240).

3   The effective communicational relationship is dealt with in the third part.

4   All texts proceed according to the paradigmatic axis (selection of an object amid others) and the syntagmatic axis (organisation of the elements among themselves). This is why we call the organisation of the exhibition's overall message the 'textual system'.

5   The whole is often limited by a system of perceptivo-motor oppositions. Thus, the 'Computers' hall of the National Museum of Science and Technology of Canada restricts the use of the wall panels almost solely to the historical section of the exhibition, while the other themes are treated mainly by mock-ups and models, or again by a series of computer terminals. The Expotec 88 exhibition: 'Journey into the Human Body', presented in Montreal, provided a homogeneous group of modules according to themes.

6   Alternatively, for example, the 'Computers' hall has only one access, which obliges visitors to do a tour of the hall to exit, unless they do not explicitly retrace their steps. Another example of this regulating space: the 'Electric' exhibit at the new Museum of Civilization in Quebec City is spatially organised in the form of a spiral; this spiral functions like an analogy of the natural movement of a whirlpool, a turbine, the nebula of the heavens, or the shell of a snail, and implicitly organises the visitor's route, whose only free movement is in the choice of not entering the 'heart' of the spiral, which is a small, audio-visual room.

7   A study undertaken at the Smithsonian Institution indicates that a significant proportion

of visitors (66 per cent) did not know where the exhibition they were seeing began (Cohen *et al.* 1977).

8 In fact, some studies of visitors showed the relative effectiveness of the conceptual organisation within the exhibition. We will deal with this later in this chapter.

9 Even if it is 'Health', an ideal theme since it unites everything, the distancing effect is still there. Expotec 88, for example, the exhibition devoted to the body and health, confronted visitors with otherness: the referents used (medical imagery, surgical instruments, hospital equipment, etc.) as well as the means of presentation (prostheses to be tried, demonstration of medical visualisation tools, etc.) were part of a universe that could only seem strange to them.

10 In the 'Electric' exhibit of the Museum of Civilization in Quebec City, on the counter-panels placed in the foreground of a series of mock-ups of people and audio-visual devices (television, slides, etc.), the choice was made to include the evolution of discovery and the applications of electricity in a temporal grid: the years, accented by notable events. These, printed in blue, are interspersed with facts, presented in red, which remind visitors of the concurrent occurrences of cultural, artistic, political and economic events and the development of electricity: noted is the launching of the Walt Disney film, *Snow White*, the arrival of Marilyn Monroe, the holding of Expo '67, the day of the excursion by John Glenn, first American astronaut to orbit the earth, etc.; so many events that have studded the pace of news. It may be added in another area that this dialectic, which the designers of the exhibition wanted, seeks above all to create a bridge between the scientific universe and the non-specialist visitor. It is validated in the preliminary evaluation used to identify these bridges amid a target public before proceeding to develop a thematic.

11 The 'Solar System' hall represents more than 65 per cent of the photographs: the 'Computers' hall gives greater space to objects (23.3 per cent), which lowers the proportion of photographs to nearly half (48.1 per cent) of the total illustrations.

12 The typology used for the illustrations is taken from the work of Jacobi (1984) on the scripto-visual dimensions of the popularisation discourse and the practical approach of the photography of Janelle (1986). The three categories of illustration are photography (conventional or treated), the graph (diagrams and registration devices), and design (humoristic or realistic).

13 Different functions are attributed to the illustrations (Janelle 1986): image-witness, image-atmosphere, image-message and image-object, depending on whether they serve as a window on the past to authenticate the existence of an object or a person, whether they are used to create an ambience and acclimatise the receiver, whether they are displayed as a complement to the text and alone carry the explanation, or whether they are a support substituting for the object.

14 The relative absence of 'treated' photographs and the small proportion of graphs stress, in a different way, the attention to transparence for the exhibition.

15 The dithyrambic discourse of the designers on the revolution of the image does not appear to hold true in the case of the scientific exhibition.

16 The anchoring function is the most common textual modality. The illustration for the 'Solar System' and 'Computers' exhibits are accompanied by a simple denominative text in nearly half of the cases (44.3 per cent and 42.0 per cent) (Schiele and Boucher 1987; Boucher 1987).

17 For both the textual systems analysed in depth, a factorial analysis of correspondences, showing the relationship of the types of illustrations, the world-referents and the modalities of linguistic–iconic juxtapositions, has put forward these relationships which we simplify, reluctantly, for the needs of our proposal.

18 Finally, even more rarely, the linguistic or sound codes function autonomously: there is modest use of music when it is not restricted to sound effects. If the use of sound tapes is increasingly widespread, the limited use of music, even in the simple function of accompaniment (diegetic value of eliminating dead time and silences) (Jacquinot 1977: 95), appears to be a characteristic of the scientific exhibition different from other types of documentary exhibitions (ethnographic, historical, etc.) which frequently provide

music for expressiveness (to create ambience) (Jacquinot 1977: 96), for diegetic value and even information-oriented music, such as folk songs, a supplementary source of information in an exhibition. The sound effects of a scientific exhibition are first of all analogical: they signify the place and its ambience; they are also sometimes arbitrary (special effects) to emphasise, suggest, evoke. This is the role, for example, of the sound of 'electric' water in the turbine.

19 Note in addition that the use of a sound track as an element of continuity tends to regulate the visit. An extreme example of this control is in the concept of the exhibition at Montreal's History Centre, which offers a 'sound and light' visit: from the entrance, the route to follow and the pace to be taken is regulated by the rate of the sound track which, synchronised with the directional lighting, indicates the room visitors find themselves in, what must be looked at and how much time must be allotted to it.

20 The statement refers to a global process which features three levels of analysis: (1) the study of physical phenomena of transmitting and receiving of sounds which pertain to the psycholinguistic approach, (2) the study of signs or imprints of the statement's declaration contained in the analysis of the conditions of actualisation of the declaration, and (3) the sense given to the global significance of a statement, by its use in a given communication situation which springs from a communication 'pragmatic' and is perceived by analysis of the language actions (Carontini 1986: 12). We will not deal with the psycholinguistic level of the declaration in the analysis of the exhibition.

21 These address signs can be personal pronouns which indicate the relationship between the protagonists of the linguistic statement or the direction of the person's observation in the visual statement. For the presentation of the declaration's parameters, we refer the reader to our synthesis in the study of the Palais de la Découverte (Schiele and Boucher 1987), which adapts the systematisation proposed by E. Carontini (1986) using the work of D. Maingueneau (1981) using our empirical process of analysis. Recall briefly that Carontini proposes, from a discussion of the proposals of Benveniste, Jakobson, Wienrich and the principal authors who have studied the visual declaration, an operational grid of analysis.

22 Benveniste (1966) called this 'the story' and it was replaced by the more general term 'narrative'. It contrasts with 'discourse', which directs the receiver of the statement through use of the address signs such as 'you', 'we inclusive or exclusive' and 'it oppositional'. The discourse positions the participants in relation to the object 'which we are talking about'.

23 Referred to then is 'referential strategy' in opposition to a 'persuasive strategy'. Note that, from the proposals of Jakobson (1963), the six constitutive factors of all actions of communication, and their corresponding functions: the exchange necessitates a sender (expressive or emotive function), a receiver (persuasive function), a message (metalinguistic function) and a channel (phatic function). These functions, depending on the predominance of one over the other, shift the communication relationship. They thus inform on the pragmatic aim of communication.

24 In terms of the temporal signs, the narrative mode is effected by the dominant use of the present intemporal, like the perspective of locution (time of occurrence of time between the 'time of the text' and the 'time of the act') (Wienrich 1973), which reduces both the possibilities of encountering the anticipations and the retrospections. In the case that concerns us, the temporal signs associated, like parameters for bringing out the image (framing of plans, depth of field, internal assembling and resulting symbolic distance), also collaborate in this detachment of the visitor.

25 In some measure, the address signs emerge from the textual system and ascribe to the visitor the role of partner in the exchange. The stater is reintroduced by specifying, in the visual or linguistic statement, a condition, an element to be observed, or a particular context. The stater presents the referent of 'what is being talked about' by using 'it oppositional'.

26 The typology of the actions of language that we have adopted is that of Searle (1972), completed by the propositions of Habermas (1979), Lyotard (1979, 1980) and Récanati (1980).

27 The non-speaker action is the expression of a certain propositional content with a certain force (promise, question, etc.) (Searle 1972).

28 Content which reveals the goal of the sender to try to have something done to the receiver.

29 Content which directs a psychological state of the sender.

30 The directive and expressive actions form part of a persuasive strategy. Their prescriptive or implicitly prescriptive statements determine the different relational interplays. The producer elements are reintroduced in the declaration by the directive and expressive acts, whose skilful formulation is directed to favouring a certain state of mind, to suggesting a behaviour or adopting a certain attitude. The position of authority, still held by the producer elements, is now found to be qualified since, depending on seductiveness (implicitly prescriptive statements), it is supported by the credibility of the sender (as condition of sincerity) (Habermas 1979). The visitor thus had to recognise the intervention of the producer elements, identify the intention followed, and submit to it 'after having been transformed by the seductive efforts of the sender' (Perraton 1987: 50). On the other hand, in the formulation of prescriptive statements, the sender commands that a receiver obey (the visitor to the exhibition).

31 Various approaches have attempted to describe them: according to Gillies (1981), the interactive devices are defined using five characteristics: (1) they are appealing; (2) they motivate for learning; (3) they enable the manipulation of certain variables; (4) they raise questions whose answers spring from the interaction with the device; and (5) they enhance the acquisition and retention of information; for Decrosse, Landry and Natali (1987) interactivity is: (1) introductory; (2) initiatory; (3) modification; (4) of programmed selections; (5) of programmed reactions; and (6) actions in real time. Note also the distinction between the 'interactivity-tool' and 'interactivity-process' of Lafrance (1986).

32 Note that the poetic function is present when the message refers back to itself (Jakobson 1963).

33 Perraton (1987) has shown that the permissive non-speaker modality of 'having-done', the essence itself of the message, actualises a 'have participated' generator of information.

34 This is Claude Julien's expression, *Le Monde Diplomatique*, January 1989, p. 22.

35 Several factors are responsible for the internal organisation of these two strategies: (1) the degree of iconicity of the devices plays a major role in the emergence of the address signs; the more the representations tend towards abstraction, the more the declarative element is manifested; (2) the condition of reception linked to the devices brings forth the receiver element which progressively takes charge of the visitor by proposing means of use in directive or prescriptive statement forms; (3) also, it is entirely logical to observe that the differential use of the text functions is a determining factor in the emergence of the receiver elements. On the one hand, the backup texts and theoretical explanation favour the registering of the producer elements which then specify the treatments which operate on the referent or which explicitly propose the observations and actions to be undertaken; on the other hand, the texts of the interactive devices are set apart from the body of the texts by means of prescriptive statements which derive from the specific set-up of this type of device.

36 See especially the work of Jacquinot (1977) on the structures of regrouping of film units.

37 Note that the syntagma is a unit of information. In the show-oriented syntagma, the assemblage is called paratactic: the elements are co-ordinated by juxtaposition or accumulation; we distinguish the simple show-oriented, by enumeration, inclusion or by synecdoche. In the demonstrative syntagma, the assemblage is called hypotactic and the elements subordinated to each other direct an operation of intellection; we distinguish the ordinary, comparative, categorial demonstrative of reception, inclusion.

38 We distinguish the embedding which joins the syntagmas in a common theme; the juxtaposition which establishes a contiguous and subordinate relationship which entails relations of antecedence and consequence between the syntagmas.

39 The allusive or transitory syntagmas, for example, advertise a content; they function

like hinges between different themes and sub-themes. Their distinctive layout (colour, graphics, volume, etc.) appeals to the visitor that one wishes to direct. It is interesting to note, in this regard, that visitors are generally unaware of these indications. Everything proceeds as if visitors interpret these syntagmas like another level of the exhibition, so they can easily pass without ill effect on the visit. The introduction panels, true modes of use, meet the same fate. Possibly it is to downplay this behaviour that the pedagogues enter the scene: they call upon, synopsise, synthesise, delineate the itineraries, encompass the visit, and direct the visitor. Frequently, 'recall' inserts present information necessary to full understanding (definition of the phenomenon of electricity or the binary principle of computer language). This process compensates for the impossibility of taking charge of the visitor's route and partially resolves the dilemma of wanting to transmit a content without wanting to control the chancy route of the visitor. This particular operation of the declarative element emphasises at a second level the dissociation between the scientists and the teacher, since the latter is manifested by secondary signs.

References

Benveniste, E. (1966) *Problèmes de linguistique générale*, Paris: Gallimard.

Boucher, L. (1987) 'Mise en scène de la science et discours d'expositions: une Étude de l'exposition "Les Ordinateurs" du Musée National des Sciences et de la Technologie d'Ottawa's, unpublished manuscript.

Carontini, E. (1986) 'Faire l'image', *Matériaux pour une Sémiologie des enonciations visuelles*, University of Quebec at Montreal: Publications Service.

Carontini, E. and Perraton, C. (1987) 'Du côté de la raison . . . ordinaire. Outils pour l'analyse des pratiques de communication', unpublished manuscript.

Cohen, M.S., Winkel, G. H., Olsen, R. and Wheeler, F. (1977) 'Orientation in a museum: An experimental visitor study', *Curator*, vol. 20, no. 2, pp. 85–97.

Davallon, J. (1986) *La Mise en exposition. Claquemurer, pour ainsi dire, tout l'Univers*, Paris: George Pompidou Centre.

Decrosse, A., Landry, J. and Natali, J.-P. (1987) 'Permanent exhibition of the Cité des Sciences et de l'Industrie de la Villette', *Explora. Museum*, no. 155, pp. 176–91.

Gillies, P. (1981) 'Participatory science exhibits in action: the evaluation of the visit of the Ontario Science Circus to the Science Museum, London: A report to the Science Museum, South Kensington', unpublished manuscript.

Habermas, J. (1979) *What is Universal Pragmatics? Communication and Evolution of Society*, Paris: Gallimard.

Jacobi, D. (1984) *Recherches sociolinguistiques et interdiscursives sur la diffusion et la vulgarisation des connaissances scientifiques*, thesis d'état, University of Besançon.

Jacobi, D. and Jacobi, E. (1985) 'Analyse sémiotique du panneau dans les expositions scientifiques', Etablissement du Parc de la Villette, unpublished manuscript, Cité des Sciences et de l'Industrie, Paris.

Jacquinot, G. (1977) *Image et pédagogie*, Paris: P.U.F.

Jakobson, R. (1963) *General Linguistic Essays*, Paris: Editions de Minuit.

Janelle, P. (1986) 'Une approche pratique de l'utilisation de la photo dans l'exposition', *Cahier Expo Media*, vol. 2, pp. 131–3.

Jurdant, B. (1973) 'Les Problèmes théoriques de la vulgarisation', unpublished manuscript, Louis Pasteur University, Strasbourg.

Lafrance, J.-P. (1986) 'L'interactivité: généalogie d'un mot à la mode', in A.M. Laulan (ed.) *L'Espace sociale de la communication*, Paris: Retz and C.N.R.S.

Lyotard, J.-F. (1979) *La Condition postmoderne*, Paris: Editions de Minuit.

—— (1980) *Deux Métamorphoses du séduisant au cinéma*, Paris: Aubier-Montaigne.

Maingueneau, D. (1981) *Approche de l'enonciation en linguistique française*, Paris: Hachette Université.

Perraton, C. (1987) 'Voir et toucher la science. Eléments pour l'analyse des stratégies communicationnelles à l'oeuvre dans le musée de science et technologie', *Cahier Expo Media*, vol. 3, pp. 14–64.

Quéré, L. (1982) *Des Miroirs equivoques*, Paris: Editions Aubier-Montaigne.

Recanati, F. (1980) 'Qu'est-ce qu'un acte locutionnaire?', *Communications*, vol. 32, pp. 190–215.

Roqueplo, P. (1974) *Le Partage du savoir*, Paris: Editions du Seuil.

Schiele, B. (1986) 'Vulgarisation et télévision', *Information sur les Sciences Sociales*, vol. 25, no. 1, pp. 189–206.

Schiele, B. and Boucher, L. (1987), 'Une exposition peut en cacher une autre. Approche de l'exposition scientifique. La mise en scène de la science au Palais de la Découverte', *Cahier Expo Media*, vol. 3, pp. 67–222.

Schiele, B. and Boucher, L. (1988) 'L'exposition scientifique: essai sur la définition du genre', *Protée*, vol. 16, no. 3, pp. 17–28.

Searle, J.R. (1972) *Les Actes de langage*, Paris: Hermann.

Wienrich, H. (1973) *Le Temps. Le récit et le commentaire*, Paris: Editions du Seuil.

13

The identity crisis of natural history museums at the end of the twentieth century

Pere Alberch

Despite the popularity of natural history museums, little is known about them by either the general public or the policy makers responsible for financing them. There are two reasons which may explain this lack of understanding. These are: (1) The many facets of the modern museum; (2) The anachronisms that permeate this type of institution which is heir to the nineteenth-century way of understanding nature.

A modern natural history museum must combine exhibitions with the conservation of collections and with research work. For more than 90 per cent of the public the museum is synonymous with its exhibitions; the function of the collection is merely to provide the institution with exhibits. Little is known about the research work. In fact, although the exhibitions are the public face of the museum, the collections are its soul, its reason for existing, whereas research is the engine which makes the centre into a dynamic and living being. Because of this it is essential that the museum fulfils its three functions harmoniously.

Collections are not merely 'jewels' for display, but rather important evidence of the richness of a national heritage. They are irreplaceable tools for work in any study on evolution or biodiversity. Collections can also be important for research in areas such as conservation, the identification of diseases, the development of natural resources, etc.

The fact that it is necessary to study the information contained in these collections means that certain types of research can only be done properly in museums. Because of this it is essential to support the latest research work in natural science museums. To promote this little known aspect of museums it is necessary to project a dynamic, vital and interesting image of the world that exists behind the shop front of the museum. The popularisation of science, by means of exhibitions, is essential if we wish not just to increase the level of knowledge of the average citizen – with a permanent education system – but also to increase public awareness of the need for the state to invest in science.

What is an exhibition in a science museum?

The traditional museum is a repository for objects which define, preserve and illustrate certain aspects of our natural or cultural heritage. In this context, a museum is defined, and its worth determined, by the items that it contains. Generally, the objects are exhibited with basic identification and very little information to allow their interpretation. Because of this, the traditional museum has been an elitist stronghold for academics, students and curious tourists. Some items may be fascinating in themselves or have intrinsic aesthetic interest (for instance the skeleton of a dinosaur which is 15 metres long or a masterpiece by Velázquez), but on the whole the more the visitor knows about the context of an item beforehand the more he will gain from seeing it. In the past fifteen years museums have attained rare levels of popularity. The Velázquez exhibition at the Prado museum, Madrid, was visited by around 300,000 people during the three months that it was open to the public in the spring of 1990. Recently an exhibition on The Celts at the Palazzo Grassi in Venice had a total of more than 700,000 visitors in under ten months. Our museum, the Museo Nacional de Ciencias Naturales in Madrid, had about 600,000 visitors to the Dinosaurs exhibition which took place between May 1990 and April 1991. More and more frequently, the success of an exhibition tends to be assessed by the number of visitors it manages to attract rather than by the quality or the quantity of items exhibited.

The Metropolitan Museum of New York was perhaps the first to use this new method of imparting culture when, in the mid-1970s, it began to organise what are known as 'blockbuster exhibits': exhibitions characterised by their spectacular nature, with aggressive publicity campaigns and massive public attendance. The aforementioned exhibitions are a clear example of this kind of show. A classic and pioneering exhibition of this type was that of the treasures from the tomb of the Egyptian Pharaoh Tutankhamun which visited the main capitals of Europe and North America, and met with great popular success.

But it would be a mistake to suppose that an exhibition which attracts around a million visitors in a few months has a public made up of experts or of people who have dedicated themselves to the study of the subject in preparation for their visit. Because of this, modern museums are no longer synonymous with their collections but, instead, play an educational role and provide a cultural offering which can compete with other options open to the individual for filling in his or her leisure hours. That is to say, the modern museum not only preserves a heritage but it also informs and entertains. In order to achieve this goal new museums have had to develop communication techniques which are increasingly sophisticated and which lead to exhibitions which are more attractive, spectacular and up to date in their way of transmitting information and motivating the visitor. To ensure success, they must be accompanied by surveys which pinpoint the type of audience the exhibition will have, and by a marketing plan whose objective is to publicise the existence of the event. The success of the exhibition at a popular level is essential to obtain private patronage, without which it would be impossible to bring such expensive projects to fruition.

Although art galleries were the first to promote this type of exhibit, it is science museums that have perfected the new exhibition techniques with singular success. Thus, in 1990 the magazine *Newsweek* was publishing the fact that, in the past decade in the United States, science museums have experienced the largest increase both in attendance figures and in the number of new centres created.

In contrast with the classical concept, a modern exhibition has stopped being a collection of objects and is becoming a type of theatrical montage with its own scenery and a script. (The exhibition–theatre analogy does, anyway, go beyond a simple metaphor; the London Science Museum, for instance, sometimes uses actors in its exhibitions.) The fundamental thing is the production: script, design, exhibiting method, etc., rather than the collections themselves. For example, some museums with great popular appeal, such as the Barcelona Science Museum, do not have collections, their specific function being to present current scientific concepts.

The aim of exhibitions in natural history museums is to give information about the history of life on earth and about geological and biological processes which are responsible for the diversity of the natural world. For this, it is necessary to present scientific concepts in a way which is accessible to the general public. This is an important challenge, especially in countries like Spain where 'culture' has basically humanist connotations. Science, despite its central role in contemporary society, is neither understood nor represented as a laudable activity. It is regarded as boring and not very aesthetic, and it is relegated to the domain of a few specialists. In the same way that the enjoyment of art is seen to be an agreeable and sophisticated activity, the appreciation of science is seen as an academic obligation, the understanding of which calls for tedious dedication and discipline. The challenge consists of converting science into something worthy and aesthetic. It definitely ought to be such since art feeds on the beauty of nature and this is what science studies.

From the exhibition of objects to the exhibition of concepts

The transformation that natural science museums are undergoing reflects the changes experienced in our perception of nature and in our method of studying it. As Michel Foucault says in his book *Les Mots et les Choses; une Archéologie des Sciences Humaines*, the history of biology can be clearly divided into three periods. Before the eighteenth century, neither natural history – nor biology – existed as disciplines. In the sixteenth century and until the mid-seventeenth century there were only exposés, for example Aldrovandi had written a *History of the Snakes and Dragons* (1639) and Gesner a *Historia Animalium*, each in the rich tradition of the medieval bestiaries in which that great three-way divide between observation, record and fable – which is so simple in appearance and so immediate – still didn't exist. Symbols were a part of things. Writing the history of a plant or an animal was the same as stating which its elements or organs were, what it resembled, the virtues attributed to it, the legends or stories in which it featured, the coats of arms in which it figured, what the ancient peoples had said about it, etc. The living being was seen to exist within a network of symbols that connected it to the world. Because of this, in the Middle Ages and the Renaissance, interest in and wonder about animals and plants was expressed in the form of a spectacle: they appeared in festivals, jousts and reconstructions of legends in which the bestiary played out its ageless fables.

'Natural history' as such – according to Foucault's proposal – appeared in 1657 with Johnston's book entitled *Historia Naturalis de quadripedibus*. In this book, description is limited to strictly observable aspects of the organism, its anatomy, diet, habits, etc. Natural history appeared once the object was separated from its symbols and observation replaced the fable. Natural history reached maturity with Linnaeus and his systematic way of describing nature. Foucault refutes the argument that botanic gardens and zoological collections emerged in the eighteenth century as a result of a new curiosity about exotic plants and animals. Their appearance was the result of a new way of appreciating the diversity of the natural world and of describing it. Legends and fables disappeared and nature came to be represented by collections of objects which, merely by their presence – without a text – projected the new vision of the world. Botanic gardens and natural history libraries were fundamental to the new science of natural history in the eighteenth century, as they represented the book of ordered structures, as well as the place where characteristics were brought together and classification was done.

It was in this context, much as happened in other countries, that the Real Gabinete de Historia Natural (the present Museo Nacional de Ciencias Naturales in its embryonic form) was created, founded by Charles III in 1752 and opened to the public in 1771. In the tradition of natural history libraries, it consisted of a collection of objects that were duly identified and classified. The quality of a collection was assessed by the variety and quantity of 'specimens' and by the clarity of the method used to classify them.

At the beginning of the nineteenth century, we find the second transformation in the field of natural science due to the work of figures such as Cuvier and Darwin: the move from natural history to biology. At the most abstract level, this transition was founded on opposing *historic* knowledge of the visible world to the *philosophical* study of invisible causes. Until about one hundred and fifty years ago biology didn't exist. The only things that had existed previously were living beings which were seen within the framework of knowledge created by 'natural history'.

Modern biology is characterised by a growing emphasis on elucidating the processes, 'the causes', of present reality; that is, study of the mechanisms, such as genetics and biological evolution, rather than mere description as an end in itself. Paradoxically, natural history museums, as their very name suggests, did not adapt themselves to the conceptual evolution that accompanied the birth of biology and because of this they became anachronistic institutions. Their exhibitions maintained, and in some cases still do, a poetic and aesthetic view which reflects a way of studying nature that ceased to exist over a century ago.

Because of this, it is not surprising that in the principal capitals of the world there exists a dichotomy between the 'Science Museum' which is modern, dynamic and revolutionary with an abundance of interactive material and plenty of funding (for example the City for Science and Industry in Paris) and the 'Natural History Museum' with its static exhibitions of stuffed animals or skeletons in glass cases, which has become a museum of a museum: that is to say, an anachronistic institution whose main interest is to generate a nostalgic curiosity for its historic past.

A strategy for creating a natural history museum for the twentieth century

The Museo Nacional de Ciencias Naturales (MNCN) in Madrid, the heir of the Real Gabinete de Historia Natural founded in 1771, was, until 1986 one of the anachronistic institutions mentioned above. During its two centuries of existence the MNCN had changed from being one of the pioneering museums in Europe, a consequence both of the quality of its collections and of the quality of the research work accomplished in it, to a centre that was failing and out of date. In 1986, the Consejo Superior de Investigaciones Científicas (CSIC), the Spanish Research Council of which the MNCN forms part, decided to close the galleries of the museum to the public and embark on an ambitious project to renovate the architecture and to restructure the exhibitions and the research departments.

The current project of renovating the exhibition in the MNCN aims to create a museum where concepts take precedence over objects. But this is not easy, as it is not obvious how to exhibit things which are invisible; the cause of the effect. With regard to this, the MNCN exhibition team are working with two strategies. The first consists of extending the range of what are recognised to be natural sciences. For example, recently our museum presented an exhibition on new techniques in molecular biology which allow the exploration of cells, their constitution and their genetic structure and also of the application of these techniques to health problems such as AIDS and cancer. Viruses and molecular biology are as much a part of natural science as are dinosaurs and ecology. An exhibition entitled The Brain; From the Art of Memory to Neuroscience, which re-examined man's perception of the brain and its functions from the Middle Ages to the present day, was presented. These types of exhibitions seek to convert the museum into a permanent education centre, a showcase for present-day science.

Another aspect of exhibiting that we hope to develop is the relationship of art to science: exhibitions where the beauty of nature is celebrated and where links are created between scientific and artistic humanism. As an example of this we can quote the temporary exhibition of the artists J. Fontcuberta and P. Formiguera entitled *Secret Fauna* (which was first seen in the prestigious New York Museum of Modern Art), and those of the American photographers, James Balog, *Survivors of Eden* and Rosamund Purcell, *Natures*.

The second strategy affects the method of exhibiting. In order to explain processes in an enjoyable way we need to resort to the most modern communication techniques. The exhibition must not have the same format as a textbook, nor must it be a substitute for one. It performs a different function, that of making the visitor into an active participant rather than a passive receiver. To achieve this objective, the modern exhibition makes great use of interactive and audio-visual elements which stimulate the visitor and urge him to explore independently. The aim is to motivate. The MNCN is preparing a permanent exhibition entitled *LIFE* which, with a budget of more than three million dollars and advice from international experts specialising in design and communication, will break new ground. The aim of the exhibition is to introduce the visitor to the mechanisms that generate and maintain the diversity of nature: themes such as replication, reproduction, energy, the relation of man to his environment, evolution, illness, death, etc.

This new vision of the aims and functions of exhibitions in museums, both of science and technology and of natural history, obliges one to re-think the type of preparation required of a specialist in scientific museum work. Exhibitions cannot be designed and organised exclusively by scientific experts in the subject but instead they need multi-disciplinary teams organised around a 'communicator', a new figure in museum work, whose main virtue is to know how to handle the most advanced design and communication techniques. The aim is to generate a cultural offering which, by the use of the museum collection in combination with interactive and audio-visual material, captures the attention of the visitor, and informs and entertains him; it must make him play an active role in the exhibition: that of the main protagonist.

Index